THE NEW
AMERICA

THE NEW AMERICA

Adlai E. Stevenson

Edited by

SEYMOUR E. HARRIS
JOHN BARTLOW MARTIN
and
ARTHUR SCHLESINGER, JR.

KENNIKAT PRESS
Port Washington, N. Y./London

THE NEW AMERICA

Copyright 1957 by Adlai E. Stevenson
Reissued in 1971 by Kennikat Press by
arrangement with Harper & Row Publishers, Inc.
Library of Congress Catalog Card No: 77-132093
ISBN 0-8046-1421-0

Manufactured by Taylor Publishing Company   Dallas, Texas

ESSAY AND GENERAL LITERATURE INDEX REPRINT SERIES

CONTENTS

III. PROGRAM FOR A NEW AMERICA

1. The Economy

2. Education

3. Health

4. Older Citizens

5. Resources and Power

6. Agriculture

7. Depressed Areas

8. Civil Liberties and Civil Rights

IV. CHOICE BETWEEN THE PARTIES

1. Broad Issues of the Campaign

2. Executive Leadership

3. Single Interest Government

4. Liberalism and Responsibility

V. THE END OF THE CAMPAIGN

VI. CREDO

EDITORS' NOTE

In addition to a selection of the more important of Governor Stevenson's speeches in the 1956 campaign, we have also included his eight "program papers," a unique contribution to American political life. It is our hope that, by putting this material between two covers, we will make it easier both for those interested in current issues and for future historians to assess the 1956 campaign and Governor Stevenson's role in it.

In order to avoid excessive duplication, we have made a number of deletions. But aside from these cuts most of the speeches are reproduced in full, except for passages dealing with local personalities and issues. We have rechecked facts and made minor editorial revisions. But what we have reproduced here is what Governor Stevenson said, as taken from the Governor's own reading manscripts.

The editors are grateful to Governor Stevenson for his co-operation in this undertaking. We want also to thank William McC. Blair, Jr., W. Willard Wirtz, Newton N. Minow, Cass Canfield, John Fischer, Alexander Heard, Frances Martin, Carol Evans, Roxane Eberlein, Ruth Harris, Julie Armstrong Jeppson and Anna Thorpe.

THE EDITORS

AUTHOR'S NOTE

This book is the record of my second campaign for the Presidency. These selections by the editors from the main speeches and papers set forth the great issues as I saw them.

These issues did not die with the 1956 election. On the contrary, today they are more alive than ever, and sooner or later the American people and their leaders will have to come to grips with them. For each of these issues demands a decision.

These decisions can be delayed a little but they cannot be evaded forever. The issues were not born of a political campaign—they grew out of the changing character of our own country, and the even more rapid changes in the world beyond our borders. They are the facts of life of the new America.

One of my keenest disappointments in the 1956 campaign was its failure to evoke any real debate of issues. In the climate of opinion which then prevailed, it was easy—and politically astute—for my opponents to brush them aside. Yet the illumination of problems, needs and dangers, and alternatives for dealing with them are the very purpose of a campaign, especially for the Presidency.

I am grateful to the editors who made these selections and arranged this volume. And I am flattered that so many people have felt that a permanent record of my presidential campaign in 1956 would have lasting value.

ADLAI E. STEVENSON

May 2, 1957

INTRODUCTION

By Arthur Schlesinger, Jr., and Seymour E. Harris

Governor Stevenson made his decision to seek the Democratic nomination a second time in the spring of 1955. Several reasons underlay this decision: his deep concern over the evident decay of our world position under the Republican administration; his feeling that we were wasting time and opportunity while grave problems accumulated at home; his belief that his own capacity to wield continued political influence depended on his accepting the personal challenge of 1956. This decision, it should be noted, was reached well before President Eisenhower's heart attack of September 24, 1955.

There was considerable discussion in the Stevenson circle about the best time to make the decision public. Former President Truman strongly urged him to announce by Labor Day; Stevenson's refusal to do this contributed to the cooling of relations between the two men. Others thought it inadvisable to announce before the new year. Governor Stevenson himself concluded that the meeting of the Democratic National Committee at Chicago in November provided an appropriate occasion. On November 15, he said:

I shall be a candidate for the Democratic nomination for President next year, which I suspect is hardly a surprise.

I shall do all I can to persuade my party to entrust that immense responsibility to me again because:

In the first place, I believe it important for the Democratic party to resume the executive direction of our national affairs.

Second, I am assured that my candidacy would be welcomed by representative people in and out of my party throughout the country.

Third, I believe any citizen should make whatever contribution he can to search for a safer, saner world.

It is of the first importance to return the executive branch of our government to the Democratic party because it is apparent that wisdom and responsibility began to reappear in the conduct of our affairs only with the return of Congress to Democratic leadership in the 1954 election.

Seldom before has the United States faced a period of greater opportunity —and of greater danger.

Our great opportunity lies in the fact that our prosperity and wealth can now be used to give all of our people the higher standards and wider opportunities which are mankind's universal dream. These are now within our reach, not simply for the favored few, but for every family in America.

Our danger lies, of course, in the ambition of a new tyranny for mastery of the world, and in Communist exploitation of the hopes and discontents of the two-thirds of mankind who now demand a larger share in the good things of life.

In partnership with our friends and allies, with confidence born of magnanimity, we must work to uproot the causes of conflict and tension and to outlaw the very means of war in this atomic age.

The task of the Democratic party is to make "prosperity and peace" not just a political slogan but an active search for a better America and a better world.

I am ready to do what I can to that end either as a worker in the ranks or at the top of the ticket if my party sees fit to so honor me.

A month later, on December 16, Senator Estes Kefauver of Tennessee announced his own candidacy for the Democratic nomination. This made a series of hard-fought primary contests the inevitable prelude to the Democratic convention in August. As a result of the primaries, Governor Stevenson's active campaign in 1956 really fell into two parts. The first part started in February and continued almost without intermission until his victory in the California primary in early June led to Senator Kefauver's withdrawal. The second part started immediately after Stevenson's nomination at the Democratic convention and continued without intermission until election day.

With the general election on top of the primaries, Stevenson had to undertake nine months of almost unremitting campaigning. During this time, he delivered about 300 speeches and traveled about 55,000 miles. It should be noted that the burden of presidential campaigning has been rapidly increasing in recent years. Thus in 1932 Franklin D. Roosevelt, the last Democratic candidate to run against a Republican incumbent, delivered in the primaries and in the general election only about 107 speeches and traveled less than 15,000 miles. Probably no campaigner in the history of the Presidency assumed so heavy a burden as Stevenson in 1956. It is a challenge both to practical politicians and to political scientists to get the primary system under control lest it become a means of killing our candidates before we elect them.

THE DEMOCRATIC CAMPAIGN STRATEGY

Well before the convention, Stevenson and his associates had begun to consider basic questions of campaign strategy. One decision was self-evident: the essence of the 1956 campaign, unlike the 1952 campaign, had to be attack. General Eisenhower and the Republicans were no longer an assaulting force to be beaten off but incumbents to be dislodged. Where in 1952 Stevenson could speak glowingly of the achievements of Democratic government and of the prospects ahead, his first task in 1956 was to persuade people that the Republicans must not be continued in office. If he could not do this, then he could not hope to induce any large numbers of people to vote Democratic. Of course, he could at the same time set forth an affirmative program—the New America—but accentuating the positive could not win by itself, especially in a time of apparent prosperity and peace.

If the Democratic candidate could not win without attacking the record of the Republican administration, where could that attack be most efficiently directed? The Eisenhower record seemed pretty vulnerable across the board; but it appeared wise to ascertain what parts of that record might be considered weakest by the voters. Considerable material was available concerning voter attitudes, ranging from public opinion polls to the analyses of experts and the impressions of professional politicians. On the whole, the various studies were consistent in their estimate of the strength and weakness of the two parties.

The essential conclusion to be drawn from these studies (a conclusion summarized in a paper prepared in July) was that the main strength of the Democratic party lay in the picture people had of it as the party of the "little guys" against the "big guys"—as the party which had fought the people's fight against the interests. The main weakness of the Democratic party seemed to be the impression that it was the party of war—the party which had presided over America's entrance into two world wars and into the recent war in Korea.

Conversely, the main weakness of the Republican party was the belief that it was the party of big business and the rich. And its main strength lay in the conviction that President Eisenhower was, above all, a man of peace, and that the Republican party was far less likely than the Democrats to involve the nation in troubling responsibilities abroad.

Given this situation, most of Governor Stevenson's advisers argued that the main emphasis should be on domestic policy. Concentration on domestic issues would renew the image of the Democratic party as the people's party, leading the nation out of depression and poverty, while too much talk about foreign policy might simply remind people that the nation had been at war several times when Democratic administrations were in power.

In any case, the Democratic strategic decision was in favor of a campaign on domestic issues. One result was the conception of the New America—a phrase Stevenson used in his acceptance address to the Democratic convention and enlarged thereafter with sympathy and imagination. Stevenson had long believed that the ideas and programs developed in the fight against depression in the thirties were inadequate to the challenge of abundance in the fifties; he had long recoiled from the existing stock of liberal clichés. Through the preceding years, he had constantly pressed for an identification of new problems and for the invention of new social ideas and policies. The New America became the symbol for a new impulse of progress, in which the attack should be directed not just at the problems of food, shelter, and employment, but at subtler questions—at expanding the opportunities for self-development, at raising the level of culture, at improving the quality of life in the new society. This meant emphasis on such issues as education, medical care, civil rights, civil liberties, the problems of children and the problems of the old.

While Stevenson enthusiastically agreed that the New America program should be the center of his campaign, he acquiesced reluctantly in the decision to minimize foreign affairs. He believed (as, indeed, did most of his advisers) that foreign policy confronted the electorate with the most important decisions it had to make in 1956; and he believed in addition (as did few of his advisers) that, if the people heard more about the alarming situation, they would listen and respond. Moreover, he had been talking domestic policy ever since February, and thought that he could speak more freshly and compellingly in the foreign field. Consequently, as the campaign wore on, the emphasis tended to shift increasingly toward foreign policy. The late October explosion in the Middle East showed how sound Stevenson's initial instinct had been.

Unfortunately, by the end of October Stevenson's views on the many complex questions of foreign policy had become lost in the uproar over two issues only: Reconsidering the draft, and suspending hydrogen bomb tests. The result, as is not uncommon in heated political campaigns, was a noisy argument over two points, not a sober discussion of the whole range of foreign policy.

The draft proposal expressed an old preoccupation of Stevenson's. He had come away from his experience in the Navy Department during the Second World War with a great dislike of the wastage of manpower by the armed services. In 1952, when some of his advisers had urged him to come out for universal military training, Stevenson had balked, and had even then expressed misgivings about continuing the draft in peacetime. The whole logic of modern military technology seemed to him to be toward a professional army, where people would stay in long enough to justify their complex and elaborate training in the use of new and newer weapons. By 1956 both the Air Force and the Navy had found the process of passing recruits through the revolving door of the draft both expensive and inadequate to their needs; they were now relying entirely on volunteers. Stevenson believed that the Army would soon reach the same point. He was convinced in addition that a more imaginative use of incentives could produce enough volunteers to keep the Army at any needed level. As a consequence, he declared before the American Legion in Los Angeles that the draft system of personnel recruitment should be reappraised in the light of changing military technology, and that a Democratic administration would bring the draft to an end as soon as consistent with national safety.

But Governor Stevenson's exposition at Los Angeles was terse and included no explanatory detail. This made it easy for the Republicans to dismiss the whole thing as a political gimmick. Moreover, many Democrats and liberals had developed a kind of Calvinism about foreign policy, which led them to believe that, if anything were burdensome and painful, it must therefore be right; and they too were dismayed by what they regarded as Stevenson's surrender to the self-indulgent proclivities of the American people. Subsequently Stevenson issued cogent and effective defenses of his proposal; indeed, no one could really disagree with what he said at Los Angeles unless his position was that the draft should be continued even when no longer required by national safety. But nothing Stevenson said later erased the impression created by his first remarks.

As for the proposal to end the testing of large hydrogen bombs, Stevenson had first mentioned this before the American Society of Newspaper Editors in April of 1956. Discussions with atomic scientists the winter before had convinced him both that the radiation problem was assuming dangerous proportions and that a cessation of H-bomb testing would leave the United States in a favorable position relative to the Soviet Union. Like President Eisenhower, he accepted the view that (as Eisenhower put it) "tests of large weapons, by any nation, may be detected when they occur." Moreover, it seemed to him essential that the United States take some initiative to break the disarmament deadlock and restore our moral leadership, especially in Asia where we dropped the atom bomb. Finally, it seemed to him imperative that the hydrogen bomb problem be brought under control before a Nasser or Peron got his hand on a bomb—a condition which the administration's disarmament expert, Harold Stassen, had declared to be imminent.

What made the H-bomb proposal a major campaign issue was less any intention on the part of the Democratic candidates than it was the need for defending the idea against the misrepresentations by Eisenhower, Nixon and Dewey. As an issue, however, it evidently had some appeal in the Far West. It had very little appeal in the East. The President's charge that Stevenson's proposal was "a theatrical gesture," the refusal of the Republican campaigners to debate or even discuss the issue on the merits, and the constant charge that Stevenson was proposing to give away our bombs were effective. On the whole, the proposal undoubtedly lost Stevenson more votes than it gained him.

In particular, along with the draft, it gave a distorted impression of Stevenson's position on foreign policy. Where he was affirming the need for new ideas in foreign policy, it looked to some as if he had become involved in trick proposals to the exclusion of more basic foreign policy issues. Moreover, there was a widespread, though wrongheaded, feeling that the two policies were inconsistent and that together they represented a weakening of American defenses in face of a continuing Communist threat. The Democrats seemed to be carrying water on both shoulders; and, though they weren't, they should not have got themselves into the position of seeming to do so. And much of the press, of course, emphasized with satisfaction the notion of political irresponsibility and desperation.

Stevenson can be consoled, however, by the certainty that in a few years both his proposals of 1956 will be regarded as self-evident. Indeed, President Eisenhower already in his Bermuda conference with Prime Minister Macmillan in March, 1957, tacitly conceded the force of the point Stevenson tried to make during the campaign about the radiological hazard in unlimited H-bomb testing, and more recently new evidence has been adduced to support it, even as disarmament talks begin in London. In March, too, a special Defense Department committee, headed by Ralph J. Cordiner, president of General Electric, recommended to Secretary Wilson an armed forces "pay for merit" program, which, according to Mr. Cordiner, would bring about great savings both in defense spending and in the use of manpower and would in time make the draft unnecessary. "The solution here, of course," concluded the Cordiner report, "is not to draft more men to stand and look helplessly at the machinery. The solution is to give the men already in the Armed Forces the incentives required to make them want to stay in the Services long enough and try hard enough to take on these higher responsibilities, gain the skill and experience levels we need and then remain to give the Services the full benefit of their skills."

If Stevenson had made foreign policy a prime issue from the start of the campaign, both the draft and the H-bomb proposals would have been placed in better perspective. Moreover, more people might have connected the Middle Eastern crisis with Republican incompetence in the conduct of foreign affairs, and thus the sudden and spectacular bankruptcy of the administration policy in the Middle East might not, as it did, have increased the passion of the people to continue the author of the policy in office.

ORGANIZATION OF THE CAMPAIGN

Running a modern presidential campaign is big business. As much as he could, Adlai Stevenson ran his own; but the demands on the candidate are unending, and they limit the amount of time he can spend on organization. His campaign manager, James A. Finnegan, was an experienced professional, who had shown in Philadelphia his capacity to work as easily with liberals and intellectuals as with ward bosses. (It may be well at this point to scotch a myth which arose during the campaign and received some newspaper currency—that the professionals and the "eggheads" were engaged in a struggle for Stevenson's soul. Nothing could be further from the truth. Finnegan and the research staff saw eye to eye on almost every issue.)

Finnegan's special field was relations with state politicians and organizations. In this area, he worked closely with the Governor's personal aide, William McC. Blair, Jr., of Illinois, a veteran of the 1952 campaign. Finnegan, Blair, James Rowe, Jr., of Washington, and Hyman Raskin of Illinois, with the counsel of Senator Clinton Anderson of New Mexico, worked out the campaign schedule.

Press relations were in the hands of Clayton Fritchey, assisted by Roger Tubby, and George Ball was in charge of the mass media. Matthew McCloskey of Philadelphia, treasurer of the Democratic National Committee, together with Roger Stevens of New York, was in charge of finance. Wilson Wyatt served as a general co-ordinator and trouble-shooter. Jane W. Dick of Chicago, Barry Bingham of Louisville, and Archibald Alexander of New Jersey ran the national headquarters of the Volunteers for Stevenson and Kefauver. Newton Minow, one of Governor Stevenson's law partners, ran the administrative details of the personal campaign organization.

The incessant pressure of a presidential campaign tends to breed personal friction, but the Stevenson campaign of 1956 (like the Stevenson campaign of 1952) had an exceptionally harmonious group of able people, working together, not without disagreement but without recrimination. Stevenson's own grace of spirit communicated itself to those who worked for him. When defeat came, it was the Governor who consoled his staff and lifted their spirits, not vice versa.

On the side of issues, the campaign had the benefit of preparations which had begun three years before. In the interval between elections, Stevenson decided to do what he had had so little opportunity to do during his four crowded years before 1952 as Governor of Illinois—he began to prepare himself systematically on the great issues both in the world and in the United States.

Traveling around the globe as well as in his own country, consulting with leaders and with ordinary people everywhere, he learned at first hand the longings of people throughout the world for peace and a share of the good things of life. He learned too the problems which confronted American policy makers in a world in revolution. Concerned as to whether the policies and programs that had been developed during the Democratic decades were obsolete or good, and whether they should be enlarged, altered or eliminated, he organized with the help of his friend, Thomas K. Finletter of New York, former Secretary of the Air Force, a group of experts to review public policy in all the principal fields. J. K. Galbraith of Harvard was particularly effective in mobilizing the talent for these meetings.

Seminars were held at irregular intervals in New York, Chicago or Cambridge, where such issues as foreign policy, foreign aid, social security, education, health, natural resources, labor, agriculture, and tax and fiscal policy were studied. Stevenson insisted upon representation of different views in the group; and the submission of a position paper was followed by a free-for-all, in which both political and academic figures, under the kindly but tough chairmanship of Finletter, took an active and sometimes vociferous part. The objective in these discussions was less to sell any particular program than to suggest the alternatives which might result from sound economic analysis and from value judgments, and especially to make clear where science ends and ideology begins. The decision about which course to take lay with the Governor.*

* It should be emphasized that the research group was not formed to promote the candidacy of Governor Stevenson. Indeed, Governor Harriman attended a number of sessions of the group. Some of its members were independents, a few may have been Republicans. The composition of the group was fluctuating, depending on the subject under discussion. The hard core of the group consisted of Thomas Finletter, J. K. Galbraith, George W. Ball, Seymour E. Harris, Arthur Schlesinger, Jr., and Willard Wirtz. Others who participated in one or more sessions included Dean Acheson, Arthur Altmeyer, William Benton, Adolf Berle, Richard Bissell, Charles Bolte, Chester Bowles, Cary Brown, Douglas

INTRODUCTION xxi

What was the gestation of a speech? By mail, by wire and by word of mouth, the candidate and his advisers received scores of suggestions as to what the issues were and how they should be treated. Congressmen, local candidates, businessmen, labor leaders, professors, students, housewives all had their ideas. Public opinion polls increased the confusion. Each locality had its own pressing problems, and this affected the character of the speech. On this basis, Stevenson and his staff made their decisions, and the process of preparation went forward.

Stevenson himself was an unusually skilled writer—better than anyone on his staff. He had long experience in speech writing, including ghost-writing for Secretary of the Navy Frank Knox during the war, as well as working in his own campaigns for Governor of Illinois in 1948, for President in 1952, and the Congressional campaign of 1954. As much as possible, he has always written his own speeches. However, no one—not even Alexandre Dumas—could write the number of speeches a modern presidential candidate has to give and at the same time do all the other things a presidential candidate is supposed to do. Nonetheless—as the newspapermen who traveled with Stevenson can testify—he worked intensively over all his speeches, even at times when he might have been better occupied talking with local politicians or making public appearances. Drafts were submitted to him, but he treated each one as if it were his own rough and imperfect first draft. In spite of the intense pressure and constant interruptions, his editorial skill enabled him—by interpolation, rearrangement and excision—to transform a page of dull copy into something which plainly bore the unique and distinctive Stevenson imprint.

Stevenson's law partner, W. Willard Wirtz, worked most closely with the Governor on speech preparation. It was his responsibility to travel with the Governor, to discuss the final drafts with him, to clear them for release and to serve as the intermediary between the Governor and the editorial staff. The editorial group functioned in Washington under the general charge of Arthur Schlesinger, Jr. An important member was John Bartlow Martin, who had worked with the Governor through the primary campaign. Others who contributed indispensably on the editorial

---

Brown, Lester Chandler, Dean Clark, Benjamin V. Cohen, Gerhart Colm, Philip Coombs, Archibald Cox, Nelson Cruikshank, Bernard DeVoto, Alexander Eckstein, John Fischer, Clayton Fritchey, Lloyd K. Garrison, Alvin Hansen, Walter Heller, Fred Hoehler, Gale Johnson, Leon Keyserling, Richard Lester, Arthur Maass, John Bartlow Martin, Wesley McCune, Max Millikan, Edward Miller, Richard Musgrave, Paul Nitze, Randolph Paul, Floyd Reeves, Beardsley Ruml, Walt W. Rostow, Paul Samuelson, Carl Shoup, Marshall Shulman, E. B. Smullyan, Philip Stern, George Stoddard, Robert Tufts, Jerry Voorhis, Wilson Wyatt.

side—some on the staff, some as volunteers—were Robert Tufts, J. K. Galbraith, John Hersey, Chester Bowles, William V. Shannon, William Lee Miller, Seymour E. Harris, David Lloyd, Charles Murphy, and Philip Stern, who was also, with Kenneth Hechler, in charge of research. Many others gave freely of time and advice, including Dean Acheson, Harry Ashmore, Adolf Berle, Stuart Gerry Brown, Benjamin V. Cohen, Philip Coombs, Elizabeth Donahue, John Fischer, Henry Fowler, Irving Fox, Lloyd Garrison, Rachel Goetz, Samuel Huntington, Lane Kirkland, Wesley McCune, Paul Nitze, Walt Rostow, S. J. Spingarn, George Taylor, Edward Trapnell, Jerome Wiesner, Robert Wood and others. When Schlesinger left Washington in the last weeks to accompany the Governor, Thomas K. Finletter added to his responsibilities in the New York campaign a general supervision of the Washington office.

The staff also included secretaries and research workers whose loyalty and capacity for work were beyond belief. These trusted members of the staff averaged twelve hours a day for over two months and sometimes worked sixteen hours a day—nothing extra for overtime, and too often long waits for their weekly checks.

It soon became apparent that the contemporary political campaign is not a good vehicle for the communication of complex ideas or arguments. This is in large part the result of "improvements" in means of communication. A hundred years ago we had the Lincoln-Douglas debates. Fifty years ago, audiences listened enthusiastically while a Bryan or a La Follette held forth in detail on, say, the problem of monopoly. Then the radio came along to shorten political speeches, first to forty-five minutes and then to half an hour. Television has further abbreviated political communication. TV experts contended in 1956 that half an hour was too long, that fifteen minutes should be the maximum for a political speech, and that five-minute or one-minute spots were most potent of all. Obviously no one can make a very thoughtful or extended analysis of any very complicated subject in fifteen minutes. Governor Stevenson had important ideas he wanted to get over to the people, especially in connection with his New America program.

Actually, he had set forth these ideas generally and in detail on repeated occasions, but still the Republican press was echoing day after day the charge that Stevenson criticized freely but had nothing to propose. Some new form had to be devised, and the result was the series of New America program papers. In the program papers Governor Stevenson could set forth at length for those who cared his thinking on a variety of subjects. This represents an innovation in campaign technology which we hope will be used often in the future. The people are surely entitled to expositions as thoughtful and complete as these papers from all men seeking the Presidency of the United States.

CONDITIONS OF THE 1956 CAMPAIGN

At home, when the campaign began, the country had experienced four years of prosperity. Abroad, the armistice in Korea meant that no American soldiers were involved on fighting fronts. It is true that the hectic flush of prosperity concealed areas of poverty in American life; and that the appearance of peace concealed a steady deterioration in our relationship to the world. But on the surface things looked good.

Ironically enough, hostilities in the Middle East only compounded the Eisenhower appeal. As someone said after the election, it was impossible to defeat a President whose aces in the hole were peace, prosperity—and war.

An important reason for the success of these varying and somewhat contradictory appeals was the domination by the Republicans of most of the means of communication in the country. The Republican capture of the government in 1952 meant that for the first time in many years the same group controlled both the national government and the great media of communications. In the ten largest cities of the country, 32 newspapers supported the Republican candidate, while only 2 supported Governor Stevenson. Eight large industrial states had 316 papers with a circulation of almost 22 million behind Eisenhower, and only 48 papers with a circulation of 2 million behind Stevenson.

In the main, the newspapers and magazines—perhaps concerned to refute Stevenson's 1952 remarks about the "one-party press"—sought to give fair *news* coverage to the Democratic candidate. But there were distressing exceptions, which became more numerous as the campaign progressed. For example, the last issue of *Life* before the election had a cover picture of Eisenhower and inside 127 column inches of space for Eisenhower and Nixon; Stevenson and Kefauver received but 51 column inches. In *Time*, the Democratic candidates stumbled and sweated in their pursuit of votes, while the Republicans remained cool and high-minded.* What Paul Douglas has called the "double-standard press" may be an even greater, because subtler, threat than the old-fashioned, unashamed one-party press.

---

* "Head bare under a hot sun, Ike welcomed his youthful guests, admonished them to search for truth and apply it, reminded them that political parties must be dedicated not to seizure of power but to ideals"; while Kefauver under the same hot sun carried in "his enormous, ever-present briefcase, stuffed with all the items that long campaign experience has taught him he needs: an extra shirt (he perspires heavily)." Do Eisenhower and Nixon sweat? Certainly they never did in the presence of *Time* readers.

But still more effective was the unprecedented immunity from close scrutiny which the Eisenhower administration had enjoyed all along. The consequence was that basic facts about our position abroad and our public affairs at home were simply not communicated to the voters—or were communicated in so muffled a way that many people missed their significance. Thus few voters were aware that our foreign affairs were in very bad shape, or that living costs were steadily rising, or that our educational system was in a crisis.

Radio and television were, on the whole, more scrupulous than the press. Yet here also were exceptions. For example, in the eleven programs of *Press Conference of the Air* preceding the election, four presented members of the Eisenhower Cabinet, one a Republican candidate for the Senate, one a Republican leader in the House, one the French ambassador, one President Nasser of Egypt, while one presented two prominent Dixiecrats and one Paul Butler, the Democratic National Chairman.

The superior wealth of the Republican party facilitated access to television and other forms of mass communication. In the report on *The 1956 General Election Campaigns* made by the Senate's Subcommittee on Privileges and Elections the Republicans reported expenditures of $20.69 million, the Democrats $11 million. The most important single campaign cost was television. The television stations and networks reported to the Senate subcommittee that in the presidential race Republicans outspent Democrats two to one.

For four years, the Republican administration had deferred to the wishes of the business community. It is hardly surprising, therefore, that the officers and directors of the 225 largest corporations were reported to Senator Gore's subcommittee as giving more than $1.8 million to the Republicans and only 6 per cent of that to the Democrats. While it is true that the political committees of labor unions reported receiving $2.6 million, most of it used on behalf of Democrats (though some labor leaders, like Dave Beck of the Teamsters, backed Eisenhower), the individual members of a mere dozen wealthy families gave more than $1 million to the Republicans.

The television situation in the 1956 campaign raises important questions for the future. The transmission of political speeches by presidential candidates through television has come to be almost indispensable to the operations of our democracy. The overriding public interest would therefore seem to lie in devising some system by which a limited amount of free television time would be made available to the parties in the interests of providing the flow of information and the equality of debate necessary for a democracy. Why, for example, should not every party which polled over 10 per cent of the vote in the previous election be granted an assured minimum of free television time—say ninety minutes a week—during the last eight weeks of the campaign?

Perhaps toughest of all, however, was the problem presented by the great and apparently indestructible popularity of President Eisenhower—a popularity which thrived under the President's prolonged immunity from newspaper criticism. It was, indeed, more than a question of popularity; it became almost a question of Eisenhower's invulnerability to the kind of candid discussion which up to this time has been normal in our democracy. People who had recognized no limits of taste or truth in their attacks on Franklin Roosevelt and Harry Truman began to act in 1956 as if statements of fact about Eisenhower—e.g., "He spends a lot of time on the golf course," or "He has had a heart attack"—were almost blasphemous. Stevenson was widely criticized for mentioning the President's health in his speech on election eve; yet many people believed this should have been the most basic issue of all.

More than this, President Eisenhower was mysteriously but effectively dissociated in the minds of many voters from the failures of the Eisenhower administration. Invariably, when a Cabinet officer blundered, it was he, not the President, who was blamed. In vain did the Democrats insist that, in the words of Andrew Jackson, the President was "accountable at the bar of public opinion for every act of his Administration." President Eisenhower did not think himself so accountable nor, judging by the results, did the majority of the people, who endorsed Eisenhower while repudiating his political party.

It seems probable, indeed, that President Eisenhower was both the symbol and the beneficiary of an apathy toward politics not matched in this country since the nineteen-twenties. This apathy is understandable enough. For twenty years, the American people had public affairs crammed down their throats. Two Presidents who regarded politics as essentially an educational process had confronted them with a series of insistent decisions. People's private lives had been invaded first by the worst depression in history, then by world war and then by an unprecedented and grueling cold war. For twenty years, they had been under unrelenting strain, emotionally and intellectually. By 1952, a good many people were in a state of emotional and intellectual exhaustion. They had "had enough" of public affairs. They yearned for a breathing spell, a period of relaxation and tranquillity.

This is precisely what Eisenhower offered. If you tell a man who

xxvi

has just won a great battle that he must forthwith fight another, he will listen without enthusiasm, however sensible your reasons may be; and he is likely to prefer the fellow who tells him to take it easy for a while. Governor Stevenson's "keenest disappointment in the 1956 campaign was its failure to evoke any real debate of issues."

If there was any doubt about the outcome, it ended the day Israel marched into the Sinai Peninsula, followed by the British and French invasion of Egypt. That President Nasser's seizure of the canal and the ensuing debacle could be traced in large measure to the blunders and provocations of Secretary Dulles and President Eisenhower made not the slightest difference. Stevenson had warned repeatedly and anxiously over many months which way we were headed in the Middle East. But to the very end the Republicans continued to assure the people that all was well. The outbreak of war in the Middle East, far from discrediting and defeating Eisenhower, started a voter stampede that converted any hope of Democratic victory into decisive defeat.

1952 vs. 1956

It has been suggested that Governor Stevenson was a different campaigner in 1956 from what he was in 1952. Even enthusiastic Stevenson supporters of 1952 have expressed disappointment over the 1956 campaign.

It is important to understand the differences between 1952 and 1956. First and most important, the essence of the 1956 campaign, for reasons mentioned above, had to be attack. Now, it is difficult to attack without attacking; and, while the logic of Stevenson's strategy seems indisputable, it nonetheless offended some sensitive people who felt that Stevenson was somehow demeaning himself by trying to win.

A second difference between 1952 and 1956 lay in the problems created for Stevenson by the prolonged primaries. This was not so much the drain on his physical energy. Stevenson, a man of surprising vitality, could bounce back quickly even after long days and weeks of exhausting travel and endless talking to large and small groups in halls, on street corners and public squares. But to fatigue must be added the fact that the primaries also interrupted his timetable and took the edge off his later campaign. He had hoped to spend the spring of 1956 traveling in strategic areas raising great issues against the Eisenhower administration. Instead he spent it in a prolonged contest with Senator Kefauver. And in the course of this, Stevenson used up a good deal of his material speaking to small groups with limited press or radio coverage. Where other politicians could repeat the same speech endlessly with apparently undiminished satisfaction, Stevenson suffered, as in 1952, from a fear of boring others and also himself, which meant that material, too often used, began to lose its freshness for him. The result was that he sometimes said wearily before large crowds in the fall the same things he had spoken with zeal and enthusiasm before a few people in the spring.

Another factor accounting for the difference between the reaction to Stevenson in 1952 and 1956 lay, of course, in the simple fact of novelty. On August 1, 1952, Stevenson was largely unknown to the American people outside the state of Illinois. By November 1, 1952, he had made himself not only a national but an international figure. Rarely in our history had any political figure burst upon the nation with such flashing brilliance. But the sense of surprise was bound to wear off, even if he or his workmanship didn't in fact change at all.

And there were differences within Stevenson himself. He sought the nomination in 1956, while he had evaded it till the end in 1952. Moreover, four years of hard evidence had persuaded him by 1956 that General Eisenhower was a far worse president than he had expected him to be in 1952. But what was equally important, we believe, was a change which intellectuals above all should have appreciated, but which evidently passed by many of them: that is, that Stevenson knew far more about national issues in 1956 than in 1952.

Perhaps some of the splendid and enduring rhetoric which ennobled Stevenson's speeches of 1952 was sacrificed this time to a sober and concrete presentation of the programs he had in mind. This, he believed, was what he owed the people whose votes he sought. Doubtless many people whose hearts had thrilled to his eloquence, wit and moral elevation were bored when they began to get technical details about a health program or the crisis in education. There was no doubt a freshness of ethical challenge about the 1952 campaign which the 1956 campaign lacked. Yet on nearly every issue his position in 1956 was more considered, informed and thoughtful than in 1952.

All these reasons—the need for attack, the heavy drain of the primaries, the greater familiarity with the Stevenson personality, the more specific and technical treatment of issues—help explain the differences in tone and impact between the two campaigns.

The Future

Sometimes in national elections defeats are more significant than victories. Thus Buchanan beat Frémont in 1856, McKinley beat Bryan in 1896, Hoover beat Smith in 1928—but a few years later the ideas of the winners were repudiated, and the ideas of the losers had conquered. A certain type of president, in avoiding trouble for the present, stores it up for the future. The standpattism of one administration makes inevitable the radicalism of the next.

From the days of Jamestown and Plymouth, America has been committed to the adventure of growth. Growth strains the structure of society. It then becomes the responsibility of political leadership to help close the gaps between the social structure and the changing world. And, when one says political leadership one means, under the American system, the Executive, the President. As Woodrow Wilson said, "His is the vital place of action, whether he accept it or not, and the office is the measure of the man —of his wisdom as well as of his force." If the President acts, then the nation has a chance to keep pace with history. If the President does not act, then he increases the number of things which crowd in upon his successor.

Our democracy seems to be doomed to progress by fits and starts. Presidential leadership which asks the people to do little more than hold the line may win elections; but, in so doing, it betrays the very conservatism it professes to exemplify. The Buchanans, McKinleys, Coolidges, representing a goodhearted and high-minded philosophy of postponement, delivered the country to their adversaries. Unless his second term turns out to be very different from his first, President Eisenhower will end in the same plight. In an epoch of rapid change, like our own, crises accumulate, both at home and abroad. If a conservative government declines to deal with them now, then a radical government will deal with them later.

As Governor Stevenson has said, the New America is not something of the future. It is here already, everywhere around us, and the only question is whether we are wise and strong enough to realize its potentialities. The New America exists in the challenge of leadership in the world—leadership to move toward justice, freedom and peace for all peoples; leadership in the Middle East, in Europe, in Asia, in Africa, in Latin America. And it exists in the challenge of leadership in our own land—leadership to enlarge liberty and opportunity for all our citizens. The challenge of the New America is children crowding into rickety school buildings; it is old people uncertainly living out the twilight of their lives; it is proud cities falling into congestion and decay; it is suburbs bravely trying to form a new basis for community living; it is Negro children seeking to attend schools and Negro adults seeking to vote—it is minority groups striving for the equality and dignity to which they are entitled as Americans; it is the fantastic technological revolution of our age, automation and electronics and atomic energy—it is all these things, and above all, it is what we as a people are prepared to do about them.

We think it may be said that Adlai Stevenson, more than anyone else, understood the magnitude of this challenge. He tried in 1956 to awaken America both to its problems and to its possibilities. He sought to explain what we must do with our abundance if we are to realize the New America—if the wealthiest nation in human history is to provide the schools, the communities, the medical care, the level of culture, the level of opportunity, the quality of life at home and the quality of leadership in the world which our people deserve and our times demand.

In making this effort, Stevenson ran up against a wall of apathy and complacency. Yet his effort was not in vain. His legacy is unmistakable. He indicated the main directions for a reconstruction of our foreign policy. He set forth concrete programs for betterment and opportunity at home. Above all, he sounded a note of ethical concern—not the copy-book moralism which passes for morality today, but a self-critical and searching comparison of what we say with what we do. He kept alive the ideals of American liberalism at a time when the nation drifted in aimless self-satisfaction. For years he has expressed the true liberal's commitment to the vindication of the individual in a massive society where mass production, mass education, mass communication and mass manipulation are grinding man into a massive conformity.

It is often said that liberalism needs new ideas and new programs—that it has subsisted too long on memories of the New and Fair Deals. While no doubt there is something in this, we are not sure that this is liberalism's central problem. What liberalism perhaps needs even more is a new and compelling vision of the decent society to enable us to revalue our lives and redirect our energies. All is not well with America today, no matter how many multitoned cars roll off our assembly lines. Rarely has a nation been at once so rich in material things and so starved for spiritual solace (and so pathetic in what presently suffices as spiritual refreshment).

The fact that our contemporary troubles tend to be spiritual rather than economic should depress only those liberals who feel that liberalism is purely a phenomenon of depression. Spiritual unemployment can be as real and as painful a fact as economic unemployment. By any reasonably sensitive barometer, the times are out of joint. The moment is surely approaching for a new forward surge of liberalism. It will probably not come, as did the New Deal, from the breakdown of the economic system. It will more likely come, as did the Progressive movement of the turn of the century, from an attempt to meet the moral needs of a people beset by psychological unrest and anxiety.

This movement—the attempt to realize the New America—is the pressing reality of the future. When the new forward surge comes, it will be evident that no one in our time did more to prepare the way than Adlai Stevenson.

I
THE CAMPAIGN BEGINS

THE NEW AMERICA

•

I accept your nomination and your program. And I pledge to you every resource of mind and strength that I possess to make your deed today a good one for our country and for our party.

Four years ago I stood in this same place and uttered those same words to you. But four years ago I did not seek the honor you bestowed upon me. This time it was not entirely unsolicited! As you may have observed. And there is another big difference. That time we lost. This time we will win!

My heart is full tonight, as the scenes and faces and events of these busy years in between crowd my mind.

To you here tonight and across the country who have sustained me in this great undertaking for months and even years, I am deeply, humbly grateful; and to none more than the great lady who is also the treasurer of a legacy of greatness—Mrs. Eleanor Roosevelt, who has reminded us so movingly that this is 1956 and not 1932, nor even 1952; that our problems alter as well as their solutions; that change is the law of life, and that political parties, no less than individuals, ignore it at their peril.

I salute also the distinguished American who has been more than equal to the hard test of disagreement and has now reaffirmed our common cause so graciously—President Harry Truman. I am glad to have you on my side again, sir! And your heart can feel what we cannot express—how much you and Mrs. Truman are beloved in this room and this country. And I must say what every Democrat has known for a generation—that your chairman here will live forever in the memories of Democrats and all who love the political institutions of this land—Mr. Sam Rayburn.

I am sure that the country is as grateful to this convention as I am for its action of this afternoon. It has renewed and reaffirmed our faith in free democratic processes.

The exalted office of the Vice-Presidency, which I am proud to say my grandfather once occupied, has been dignified by the manner of your selection as well as by the distinction of your choice. Senator Kefauver is a great Democrat and a great campaigner—as I have reason to know better than anybody!

If we are elected and it is God's will that I do not serve my full four years, the people will have a new president whom they can trust. He has

Acceptance Speech to the Democratic National Convention, Chicago, August 17, 1956.

3

dignity, he has convictions, and he will command the respect of the American people, of the world.

Perhaps these are simple virtues, but there are times when simple virtues deserve comment. This is such a time. I am grateful to you for my running mate—an honorable and able American—Senator Estes Kefauver.

And may I add that I got as excited as any of you about that photo finish this afternoon—and I want to pay my sincere respects too to that great young American statesman, Senator John Kennedy of Massachusetts.

When I stood here before you that hot night four years ago we were at the end of an era—a great era of restless forward movement, an era of unparalleled social reform and of glorious triumph over depression and tyranny. It was a Democratic era.

Tonight, after an interval of marking time and aimless drifting, we are on the threshold of another great, decisive era. History's headlong course has brought us, I devoutly believe, to the threshold of a New America—to the America of the great ideals and noble visions which are the stuff our future must be made of.

I mean a New America where poverty is abolished and our abundance is used to enrich the lives of every family.

I mean a New America where freedom is made real for all without regard to race or belief or economic condition.

I mean a New America which everlastingly attacks the ancient idea that men can solve their differences by killing each other.

These are the things I believe in and will work for with every resource I possess. These are the things I know you believe in and will work for with everything you have. These are the terms on which I accept your nomination.

Our objectives are not for the timid. They are not for those who look backward, who are satisfied with things as they are, who think that this great nation can ever sleep or ever stand still.

The platform, the program you have written is, I think, more than a consensus of the strongly held convictions of strong men; it is a signpost toward that New America. It speaks of the issues of our time with passion for justice, with reverence for our history and character, with a long view of the American future, and with a sober, fervent dedication to the goal of peace on earth.

Nor has it evaded the current problems in the relations between the races who comprise America, problems which have so often tormented our national life. Of course there is disagreement in the Democratic party on desegregation. It could not be otherwise in the only party that must speak responsibly and responsively in both the North and the South. If all of us are not wholly satisfied with what we have said on this explosive subject, it is because we have spoken the only way a truly national party can.

In substituting realism and persuasion for the extremes of force or nullification, our party has preserved its effectiveness, it has avoided a sectional crisis, and it has contributed to our national unity as only a national party could.

As president it would be my purpose to press on in accordance with our platform toward the fuller freedom for all our citizens which is at once our party's pledge and the old American promise.

I do not propose to make political capital out of the President's illness. His ability personally to fulfill the demands of his exacting office is a matter between him and the American people. So far as I am concerned that is where the matter rests. As we all do, I wish deeply for the President's health and well-being.

But if the condition of President Eisenhower is not an issue as far as I am concerned, the condition and the conduct of the President's office and of the administration are very much an issue.

The men who run the Eisenhower administration evidently believe that the minds of Americans can be manipulated by shows, slogans and the arts of advertising. And that conviction will, I dare say, be backed up by the greatest torrent of money ever poured out to influence an American election—poured out by men who fear nothing so much as change and who want everything to stay as it is—only more so.

This idea that you can merchandise candidates for high office like breakfast cereal—that you can gather votes like box tops—is, I think, the ultimate indignity to the democratic process. But we Democrats must also face the fact that no president and no administration has ever before enjoyed such uncritical and enthusiastic support from so much of the press as this one.

But let us ask the people of our country: To what great purpose for the Republic has the President's popularity and this unrivaled opportunity for leadership been put? Has the Eisenhower administration used this opportunity to elevate us? To enlighten us? To inspire us? Did it, in a time of headlong, world-wide, revolutionary change, prepare us for stern decisions and great risks? Did it, in short, give men and women a glimpse of the nobility and vision without which peoples and nations perish?

Or did it just reassure us that all is well, everything is all right, that everyone is prosperous and safe, that no great decisions are required of us, and that even the Presidency of the United States has somehow become an easy job?

I will have to confess that the Republican administration has performed a minor miracle—after twenty years of incessant damnation of the New Deal they not only haven't repealed it but they have swallowed it, or most of it, and it looks as though they could keep it down at least until after the election.

I suppose we should be thankful that they have caught up with the New Deal at last, but what have they done to take advantage of the great opportunities of these times—a generation after the New Deal?

Well, I say they have smothered us in smiles and complacency while our social and economic advancement has ground to a halt and while our leadership and security in the world have been imperiled.

In spite of these unparalleled opportunities to lead at home and abroad they have, I say, been wasting our opportunities and losing our world.

I say that what this country needs is not propaganda and a personality cult. What this country needs is leadership and truth. And that's what we mean to give it.

What is the truth?

The truth is that the Republican party is a house divided. The truth is that President Eisenhower, cynically coveted as a candidate but ignored as a leader, is largely indebted to Democrats in Congress for what accomplishments he can claim.

The truth is that everyone is not prosperous. The truth is that the farmer, especially the family farmer who matters most, has not had his fair share of the national income and the Republicans have done nothing to help him—until an election year.

The truth is that 30 million Americans live today in families trying to make ends meet on less than $2,000 a year. The truth is that the small farmer, the small businessman, the teacher, the white-collar worker, and the retired citizen trying to pay today's prices on yesterday's pension—all these are in serious trouble.

The truth is that in this government of big men—big financially—no one speaks for the little man.

The truth is not that our policy abroad has the Communists on the run. The truth, unhappily, is not—in the Republican President's words—that our "prestige since the last World War has never been as high as it is this day." The truth is that it has probably never been lower.

The truth is that we are losing the military advantage, the economic initiative and the moral leadership.

The truth is not that we are winning the cold war. The truth is that we are losing the cold war.

Don't misunderstand me. I, for one, am ready to acknowledge the sincerity of the Republican President's desire for peace and happiness for all. But good intentions are not good enough and the country is stalled on dead center—stalled in the middle of the road—while the world goes whirling by. America, which has lifted man to his highest economic state, which has saved freedom in war and peace, which saved collective security, no longer sparks and flames and gives off new ideas and initiatives. Our lights are dimmed. We chat complacently of this and that while, in Carlyle's phrase, "Death and eternity sit glaring." And I could add that opportunity, neglected opportunity, sits glaring too!

But you cannot surround the future with arms, you cannot dominate the racing world by standing still. And I say it is time to get up and get moving again. It is time for America to be herself again.

And that's what this election is all about!

Here at home we can make good the lost opportunities; we can recover the wasted years; we can cross the threshold to the New America.

What we need is a rebirth of leadership—leadership which will give us a glimpse of the nobility and vision without which peoples and nations perish. Woodrow Wilson said that "when America loses its ardor for mankind it is time to elect a Democratic President." There doesn't appear to be much ardor in America just now for anything, and it's time to elect a Democratic administration and a Democratic Congress, yes, and a Democratic government in every state and local office across the land.

In our hearts we know that the horizons of the New America are as endless, its promise as staggering in its richness as the unfolding miracle of human knowledge. America renews itself with every forward thrust of the human mind.

We live in a second industrial revolution; we live at a time when the powers of the atom are about to be harnessed for ever-greater production. We live at a time when even the ancient specter of hunger is vanishing. This is the age of abundance! Never in history has there been such an opportunity to show what we can do to improve the quality of living now that the old, terrible, grinding anxieties of daily bread, of shelter and raiment are disappearing. With leadership, Democratic leadership, we can do justice to our children, we can repair the ravages of time and neglect in our schools. We can and we will!

With leadership, Democratic leadership, we can restore the vitality of the American family farm. We can preserve the position of small business without injury to the large. We can strengthen labor unions and collective bargaining as vital institutions in a free economy. We can, and our party history proves that we will!

With leadership, Democratic leadership, we can conserve our resources of land and forest and water and develop them for the benefit of all. We can, and the record shows that we will!

With leadership, Democratic leadership, we can rekindle the spirit of liberty emblazoned in the Bill of Rights; we can build this New America where the doors of opportunity are open equally to all, the doors of our factories and the doors of our schoolrooms. We can make this a land where opportunity is founded on responsibility and freedom on faith, and where nothing can smother the lonely defiant spirit of the free intelligence. We can, and by our traditions as a party we will!

All these things we can do and we will. But in the international field the timing is only partially our own. Here the "unrepentant minute," once missed, may be missed forever. Other forces, growing yearly in potency, dispute with us the direction of our times. Here more than anywhere guidance and illumination are needed in the terrifying century of the hydrogen bomb. Here more than anywhere we must move, and rapidly, to repair the ravages of the past four years to America's repute and influence abroad.

We must move with speed and confidence to reverse the spread of Communism. We must strengthen the political and economic fabric of our alliances. We must launch new programs to meet the challenge of the vast social revolution that is sweeping the world and that has liberated more than half the human race in barely a generation. We must turn the violent forces of change to the side of freedom.

We must protect the new nations in the exercise of their full independence; and we must help other peoples out of Communist or colonial servitude along the hard road to freedom.

And we must place our nation where it belongs in the eyes of the world —at the head of the struggle for peace. For in this nuclear age peace is no longer a visionary ideal. It has become an absolute, imperative, practical necessity. Humanity's long struggle against war has to be won and won now. Yes, and I say it can be won!

It is time to listen again to our hearts, to speak again of our ideals, to be again our own great selves.

There is a spiritual hunger in the world today and it cannot be satisfied by material things alone—by better cars or longer credit terms. Our forebears came here to worship God. We must not let our aspirations so diminish that our worship becomes rather of material achievement and bigness.

For a century and a half the Democratic party has been the party of respect for people, of reverence for life, of hope for each child's future, of belief that "the highest revelation is that God is in every man."

Once we were not ashamed in this country to be idealists. Once we were proud to confess that an American is a man who wants peace and believes in a better future and loves his fellow man. We must reclaim these great Christian and humane ideas. We must dare to say again that the American cause is the cause of all mankind.

If we are to make honest citizens of our hearts, we must unite them again to the ideals in which they have always believed and give those ideals the courage of our tongues.

Standing as we do here tonight at this great fork of history, may we never be silenced, may we never lose our faith in freedom and the better destiny of man.

Good-by—and I hope we can meet again in every town and village of America.

TWENTY-EIGHT YEARS OF DEMOCRATIC AND TWENTY-EIGHT YEARS OF REPUBLICAN ADMINISTRATIONS

•

I come here tonight to summon you Democrats to the cause of freedom, the cause of human welfare, and the cause of peace.

And I summon all Americans who believe greatly in these things to join with us. We claim no monopoly on the ideals we assert. They are America's ideals. The victory we seek is not just for a party; it is for a people.

But we do claim that this victory will come only to the bold and the brave, to those who are willing to work to make democracy's ideals come true in the lives of every man and woman and child in America—yes, and in the world. This is our Democratic goal. This is the victory we seek in November.

And I am going to fight for it with everything I have!

Why is President Eisenhower the first President in this century to lose

From a speech at Harrisburg, Pennsylvania, September 13, 1956.

control of Congress in his first elected term? I think it is because the fog is rising, the fog of half-truths and amiable complacency—and people perceive that all is not well in Washington and the world.

In the few minutes I have I want to tell you a little about Washington and the world and what is at stake, as I see it, in this 1956 election.

First, our Republican friends have been suggesting in one way or another that there are no real issues between the parties. And they contrive this remarkable transformation by talking—now that it is election year again—like Democrats.

Well, when someone says to me that the two parties' programs are just about the same, I say that so are two checks, signed by different people. The question is which one can be cashed and which one will bounce.

And I say that for 150 years, a check by the Democratic party, written out to the American people, has been worth its face value. We say what we mean. We mean what we say. And the record proves it.

This is 1956—the fifty-sixth year of the twentieth century. America has spent twenty-eight of these years under Democratic government, twenty-eight years under Republican.

During those Democratic years we abolished child labor, commenced unemployment compensation, old-age and survivors insurance and minimum wages, made collective bargaining work, guaranteed bank deposits, financed homeownership, started public housing, put a floor under farm prices, set up TVA and REA, protected investors through the Securities and Exchange Commission, and consumers through the Federal Trade Commission, and lifted the nation from the rubble of bankruptcy and despair to a great plateau of abundance.

And, most of all, it was under Democratic leadership that this nation met and defeated the greatest threats to individual liberty and national freedom in modern history—from the Kaiser, Hitler, Tojo, and Stalin. And in those Democratic years we pressed toward ultimate peace and security through the League of Nations, the United Nations, the Marshall Plan, NATO, the Point Four Program.

These are only a few of the things we did during our twenty-eight years —not we Democrats; but we Americans under Democratic leadership.

And what did the Republicans do in their twenty-eight years of leadership? Well, there were, to be sure, some accomplishments that must not be dismissed lightly. But they don't even compare with these I have mentioned. And that's why I say that to get things done America will once again turn to Democratic leadership.

Indeed, it is a central issue in this election—whether America wants to stay on dead center, mired in complacency and cynicism; or whether it wants once more now to move forward—to meet our human needs, to make our abundance serve all of us and to make the world safer—in short, to build a New America.

The Republicans pose the issues of this campaign in terms of slogans —"peace, prosperity, progress."

I pose these issues in terms of facts—the grim facts of America's unmet human needs, the facts of a revolutionary world in the hydrogen age.

Here are some facts:

In four years—four years of wealth and abundance—our government has let the shortage of schoolrooms and teachers get worse. It has done almost nothing to stop the slum cancer which today infects 10 million American dwellings. And juvenile delinquency, which breeds in slums and poor schools, has increased at a frightening rate.

We have done nothing to help the lot of the poor and of our older people, most of whom must now subsist in a penury that gets worse as the cost of living climbs to the highest point in our history.

We have done precious little to aid the fight against cancer, arthritis, mental disease and other crippling and killing diseases, or to make up the shortage of doctors and nurses.

We have watched higher costs and lower prices close on the hapless, helpless farmer whose only offense is that he has done his job too well.

And the small businessman is now backed to the wall.

Instead of turning our natural resources—our rivers, lands and forests—to the public good, we have seen them raided for private profit.

And the facts of our progress toward peace are even more sobering. The Soviets have advanced, while we have fallen back, not only in the competition for strength of arms, but even in the education of engineers and scientists. Millions of people have moved more toward the false promises of Communism than the true faith in freedom. And today there is doubt in the world about whether America really believes in the freedom which is our birthright and the peace which is our greatest hope.

Why has all this happened?

It has happened because for four years now we have had a government which neither fully understands nor wholly sympathizes with our human needs or the revolution that is sweeping the world.

The Republican administration took office on the pledge to make it a businessman's government. Well, that's one pledge they kept. President Eisenhower filled two out of every three top-ranking offices in his administration with men whose lives have been spent representing business, mostly big business.

Then—partly by choice, partly by a necessity we regret—President Eisenhower turned over to these men of limited interests and experience still more of the powers of government.

Where their interests are involved—cutting taxes for the well-to-do, turning our natural resources over to private companies, chipping away at TVA with Mr. Dixon and Mr. Yates—the men in the Cabinet and the White House have been highly effective.

But where human interests are concerned—the interests of the young and the old, the workman, the farmer and the little fellow—where the need is to wipe out poverty, or to build schools and hospitals, to clear slums, even to distribute the Salk vaccine—there no one leads.

And when all the world read with dismay Mr. Dulles' boasts about how close he had brought us all to atomic war, the President of the United States said that he had not had time to read it!

Now, I respect Mr. Eisenhower's good intentions. I have even been accused of undue moderation toward his administration. And certainly the Democrats in Congress have constantly rescued the Republican President from his own party.

Everyone shares in sympathy for the circumstances which have created a part-time Presidency. But we cannot understand—and we will not accept —turning the government over to men who work full time for the wrong people or a limited group of people.

And the plain truth is that this situation would get worse, not better; because what influence the President has with the Republican leaders in Congress has depended on his running again.

But from here on the future of Republican leaders will depend not on Mr. Eisenhower, but on the Republican heir apparent, Mr. Nixon. And the Vice-President seems to sail downwind no matter which way the wind blows.

These are stern facts. To ignore them is perilous. They are the reasons America's human needs go today unmet. Nor will they be met so long as the President is not master in his own house.

I firmly believe that America does not want to rest on dead center, that it wants—fervently—to move forward again to meet these needs. And I firmly believe that a leadership that will ask Americans to live up to the best that is in them will carry us across the threshold of the New America that now opens before us.

I think America wants to be called on to build the schoolrooms and train the teachers our children so desperately need.

I think America wants to be called to clear away the slums and bring basic decency to millions of American families.

I think America wants to attack relentlessly the vast realm of human pain, and lift from those hit by serious accident or illness at least the added burden of grinding debt.

I think America wants to give to the lives of people when they grow old the dignity and meaning they yearn for and deserve.

As I have in the past, I will lay before you, in as full detail as a campaign permits, proposals for meeting our needs. And we will talk soberly about their cost and ways and means of approaching them in a responsible manner.

Most of all we want peace. Whatever we can do here at home will be meaningless unless the world is such that what we do can endure.

When we are spending $40 billion a year for defense, when the peace the Republicans boast about looks more fragile by the moment, when the hydrogen bombs and the guided missiles are multiplying, when Communist influence is spreading among restless millions, when we can lose the cold war without firing a shot, then I say that most of all America is anxious about peace and security.

It is not enough to pile pact on pact, weapons on weapons, and to totter dangerously from crisis to crisis. There must be a call to war against the poverty, the hunger, the nothingness in people's lives that draws them to Communism's false beacon.

We must guide the hopes of mankind away from the blind alleys of extreme nationalism or bogus Communist internationalism. We must turn them instead to an ideal of partnership between the nations in which disputes are settled by conciliation, not violence, and in which the weapons of death are limited and controlled. We Americans have never been and we will never be a nation content just to count today's blessings.

We have confidence in ourselves, confidence that we can build what we have to build, grow as we have to grow, change as we must change, and play our full part in the making of a New America and a better tomorrow for ourselves and all mankind.

Our plan for twentieth-century man is not just for his survival, but for his triumph.

If I were to attempt to put my political philosophy tonight into a single phrase, it would be this: Trust the people. Trust their good sense, their decency, their fortitude, their faith. Trust them with the facts. Trust them with the great decisions. And fix as our guiding star the passion to create a society where people can fulfill their own best selves —where no American is held down by race or color, by worldly condition or social status, from gaining what his character earns him as an American citizen, as a human being and as a child of God.

So I say let us be up and doing, probing ceaselessly for solutions of today's problems and the new ones tomorrow will find on our doorstep. And if you share my view, the Democratic view, that this election is a summons to a sleeping giant, then I hope you will join us to make that summons clear and strong on election day—and help us march forward toward the New America.

II

FOREIGN POLICY, DEFENSE
AND THE H-BOMB

1. Foreign Policy

2. H-Bomb

3. Draft, Disarmament and Peace

4. Foreign Aid

I

Foreign Policy

H-BOMB, DEFENSE AND FOREIGN POLICY
●

I have often confessed that I am a frustrated newspaperman. So you will understand the personal feelings that crowd in upon me as a renegade journalist turned politician rises to address this austere society.

Yet I have never thought that my transformation from newspaperman to politician involved very radical changes. After all, newspapermen—and especially editors—have much in common with politicians, though you may not perhaps be as ready to acknowledge this resemblance as we are. We all have messages to put over. We all deal in words. At our worst we all falter in the face of temptation to dissemble and deceive. At our best we all like to think that we elevate the national discourse and clarify the issues of our age.

But if we are going to rise to this high responsibility, we must have the information on which sound judgment is based. I know that you gentlemen are much concerned about improving the quantity and quality of the information the nation gets about the great issues of our time. I know something about the good work of your Freedom of Information Committee, and I was pleased to hear its praise from Congressman Moss for helping strengthen the awareness in federal agencies of the "public's right to know." The American people are in your debt for these efforts.

But the very need for a Freedom of Information Committee points to a danger. Government secrecy, as your president, Mr. Kenneth Macdonald, has said, has become "entrenched behind a host of statutes and

Address to American Society of Newspaper Editors, Washington, April 21, 1956.

regulations." Indeed, one of the most serious criticisms I would make of this administration is that it has had so little respect for the public's right to know. We have to rethink the whole question of governmental secrecy, for without facts democracy dies at the roots. And we have not only been denied facts we ought to have, we have all too often been deliberately, intentionally misinformed. We have been sold rather than told. That is a long and dangerous step toward being told what we are permitted to think.

Peace and security are the nation's most important business. Yet nowhere has our government told us less and kidded us more. It has used foreign policy for political purposes at home. Unwilling to admit its failures, it has been unwilling to take us into its confidence. Reverses have been painted as victories. And if the administration has not succeeded in misleading the enemy, it has succeeded wonderfully well in misleading us.

When the Eisenhower administration first came to power, there was considerable talk about "operation candor"—they were going to tell us the facts of international life and national defense. But since then "operation candor" has been replaced by "operation bromide"—by vague and comforting assurances to allay anxiety and persuade us that we were comfortably ahead in the armaments race and had the love and esteem of our fellow men.

Was Secretary Dulles informing us or misleading us when he told a House committee on June 10, 1955, that the Soviet Union was "on the point of collapsing"? Was he giving us the facts when he said last November 29 that "we have the initiative, very distinctly" in the Middle East and in South Asia? Was he serious when he told the Senate Foreign Relations Committee as recently as February 24 that the free world is in a stronger position than it was a year ago and that the new Soviet economic and political challenge was a confession of failure? Was he the responsible Secretary of State of the greatest power in the world when he recently boasted that he and the President had conducted the nation three times to the brink of war and then averted catastrophe by his own peerless statesmanship?

We must do better than this. Underlying every other freedom, especially freedom of the press, is the freedom to know, to know the facts, especially the facts about our own prospects for life or for death.

Given the facts, Americans will not retreat in confusion or dissolve in terror, but will respond with determination to do whatever is necessary to assure the nation's safety.

And it is about some of the things which I think we must do and not do to ensure the nation's safety that I want to talk with you today.

Let me commence with a speech President Eisenhower made to this society here in Washington on "The Chance for Peace" exactly three years ago. It endorsed the principles which had guided American policy since 1945 under President Truman; it placed the blame for the fears that gripped the world squarely on the Soviet government, and Stalin, who had died a few weeks earlier; and it held out to the new Soviet rulers a chance to work with us in building a hopeful future for mankind. You hailed it in your papers as the authentic voice of leadership in the new administration. Your reporters described the response as one of "universal acclaim."

What has happened? What has gone wrong since that speech?

But, first, let us try to recall hurriedly the context of that speech— what our position was three years ago when it was delivered.

You will recall how, in one act of constructive statesmanship after another, President Truman's administration met the postwar challenges and crises.

The United Nations and a new international order came into existence with tireless American encouragement.

Western Germany was forged into a strong nation, with a democratic constitution and a self-supporting economy.

Japan was re-established with a humanitarian constitution dedicated to the arts of peace.

In 1947, when Russian power threatened the Eastern Mediterranean, the Truman Doctrine was proclaimed and Greece and Turkey were saved.

Berlin was saved by decisive action to break the blockade.

Then there followed in dramatic succession the Marshall Plan—a bold act of statesmanship that revived the economy, the self-esteem and defenses of Western Europe, to their benefit and ours; President Truman's Point Four Program, which gave new hope to the underdeveloped nations and underprivileged peoples of the world; the North Atlantic Treaty Alliance, which confronted Russia in the West not only with economic strength but the military potential of the great coalition.

Those were great, creative years in American foreign policy. Years of achievement. Years of success.

Then, in 1950, war came to Korea. A psychopathic Stalin challenged world democracy and the United Nations. Under the decisive leadership of President Truman, that threat was stopped in its tracks. The United

Nations was saved and a third world war was prevented.

This is a record in foreign affairs that we, as Americans, can all be proud of, regardless of party. In those years we confidently, courageously took the political and the moral leadership of the free peoples of the world. Compare that extraordinary outburst of creativity with the sterility of the past three years—a sterility which even the exuberance of Mr. Dulles' slogans cannot disguise.

We desperately need today a rebirth of ideas in the conduct of our foreign affairs. I would urge you, three years after that speech by the President, to think a little about America's position in the world today.

Is the United States more secure or less than it was three years ago?

Are our relations with our allies stronger or weaker? Is the mounting criticism of the United States, from Britain and France and Iceland and Turkey, in the West, to Japan and Formosa and Pakistan and Ceylon, in the East, really without foundation and justification?

Does our Secretary of State enjoy the trust, the respect and the confidence of the peoples and governments of the free world?

Is the moral position of the United States clear and unambiguous and worthy of us and our real aims? Is the image of the United States one that inspires confidence, respect and co-operation?

Do you think we are winning or losing ground in the competition with the Communist world?

I very much hope that the President will address himself to these vital questions when he speaks to you tonight. For these are the vital questions of our day. And the fact that such questions must be asked three years after his speech of 1953 shows, I fear, what all the world has discovered—that our admirable sentiments mean little when unsupported by positive and sustained action. Virtuous words are easy, but they are no substitute for policy.

The fact is that that speech never really served as a guide to policy. The tone it set found few echoes in what the President or the Vice-President or the Secretary of State and the Secretary of Defense did in the months that followed.

This is too bad. Our position in the world, I believe, would have been vastly different had we followed the guide lines laid down here before this society three years ago.

Now, where are we today—at this period of an extraordinary age which has witnessed the coincidence of three revolutions:

1. The technological revolution that has split the atom, devastated distance and made us all next-door neighbors.

2. The political revolutions that have liberated and subjugated more peoples more rapidly than ever before in history.

3. The ideological revolution, Communism, that has endangered the supremacy of Western ideas for the first time since Islam retreated from Europe.

It is against this background of violent, sudden change in all directions that the drama—or melodrama—of foreign policy must be played. This is a time of change in world affairs. The peoples sense it, even if the statesmen don't, for the peoples are, in a deep sense, forcing change. No one knows just where these changes will lead.

The administration has been slow to respond to this new mood. The Russians, on the other hand, have exploited it adroitly. Their objectives, we are told almost every day, have not changed. Of course they haven't. No one said they had. The Soviet rulers frankly state that their goal is a Communist world. But they have changed their approach; and we have not changed ours.

I seem to recall a slogan from 1952—something about "It's time for a change." It is indeed time for a change—in a number of ways—especially in foreign policy. Our old policies are no longer adequate in the new situation. At least they are not if reports from all around the world are to be believed, and I think they are. From every corner of the globe your reporters are saying what has been apparent for a long time—that U.S. policy is rigid, unimaginative and fails to take advantage of new opportunities. And the realities of our situation bear little resemblance to the press releases.

I do not propose to chronicle here the whole long list of tension points in the world today. We know their names: Israel, Algeria, Formosa, Indochina, and Indonesia, Kashmir, Cyprus, and now the whole NATO area.

What is more basic and ominous and infinitely harder for us to accept is that in these last three years the United States has come dangerously close to losing, if indeed it has not lost, its leadership in the world—economically, militarily, and worst of all, morally. On all three of these fronts we have manifestly lost the initiative—and that is the prelude to the loss of leadership itself.

It is tragic irony that the people of America, who believe more firmly and fervently in peace and human freedom than anyone else, are not recognized as their sympathetic friend by the millions of mankind who are struggling out of the poverty and squalor and colonial bondage of ages. Instead it is Communist imperialism which has enslaved scores of millions in a decade which is usurping the role.

And only a few years back we seemed to those people the hope of the earth. America had gained freedom itself through revolution against European colonialism. Our great documents, from the Declaration of Independence to the Atlantic Charter, had spoken the aspirations of independence and growth. Our own colonial policies had been generous and forbearing. Our great leaders had affirmed the ideals of freedom with an eloquence that had won the allegiance of men and women everywhere. It was to us that new nations instinctively looked for sympathy, for support and for guidance.

Yet today, in the great arc from North Africa through Southeast Asia, the Russian challenge is developing rapidly and with great flexibility and force. Everywhere people seeking a short cut to raise their own standards of life are told that the Soviet Union alone has mastered the secret of converting a peasant economy into a modern industrial state in a single generation.

In the meantime, we, whose position is fundamentally decent and honorable and generous, have so mismanaged ourselves of late that we must now try to prove that we love peace as much as the Russians, and are as concerned with the problems of economic development and national independence as they are. It is fantastic but true.

Today the peoples of the proud, poor, new nations can find little in official United States policy which seems addressed to them and their problems, little which holds out promise of contributing to their social and national self-fulfillment.

Why is this?

It is compounded of many factors. One is the price we have been paying ever since the bomb was dropped on Hiroshima. The world is on edge and wants to blame somebody for not being able to sleep at night. And since America dropped the first bomb on Asians, and then the Japanese fishermen were burned, America has been unfairly suspected of caring precious little about Asians and peace.

False and unfair as this is, we contribute to it in many ways.

On the one hand, we exhort the world about the virtues of the United States. On the other hand, most of our official dealings seem to be in terms of military threats, military alliances and military values. During the 1952 campaign, General Eisenhower and Mr. Dulles talked loosely about the liberation of the satellite countries. Since then the administration has noisily "unleashed" Chiang Kai-shek, huffed and puffed about Indochina, threatened massive atomic retaliation, and scolded, boasted and bluffed—while at the same time presiding over the reduction of our armed strength. And all this has been more visible outside the United States than inside.

At a time when the new leadership in Russia has been very successfully playing on the universal desire of people everywhere for an end of the cold war tensions, the administration has clung stubbornly to its military emphasis on pacts, foreign aid, trade and international exchanges of all kinds. Much of the world has come to think of us as militarist, and even a menace to peace. In a survey last year in Calcutta people thought the United States more likely to start a war than Russia in the ratio 19 to 1.

Also, on the question of colonialism the administration has done nothing to evolve a reasoned and sound American position, linked to our own traditions as well as to respect for our friends and a due concern for world stability. In the absence of a rational attitude, we have floundered, trying to be all things to all people and thereby antagonizing everyone.

We have persisted in construing the Communist threat to the underdeveloped world as essentially military. For people hungering after economic growth, we offer SEATO and place a defense effort ahead of the struggle against poverty. For people hungering after national independence, we offer little more than a policy of insensitive arrogance—witness the official derision of the Bandung Conference and the clumsy reference to Goa.

We had earlier this month, at Mr. Dulles' press conference on April 3, a pitiful summation of all this—and a revealing commentary on the cause of so much of it. Asked to comment on the present state of the reputation of the United States in the world, Secretary Dulles answered, and I quote from the *New York Times* report, that he "agreed that the United States was being criticized all over the world, but concluded that this was a fine 'tribute' to the United States because it proved nobody was afraid to criticize us."

This, of course, is dangerous nonsense. For what this criticism reflects is the infinitely sterner, more ominous fact that we have lost the moral initiative—and the rest of the world knows it.

Equally sobering is the realization that we are also losing the military advantage. Three years ago the United States had a clear margin of military superiority in the field of air-atomic power—in the production of the new weapons and in our capacity to deliver them. Today we have lost that margin of superiority.

It was, of course, inevitable that when the Soviet Union built its stockpiles to a certain level the fact that we retained a lead in the number of weapons would lose significance, and that an atomic stalemate might require us to develop more conventional forces. But it was not inevitable that we should fall behind in our air strength and in weapon development.

I trust I've made it clear that armed might should not stand as the symbol of our foreign policy. But military power is diplomacy's indispensable partner during this period when the ramparts of peace are still to be built and genuine arms control is still in the future.

To summarize: Three years ago this nation was looked to by all the free world as equipped by faith, history, accomplishment and authority to lead the peoples of the world to the promised land of security and peace. That is no longer the case. And we must squarely face the fact that there is no time to lose in re-examining and in redefining our policy to meet the challenge of today.

I know well the willfulness of the forces which affect the conduct of a nation's foreign policy. I make no pretense that there are one or two or three sure steps which would solve our problems. Wars may be won by secret weapons, but there are no secret weapons which will guarantee peace.

But I recognize the obligation to measure criticism by affirmative suggestion. So let me make some suggestions which are inherent, I think, in what I have said.

First of all, a decent respect for the opinions of others is still a basic requirement of a good foreign policy. Foreign policy is not only *what* we do, it is *how* we do it. The wisest policy will be poisonously self-defeating if mishandled. Smugness, arrogance, talking big are poison. Impulsive, abrupt actions create the impression that we are impulsive and abrupt. The restoration of composure, confidence and an impression of knowing-what-we-are-about is thus of first importance.

We want to be recognized not as bold, but as prudent, and that rules out boasting about brinks and the like. We want to be recognized as sensitive to the implications of modern warfare, and that rules out talk of massive retaliation. We want to be recognized as responsible, and that rules out trying to reconcile the irreconcilable wings of the Republican party. We want to be regarded as reasonable, and that rules out nonsense about the imminent collapse of the Soviet system. And we must reveal that craving for peace which is the true heart of America.

Second, I believe we should give prompt and earnest consideration to stopping further tests of the hydrogen bomb, as Commissioner Murray of the Atomic Energy Commission recently proposed. As a layman I hope I can question the sense in multiplying and enlarging weapons of a destructive power already almost incomprehensible. I would call upon other nations, the Soviet Union, to follow our lead, and if they don't and persist in further tests we will know about it and we can reconsider our policy.

I deeply believe that if we are to make progress toward the effective reduction and control of armaments, it will probably come a step at a time. And this is a step which, it seems to me, we might now take, a step which would reflect our determination never to plunge the world into nuclear holocaust, a step which would reaffirm our purpose to act with humility and a decent concern for world opinion.

(After writing this last week down south, I read last night in Philadelphia that the Soviet Union has protested a scheduled H-bomb test. After some reflection I concluded that I would not be intimidated by the Communists and would not alter what I had written. For this suggestion is right or wrong and should be so considered regardless of the Soviet.)

Third, we should seriously consider basic revision of our method of giving aid; specifically, we should, I think, make greater use of the United Nations as the economic aid agency. We should try to remove economic development from the arena of the cold war. We believe, to be sure, that anything which strengthens economic growth, national independence, human welfare and democratic processes will improve a nation's resistance to the virus of Communism. But our first purpose is human betterment, and anything else is a by-product.

Also, if we propose to make economic aid most effective, we will have to stop demanding that recipient nations pass loyalty tests, and stop using our money to bribe feeble governments to set up rubber-check military pacts which will bounce as soon as we try to cash them. Rather we must convince the peoples of the underdeveloped world that we want no dominion over them in any form, and that we look forward to the end of colonialism in the world.

I don't believe we have explored all possible uses of our agricultural surpluses as raw materials of diplomacy. Surely there are ways of using our abundance, not as an embarrassment but creatively as part of a comprehensive plan of foreign assistance.

There is, too, the vast potential in peaceful use of atomic energy. It will be our ultimate ironical failure if the Soviet Union rather than the United States should provide the underdeveloped needful nations with atomic power. Our mastery of the atom, our willingness to make it mankind's public utility, should be one of our greatest contributions to human betterment.

I emphasize again, however, that all the bushels of wheat and the nuclear reactors and dollars in creation will do us little good if they seem only to be the bait with which a rich but uncertain nation seeks to buy protection for itself. If our attitude is wrong, no amount of money can do the job; and if our attitude is right, less money will go further.

These poor nations have discovered that poverty, oppression and disease are not the immutable destiny of man. They mean to improve their lot and quickly—by the methods of consent, our Western way, if possible. But if they can't, they will turn away from us—to forced labor and forced savings, the totalitarian way—because they mean to industrialize one way or another.

If the United Nations administered economic development funds supplied by its members, it would strengthen international co-operation and the United Nations. It would remove economic development from the arena of the cold war. It would permit objective priorities on the needs of various backward sections of the world. It would stop competitive bidding. And if contributions were apportioned according to the existing formula, for each dollar contributed by the United States two dollars would be contributed by other UN members.

And, finally, it would involve the Soviet Union in responsible international co-operation all over the world. As it is now, there is nothing to prevent Russian penetration anywhere on a unilateral basis to serve its separate ends.

The Soviets refused to participate in a similar arrangement when we proposed the Marshall aid program in 1948. But that was Joseph Stalin —of now dishonored memory. And if his heirs should similarly reject multilateral economic assistance, the implications would be clear to all the world.

In this connection, a first step in this direction might well be taken in the Middle East, it seems to me. We all welcome the good news that a partial cease fire agreement has been arranged.

But there are many tasks ahead, of course, before any genuine peace in that area can even be foreseen. Without reciting them here, let me just suggest that a co-ordinated attack on poverty in the Middle East might well be a profitable field for a United Nations economic program such as I have suggested.

Finally, it seems to me that any aid program we devise will be effective only as it expresses a healthy relationship between free and self-respecting peoples. We must show that we care about others in the world. not as bodies we would hurl into the military breach, but as men and women and children who we hope will live lives of dignity and fulfillment.

So long as we overmilitarize our international thought and statement, so long as we picture the differences between Russia and the West as part of a great military contest, hot or cold—for so long will our efforts prove futile and our motives suspect. For there is little about that struggle which penetrates the minds and hearts of the people of Asia or Africa.

Let us, rather, rally the nations for a world-wide war against want. And let us then—for men do not live by bread alone—identify what we do in the world with the one export which we can offer as no one else can. I mean liberty, human freedom, independence, the American idea—call it what you please—which is more precious and more potent than guns or butter.

For from the word "go"—which is to say, from our very first national statement in 1776—America spoke for freedom in terms so inspiring, so sublime and so inexorably appealing to men's consciences that the Old World was shaken to its foundations. Tyrannies dissolved; hope sprang up like a fresh breeze; movements of liberation mushroomed. This was the greatest foreign aid program in history and no one has ever improved on it or ever will.

We have drifted and stumbled long enough. It is time to restore the true image of America, once so well known and well loved, which gave birth to the Declaration of Independence and the Four Freedoms —a nation marked, not by smugness, but by generosity; not by meanness, but by magnanimity; not by stale conservatism and a weary reliance on dollars and arms, but by broad vision and moral and social passion.

It is time to regain the initiative; to release the warm, creative energies of this mighty land; it is time to resume the onward progress of mankind in pursuit of peace and freedom.

FOREIGN POLICY

•

I want to talk with you about the most serious failure of the Republican administration. I mean its failures in conducting our foreign policy. For, although its failures have been serious here at home, in serving the cause of peace they are far more serious.

From a speech at Cincinnati, Ohio, October 19, 1956.

I'm not going to spend much time on the Secretary of State, Mr. Dulles. Under our Constitution, the President conducts America's relations with the rest of the world, and he is responsible for them, and for his Secretary of State.

But I cannot refrain from commenting on Mr. Dulles' special contribution to our public life—you might almost call it Mr. Dulles' one new idea. I mean his habit of describing every defeat as a victory and every setback as a triumph.

We would all be better off with less fiction and more plain speaking about our foreign affairs.

The Republican candidate has a list of successes he likes to recite. And let us acknowledge such successes as we have had and be thankful for them.

But there is, unfortunately, another list.

This other list shows that Korea is still divided by an uneasy armistice line and still costs us hundreds of millions of dollars in economic and military aid.

The richest half of Indochina has become a new Communist satellite, and, after loud words and gestures, America emerged from that debacle looking like a "paper tiger."

Communism and neutralism have made great gains in Ceylon and Burma and Indonesia in the past year or so.

In India, which may be the key to a free Asia, we will have had four ambassadors in three and a half years—provided the administration gets around to filling the vacancy which has existed since last July. And that is a very poor way of showing our concern for the second largest and one of the most influential countries in the world.

In Western Europe, when the idea of a European defense community collapsed, we heard no more about Mr. Dulles' threatened "agonizing reappraisal," and meanwhile the declining influence of NATO has stirred widespread concern.

The Cyprus dispute has gravely disturbed the relations between three of our valued allies. Yet, so far as I can discover, we have been of no help in settling that dispute.

Iceland is insisting on the withdrawal of our forces from the key base we built there.

America's relations with its oldest and strongest allies, Britain and France, are more fragile than they have been in a generation or more.

And the Republican candidates say that "all is well," that Communism is "on the run," that "American prestige has never been higher," that peace is secure!

I do not mean to criticize the compromises that have been made. But, I severely criticize this effort to mislead the people, to describe an armed truce as peace, to gloss over serious difficulties, to obscure the grim realities, to encourage the people not to know the truth.

Now, what are the realities?

We live at a watershed of history—and no man knows in what direction the elemental forces that are loose in the world will turn.

This much is plain: the West, so long the dominant force in world affairs, has now gone on the defensive, drawing back little by little from positions long established in the rest of the world, particularly in Asia and Africa.

At the same time the Communist sphere has been growing, as it welded Communist ideology to modern technology to forge a powerful weapon for expansion.

And there is a third area or group—of peoples who have recently won or who are struggling to win independence, to gain control of their own futures, to escape from poverty, to win a place for themselves in the sun.

Though we have great influence—as much as any other power, or more —we can no more, alone, control the forces at work than we can make the seas do our bidding. For our power, like all power, is limited. We are rich, but there are only 168 million of us and we have 2.5 billion neighbors. Our power is necessarily in conflict with the power of others who do not share or only partly share our aspirations.

The end of this conflict cannot be foreseen, nor the victor. History knows no sure things! But we do know that we have not been doing well these past few years.

We need to be called to labor, not lulled with rosy and misleading assurances that all is well. Leadership which fails in this is leadership to disaster.

Yet a few nights ago the Republican candidate sought to make political capital out of a crisis that could engulf the world. Wars have begun over matters of far less moment than the Suez dispute—for the canal is a lifeline of the world.

I have refrained until now from commenting on the Suez crisis. But the Republican candidate has introduced it, in a highly misleading way, into the campaign.

A week ago he came before that so-called press conference on television arranged by advertising agents of the Republican campaign evidently more for adulation than for information. He announced that he had "good news" about Suez.

But there is no "good news" about Suez. Why didn't the President tell us the truth? Why hasn't he told us frankly that what has happened in these past few months is that the Communist rulers of Soviet Russia have accomplished a Russian ambition that the czars could never accomplish? Russian power and influence have moved into the Middle East—the oil tank of Europe and Asia and the great bridge between East and West.

When the historians write of our era they may, I fear, find grim irony in the fact that when Russian power and influence were for the first time being firmly established in the Middle East, our government was loudly, proudly proclaiming our victorious conduct of the cold war and the President reported good news from Suez.

This reverse was not inevitable. I cannot remember any other series of diplomatic strokes so erratic, naïve and clumsy as the events of the past few years through which Russia gained welcome to the Near and Middle East.

The trouble is that neither there nor anywhere else has the administration shown any real capacity to adjust its policies to new conditions. Three and one-half years have passed since Stalin's death. It is now fourteen months since the Geneva Conference at the Summit. And I ask the Republican candidate to tell us of a single new idea that has emerged from Washington for meeting the new Soviet challenge.

Instead of fresh ideas and creative thinking about the great struggle of our century, our approach to world affairs has remained sterile and timid. It has remained tied to old methods, old thinking, and old slogans.

It won't work.

I believe that the President knows this. I think it was this realization that led him, three years ago, to think seriously of forming a new political party. For the central fact is that the leader of the Republican party cannot possibly deal with the problems of today's world! Does that sound startling? If the President called now for the action which is needed in the conduct of our foreign affairs, it would split the Republican party right down the middle—with the election only three weeks away. For the Republican party has been hopelessly divided over foreign policy ever since the League of Nations battle and the triumph of the isolationists thirty-five years ago.

The right to criticize—fairly, honestly, responsibly—is deeply rooted in the American political tradition. We cannot deal intelligently with problems unless we first recognize that they exist and ask ourselves what mistakes we made. Honest self-criticism is still the not-so-secret weapon of democracy.

There goes with criticism a clear responsibility to state a constructive alternative. What will a Democratic administration do to meet the challenge of our times? How will a Democratic foreign policy differ from the Republican?

Let me say at once that I have no slick formula, no patent medicine, to cure our problems. The difficulties which face American policy makers in all parts of the world are deep-rooted and complex. And this will continue to be so regardless of who wins in November.

But it is equally true that there is much that can and must be done.

First, our entire military establishment must be re-examined to determine how we can best build and keep the forces we need for our national security.

There is much evidence that we don't have the military establishment we need now. The problem is, I think, less one of money than adjusting our thinking and planning to the revolutionary changes in weapons and in world relationships.

Among other things, I have suggested a restudy of the Selective Service system to find, if possible, some better way of meeting our manpower requirements than the draft with its rapid turnover.

I have been surprised that the Republican candidate has reacted so violently to my suggestion that this ought to be considered. I thought that it was hardly open to debate that we need to find a better way of obtaining the mobile, expert, ready forces we need in the handling of the new weapons and the new tactics of the new military age. My suggestion, I should like to add, was aimed at stronger, not weaker, forces.

Second, I would propose—in view of the unthinkable implications of modern warfare—that disarmament should be at the heart of American foreign policy.

I have suggested that we could initiate a world policy of stopping the exploding of large-size nuclear bombs—the H-bombs. This appears to be a safe, workable, reliable proposal.

I call your attention to the fact that the other powers concerned have stated that they are prepared to act.

If we bring this about, all mankind will be the gainers. And I think that we, the United States, should once more assert the moral initiative which many wait and pray for to break out of the deadly deadlock which has blocked all progress toward arresting the arms race that imperils us all.

I am not dogmatic about this or any other proposal. Honest and open debate may suggest better ways. I think the heart of the issue is a weighing of different risks. The risk of permitting the arms race to continue unchecked seems to me most serious in view of the furies that have been unleashed. The world has had the last great war that civilization can afford. We must, if it is humanly possible, make a fresh start for peace and reason.

Next, I propose that we act, and act fast, to meet the challenge of the underdeveloped countries. The choices these nations make may well determine the future of freedom in the world.

We must do better than we have been doing. And the way to begin is to understand the hopes and fears of these peoples and to work out with them new relationships based on co-operation and trust and mutual respect. I might add that, in my judgment, the spirit of these new relationships is more important than an expansion of economic aid.

I believe, too, that we must breathe new life into the Atlantic Community. NATO has served and will, in some form, continue to serve an essential need for collective security. But let us recognize clearly that co-operation in defense implies and demands co-operation in political and economic affairs as well. And in the neglect of these matters lies the explanation of the declining vigor of the alliance.

Again, I propose a fresh approach to the problems of world economics. This new approach must take account of the almost universal desire for economic development and must rest solidly on the principle of mutual advantage. I am more interested in practical measures than in global plans for solving all the world's problems by some master stroke. I am impressed, for example, by the possibilities of a world food bank as a means of aiding economic development and putting our agricultural surpluses to work.

Finally, and perhaps most important, I propose that the American government deal openly, frankly, honestly with the American people. I think that in the name of security we have been sweeping far too many things under the rug. We have drawn a paper curtain between the American people and the world in which they live.

It is easy—and when mistakes have been made or reverses suffered, it is all too inviting—to use the excuse of security for not telling the people the facts.

Some things must be kept private, but a democratic government must never forget that it is no wiser and no stronger than the people whose servant it is. The sources of information are the springs from which democracy drinks. These waters alone can nourish and sustain us in a free way of life.

This seems to me the central point, for unless the American people are given the information required to understand the needs of this tempestuous, turbulent period when the swirling waters of three revolutions are converging, they will listen to demagogues who promise quick and easy solutions. But the ideological revolution of Communism cannot be met by quick and easy solutions. Neither can the political revolution of the oppressed and the newly independent peoples, or the historic revolution of technology throughout the world.

I ask your support not because I offer promises of peace and progress, but because I do not. I promise only an unending effort to use our great power wisely in pursuing the goal of peace—in full knowledge that as soon as one problem is brought under control, another is more than likely to arise.

I ask your support not because I say that all is well, but because I say that we must work hard, with tireless dedication, to make the small gains out of which, we may hope, large gains will ultimately be fashioned.

I ask your support not in the name of complacency, but in the name of anxiety.

We must take the world as we find it and try to work in the direction of peace. We did not want a contest with world Communism, but the contest is upon us. The first and in some ways the most difficult task is to recognize this fact of contest. General George Marshall used to warn his colleagues not "to fight the problem," but to deal with it. That is good advice for us today. If we try to hide the problem from our own minds, to pretend that it does not exist, to wage our political contests here at home in terms of misleading promises, we will be fighting the problem and we will fail.

Peace is our goal. I am in politics as a result of a personal decision to do what I could to help in building a peaceful world. That decision carried with it an obligation—the obligation to talk sense, to tell the truth as I see it, to discuss the realities of our situation, never to minimize the tasks that lie ahead.

I don't know whether that is the way to win in politics, but it is the only way I want to win. For, if you entrust me with the responsibility of power, I do not want to assume that power under any false pretenses nor do I want you to labor under any misapprehensions. To do otherwise would be not only to mislead you, but to make my own task almost impossibly difficult, for I would not have won your support on the basis of an understanding between us about the needs we face and the demands they place upon us.

To achieve such understanding seems to me to be the true function of politics.

MIDDLE EAST

•

The President spoke to you about the Middle East crisis last night. The networks have been good enough to accord me time to speak tonight, and I want to tell you how this crisis came about, this crisis which is so threatening to peace and to our interests in this strategic area.

This matter should be above politics—if anything can be a few days before election—because all Americans suffer from any failure of our foreign policy, and from war anywhere in the world; for in this hydrogen age war is contagious.

I have only a few moments, so let me hastily sum up the central facts of the situation. I can find no better way to do this than to read you a sentence from a special dispatch from Washington in today's *New York Times:* "The United States has lost control of events in areas vital to its security. This is the main conclusion of serious and well-informed men here tonight concerning the United States' role in the Middle East crisis."

The condition which confronts us is stark and simple—our Middle-Eastern policy is at absolute dead end. And the hostilities going on tonight in which Israel, Egypt, Britain and France are involved reflect the bankruptcy of our policy; and they have given the Soviet Union two great victories.

The first Communist victory is the establishment in the Middle East of Russian influence.

The second Communist victory is the breakdown of the Western alliance. This has been a supreme objective of Soviet policy since the end of the Second World War.

As the climax, the United States finds itself arrayed in the United Nations with Soviet Russia and the dictator of Egypt against the democracies of Britain, France and Israel.

A foreign policy which has brought about these results—which has benefited Communism and has cut our own country off from our democratic friends—is a foreign policy which has failed.

A telecast at Buffalo, November 1, 1956.

And, at a time when the uprisings in Poland and Hungary are opening the Soviet world to freedom, the strategic Middle East is opening to Communist penetration.

I have three points to make tonight.

The first is that this series of failures could have been averted—that they were in great part the result of ill-considered and mistaken policies of this administration.

The second is that this administration not only made mistake after mistake in its Middle Eastern policy, but has withheld the consequences from the American people.

The third is that there are many things which might have been done in the past year to avert war in the Middle East.

The Middle East is one of the most important strategic areas in the world. It has three-quarters of the world's known oil reserves, and it controls the land, sea and air communications linking three continents. All nations which have sought world domination have wanted to control the Middle East.

When President Eisenhower came to office in January, 1953, Communist influence in the Middle East was at a low ebb, and the area was more free of violence than it had been in years.

Things changed.

Secretary of State Dulles began by giving General Naguib—Colonel Nasser's predecessor—a pistol as a personal gift from President Eisenhower. The fateful symbolism of this gift was not lost upon Israel or the Arab states. It was the token of a new policy called "impartiality" between the Arab states, on the one hand, and, on the other, the new democracy of Israel whom they had vowed to destroy and whom we and the United Nations were pledged to defend.

Following this, and pursuing the new policy of trying to build up Nasser as a bulwark of stability in the Middle East, the United States pressured the British to evacuate their great military base along the Suez Canal without making any provision for international control of the canal.

Then Mr. Dulles fanned the flames of ambition, nationalism and rivalry in the Middle East with the so-called Baghdad Pact as a defense against Russia. But its military advantages were far outweighed by its political disadvantages. And it was particularly offensive to Nasser—the very man whom we had been trying to build up.

Then in 1955 Colonel Nasser's negotiations for some arms from the United States bogged down in everlasting haggling. And so he negotiated an arms deal with the Communists.

We not only failed to stop the introduction of Communist arms into the Middle East, but we refused to assist Israel with arms too. We also refused to give Israel a guarantee of her integrity, although we had given such guarantees to others.

And in the meantime we dangled before Colonel Nasser the prospect of financial aid for building a great dam on the Nile.

In time, the bankruptcy of the Eisenhower administration's policy began to become evident even to Mr. Dulles. It became clear that Colonel Nasser was not a bulwark of stability, but a threat to peace in the Middle East. Thereupon President Eisenhower abruptly and publicly withdrew the aid he had led Colonel Nasser to expect.

As anyone could have foreseen, Colonel Nasser promptly retaliated by seizing the Suez Canal.

Driven by our policy into isolation and desperation, Israel evidently became convinced that the only hope remaining was to attack Egypt before Egypt attacked her. So she took her tragic decision.

Here we stand today. We have alienated our chief European allies. We have alienated Israel. We have alienated Egypt and the Arab countries. And in the UN our main associate in Middle Eastern matters now appears to be Communist Russia—in the very week when the Red Army has been shooting down the brave people of Hungary and Poland. We have lost every point in the game. I doubt if ever before in our diplomatic history has any policy been such an abysmal, such a complete and such a catastrophic failure.

It is bad enough to be responsible for such a disastrous policy. I think it is almost worse in a democracy to try and conceal the truth from the people. But this is what the Eisenhower administration has done systematically with regard to the situation in the Middle East.

It was only a few days ago—on October 12—that President Eisenhower himself said in a political telecast: "I've got the best announcement that I think I can possibly make to America tonight. The progress made in the settlement of the Suez dispute this afternoon at the United Nations is most gratifying. . . . It looks like there's a very great problem that's behind us."

And the next day Vice-President Nixon gave his views. "We have kept the peace," Mr. Nixon said, "and it appears that Mr. Eisenhower's tolerance and wisdom and leadership will serve to avert armed conflict in that part of the globe."

Either the President and the Vice-President did not know how serious the situation was in the Middle East or they did not want the American people to know—at least, not till after the election.

And only last Sunday—just four days ago—Mr. Dulles said in a television interview that the United States, Britain and France "have developed a common policy, and I think it's amazing the degree to which we have had a common policy. . . . And the fact that there are certain minor superficial difficulties as to details about just how you handle tolls or how much is going to get paid to Egypt and how much isn't doesn't detract from the fact that we have a common policy."

The "superficial difficulties" of Sunday became pretty formidable by Tuesday, when Britain and France broke with the United States in the UN.

This is but a brief summary of this sorry chapter, but I think it demonstrates that the Middle Eastern policy of our government in Washington was blundering and mistaken, and that it has compounded its blunders by a consistent policy of misleading the American people into believing that all was well in the world.

But the question now is what to do about it.

A year ago, on Armistice Day, 1955, I discussed the Middle Eastern crisis in a speech at Charlottesville, Virginia. I pointed out the growing dangers in the area and suggested that United Nations guards should patrol the areas of violence and collision and keep the hostile forces apart. I said that it would take decisive acts of statesmanship to head off all-out war in the Middle East.

As late as the summer of 1955 at the Geneva Conference, if the President had taken an insistent stand against the shipment of Communist arms to Egypt, I am convinced that the Communists would not have risked arming Egypt as they have.

Had the Eisenhower administration taken a firm stand in the Middle East, had it aided Israel with arms and territorial guarantees, we might, I believe, have been able to prevent the present outbreak of hostilities. And if this government had not alternately appeased and provoked Egypt, I do think that we would command more confidence there and in the Arab world.

But all this is behind us. What can we do now to deal with the crisis in front of us?

It appears that President Eisenhower is now approaching this problem by trying, very properly, to check military action. But this will only restore the situation that existed up until four days ago. I say this betrays a complete lack of understanding of the crisis. The situation of four days ago was one when events were threatening strangulation of our European allies, the destruction of Israel, and increasing control of the Middle East by Communist Russia. Just to restore that situation would be another setback for the West.

I would not condone the use of force, even by our friends and allies. But I say that we now have an opportunity to use our great potential moral authority, our own statesmanship, the weight of our economic power, to bring about solutions to the whole range of complex problems confronting the free world in the Middle East.

The time has come to wipe the slate clean and begin anew. We must, for a change, be honest with ourselves and honest with the rest of the world. The search for peace demands the best that is in us. The time is now. We can no longer escape the challenge of history.

THE PRESIDENT DOES NOT RUN THE STORE

•

Well, the campaign is drawing to a close.

Tomorrow the politicians will at last fall silent—and the people will speak.

You have had to endure quite a lot of political talk already—and not all of it has been honest talk.

There is no reason why political talk shouldn't be honest. After all, politics is the means by which a democracy solves its problems. Nothing is more essential than responsible politics to the successful working of a free state.

One thing Estes Kefauver and I have tried to do in this campaign is to practice responsible politics—to talk sense to the American people.

We have not tried to kid you, to fool you or to deceive you.

But it seems to me that the effort to kid the people, to fool the people, to deceive the people has been the essence of the Republican campaign.

I think you here in Minnesota know what I mean, since you have to suffer more than your share of Republican deceit.

I don't know whether it is a compliment or an insult that so much should have been concentrated in Minnesota.

Secretary Benson came to Minnesota and said that farm prices would rise—and they promptly fell. They have fallen 3 per cent in Minnesota in the last month.

And President Eisenhower came to Minnesota and said that the price

From a speech at Minneapolis, November 5, 1956.

adjustment period was over—and a few days later, the Department of Agriculture reported the fourth straight monthly decline in farm prices.

And Vice-President Nixon came to Minneapolis and said—and I quote —"There will be no war in the Middle East." And you know what happened then.

When the Republican leaders say these things, you can draw only one of two possible conclusions. Either they don't know any better—in which case they shouldn't be in responsible office. Or they do know better—and have decided not to tell you the truth—and in this case there is even less argument for them.

On the national level, of course, they are overflowing with a pretense of virtue. Even the Vice-President has put away his switchblade and now assumes the aspect of an Eagle Scout. But, down at the grassroots, the Republicans haven't changed.

The President continues to act as if he had a monopoly on all the virtue in the country.

How do you reconcile the fact that the President holds forth in the pulpit while his choirboys sneak around back alleys with sandbags?

The answer must be clear. The answer is that the President doesn't know what's going on—and doesn't care enough to find out.

The answer is that the President doesn't run the store.

When Mr. Eisenhower doesn't run the store at home, it's bad enough. You know what it has meant for the farmers. The Eisenhower policy has been to throw the American farmer onto the mercy of the market, the weather and the processors—and four more years of this kind of farm relief will relieve the farmer of everything he has.

But when he doesn't run the store in foreign affairs, it is disastrous. Presidential negligence on questions of peace and war may plunge the whole world into the horror of hydrogen war.

And negligence is precisely what we have been getting.

Let us remember President Eisenhower's role in the making of our Middle Eastern policy. In February of this year, the Eisenhower administration started to send a shipload of tanks to Saudi Arabia. This was at the time that we were declining to send arms to Israel. When protests mounted, the administration first embargoed the shipment. And while it was trying to decide what to do, where was the President of the United States? On February 17, he played golf. On February 18, he shot quail. On February 22, when the ban was finally removed, the President shot eighteen holes of golf.

If the confusion over the Saudi Arabian tanks proved anything, it proved the need for some firm direction of our Middle Eastern policy. But did we get it? Toward the end of March, as the situation grew worse, Prime Minister Eden sent the President an urgent message about the Middle East. But some days later the President, when asked about it in a press conference, said, "I can't recall how long it has been since I have had a letter from the Prime Minister."

On April 9, the White House announced: "The President and the Secretary of State regard the situation [in the Middle East] with the utmost seriousness." On the same day, the President began a golfing vacation in Georgia. When Egypt took over the Suez Canal in July, the President was at Gettysburg; on August 4, when the *New York Times* called the Suez impasse the "gravest challenge to the West since Berlin and Korea," the President played golf. On August 11, when Britain rejected Communist proposals for a Suez conference, the President played golf. As the crisis mounted toward the end of August, the press reported that the President, now at Pebble Beach, California, "golfed happily at one of America's toughest and most beautiful courses."

Now, no one begrudges the President his recreation, but peace is a full-time job.

Obviously something has gone out of our foreign policy in these Republican years—consistency, boldness, magnanimity—some instinct for leadership in a free world that begs for rescue from anarchy and disintegration.

Even the seizure of the Suez Canal by Nasser caught us by surprise, for our Secretary of State—whose erratic treatment of Egypt had precipitated this seizure—was out of the country and the President was on holiday.

And now we hear that the President of the United States first learned of the British and French ultimatum in the Middle East from newspaper reports!

And even when we have been forewarned, we have still failed to act.

Our government knew about the impending arms deal between Egypt and the Communists a full month before President Eisenhower met with the Russian leaders at Geneva. Yet our President made no protest of this action which gave the Russians the foothold in the Middle East which the czars vainly sought for three centuries. If there had been less hearts and flowers and more firm talk at Geneva, the Communists would never have dared to arm Egypt, and the tragic war that is raging in the Middle East today could have been avoided.

The last four years have presented America and the free world great opportunities to exploit weaknesses in the Communist ranks and advance the cause of peace.

But this administration has failed to take advantage of them.

The death of Stalin caught us off guard.

The uprisings in East Berlin caught us off guard.

The uprisings in Poznań caught us off guard.

The most recent revolts in Poland and Hungary obviously caught us off guard.

When there was a danger of the Communists taking over Greece and Turkey, our government responded with the Truman Doctrine.

When the Russians threatened our position in Berlin, President Truman reacted with the dramatic Berlin Airlift.

And when Communist aggression in Korea challenged the principle of collective security, President Truman led the free world in halting Red aggression in its tracks. His response was immediate; it was decisive; and it was courageous.

President Truman knew that the United States cannot survive in the world of today without friends and allies. He treated our allies with courtesy and respect. And when the United States gave its word, that word was kept.

But in the last four years we have treated our allies and our would-be allies as junior partners. We have bullied them and threatened them. And, what is worse, we have deceived them. The result is that we have lost our closest and best friends, and what friends have we won? Russia? Egypt? Of course not.

The keystone of our American foreign policy has been our co-operation with the great Western democracies of Great Britain and France, and now that foundation of the free world strength is crumbling.

What we have had in the last four years is a rigid policy for foreign affairs and a flexible policy for farm prices!

I say it's time for a change!

This has been a critical week for America. Our foreign policy has collapsed in the Middle East. Our Western alliance with Britain and France, upon which our peace and security have largely depended, has been shaken to its foundations. With the West divided, Russian tanks are now crushing freedom in Hungary, and there is war in the world—in a very dangerous place.

This is the harvest of the errors of the Eisenhower-Dulles policy, which have been pointed out time and again, step by step.

After the war, Stalin, at the peak of his power, tried to break into the Middle East, but was stopped cold in Iran and again in Greece and Turkey by a brave and courageous President—Harry Truman. Now, thanks to our incredible backing and filling, the Egyptians have turned to Russia, and

Soviet influence is spreading through the Middle East and exploiting the new Arab nationalism. Meanwhile, our democratic friend, Israel, has lashed out in desperation.

Russian influence in the Middle East is sinister enough; but more alarming is the fact that there has now opened up a fateful split between the United States, on the one hand, and England and France, our oldest and strongest allies. While we deplore the use of force by Britain and France in Egypt, we dare not overlook the fact that the preservation of our security, the preservation of NATO, indeed the preservation of the United Nations itself, will depend on re-establishing the basis of mutual confidence between us.

And America reached the summit of foolishness when Mr. Nixon hailed the collapse of our alliance as "a declaration of independence that has had an electrifying effect throughout the world."

The separation of the United States from its democratic allies may delight Mr. Nixon. And it also certainly delights the Russians, who have been trying to do just that for many years. But it is a deadly threat to our future security.

Moreover, with the Atlantic Alliance divided and incapable of firm and united action, the Red Army has rolled back into Hungary to crush the rebellion. Fumbling and uncertain, the Eisenhower administration even delayed the efforts of other nations to help the people of Hungary in the United Nations.

Early yesterday morning I sent President Eisenhower a telegram urging that we call upon the United Nations Peace Observation Commission for possible help to Hungary and other satellites struggling for their freedom. The commission would send teams of United Nations observers into those parts where their presence might help the situation. I am gratified that the Eisenhower administration has embodied this suggestion in the resolution which it submitted Sunday afternoon.

It is ironical that Marshal Zhukov is directing the Red Army's effort to crush freedom in Hungary—the same Marshal Zhukov of whom President Eisenhower said last year that he was "intensely devoted to the idea of promoting good relations between the United States and the Soviet Union." That was at the Geneva Conference, which Mr. Eisenhower ended by assuring us that the Russian leaders "desired" peace as much as we did.

For years the Eisenhower administration has been assuring us periodically that all is well, that we have the Communists on the run, that America is master of the situation, that our prestige was never higher, and that there was nothing that another slogan, another brink, another trip by Mr. Dulles, or another smile by Mr. Eisenhower couldn't cure.

We have had enough of this nonsense. For three years we have been retreating, confidence in America has been declining, and now our world policy is in ruins.

While everyone respects Mr. Dulles for his heroic efforts, and everyone, especially old friends like myself, lament his illness at this critical period and earnestly hope for his speedy recovery, let us face the fact that in the future we must have more candor and realism.

It is clear that the events in Eastern Europe and the Middle East are symptoms of a vast new upheaval in the balance of world power. This upheaval is a challenge both to the free world and to Communism. At this point we are losing out in this contest. We are losing because our friends and allies no longer trust our leadership. And we are losing because our foreign policy is rigid and stale.

Re-establishing the solidarity of the West is our most urgent business. The United States, as it has been said so well, is the one great power that can take the lead to save the world from this creeping anarchy and disintegration. Mr. Dulles obviously can't do it. Mr. Nixon applauds the collapse of our alliance. President Eisenhower appears to be isolated, uninformed and interested only intermittently.

But we must get on with the job before our margin of time runs out. And there may not be much left.

When we think of the Hungarians and Poles sacrificing their lives to gain their country's freedom, we must prize more than ever our own good fortune in being able to choose our government freely at the polls.

The ballot is only a scrap of paper—but it is still the most powerful weapon on earth. It is the shield and the sword of the free. It is your children's insurance policy. It is our key to the future.

The ballot, like all our other rights and liberties, was won in hard struggle. John Adams said in 1777, "Posterity! You will never know how much it cost the present generation to preserve your freedom! I hope you will make good use of it. If you do not, I shall repent in heaven that I ever took half the pains to preserve it."

I do not think we have forgotten what freedom cost those men. An American election is a reaffirmation of our freedom. It is proof anew of our enduring trust in the wisdom of the people.

And when we vote tomorrow—and vote Democratic—it will be our vote of confidence in the wisdom—not of one man or one group of men—but in all the people.

2

H-Bomb

TESTING BOMBS

●

Thirteen years ago this winter I was in Italy. The war was on, and it was a wet, cold, ugly winter. It seems a long time ago. Our men were fighting their way up a valley whose name none of you will remember—unless you happened to be one of them. The Liri Valley it was called. It was a place of mud and blood.

I served through the war as personal assistant to the Secretary of the Navy, Frank Knox. And what I saw and experienced there in the Liri Valley was nothing very out of the ordinary—as war goes and as I saw it in the Pacific and Europe. I mention it now only because I think it was there that I decided that after the war I would do what I could to help in mankind's eternal search for peace.

For it was painfully clear, there in the Liri Valley, that civilization could not survive another world war. And that fact became even more clear on the day the first atomic bomb exploded over Hiroshima.

So, after the war, I served for several years with the American Delegation in the early days of the United Nations, both here and abroad. And that, in turn, led me into politics and brought me here tonight.

And now, thirteen years after that decision in Italy, I come before you to talk a little about the cause which means more to all of us than anything else—the cause of peace.

We are caught up today, along with the rest of the world, in an arms race which threatens mankind with stark, merciless, bleak catastrophe.

It is no accident that the instinct of survival which is common to all men and all nations is slowly but surely compelling the most practical and

From a television broadcast from Chicago, October 15, 1956.

hardheaded statesmen to give increasing heed to the prevention and abolition of war. In this nuclear age peace is no longer merely a visionary ideal, it has become an urgent and practical necessity.

Yet we dare not tear down and abandon armed deterrents to war before we devise and secure other and more effective guaranties of peace. Great and law-abiding nations cannot leave their security at the mercy of others. We have learned that unilateral disarmament invites rather than deters aggression.

So, until there is world-wide agreement on an effective system of arms reductions with adequate safeguards, we must maintain our national defense and the defenses of the free world.

I am not only opposed to unilateral disarmament, but I have felt that we should not put too many of our eggs in the atomic and hydrogen basket. I have felt that we should try to maintain sufficient balance, flexibility and mobility in our armed strength so that we will not be forced to choose between appeasement and massive retaliation, between too little and too much, between submission and holocaust.

Effective disarmament means universal disarmament—an open world, with no secret armies, no secret weapons, and, in effect, no military secrets. Responsible statesmen do not risk the security of their countries for hopes which may prove illusory or promises that are worthless.

But nations have become so accustomed to living in the dark that it is not easy for them to learn to live in the light. And all our efforts to work out any safe, reliable, effective system of inspection to prevent evasion of arms agreements have been blocked by the Soviet rulers. They won't agree to let us inspect them; we cannot agree to disarm unless we can inspect them. And the matter has been deadlocked there for eleven years.

Yet if we are going to make any progress we must find means of breaking out of this deadly deadlock. We must come forward with proposals which will bear witness to our desire to move toward and not away from disarmament.

It was with this hard, urgent need in mind that I proposed last spring that all countries concerned halt further tests of large-size nuclear weapons —what we usually call the H-bombs. And I proposed that the United States take the lead in establishing this world policy.

I deliberately chose to make this proposal as far removed as possible from the political arena. It was made four months before the party conventions. It was made to the American Society of Newspaper Editors. It was made without criticism of the present administration's policy for H-bomb development.

Others—and not I—have chosen to make this proposal for peace a political issue. But I think this is good. After all, the issue is mankind's survival, and man should debate it, fully, openly, and in democracy's established processes.

Because there has been only negative criticism of this proposal from the Republican candidates in this campaign, I want to return to it tonight.

These are the reasons why I think the time is ripe and there is an insistent necessity for the world to stop at least the testing of these terrifying weapons:

First, the H-bomb is already so powerful that a single bomb could destroy the largest city in the world. If every man, woman and child on earth were each carrying a 16-pound bundle of dynamite—enough to blow him to smithereens and then some—the destructive force in their arms would be equal to the force of one 20-megaton hydrogen bomb, which has already been exploded.

Second, the testing of an H-bomb anywhere can be quickly detected. You can't hide the explosion any more than you can hide an earthquake.

As the President has stated: "Tests of large weapons, by any nation, may be detected when they occur." In short, H-bomb testing requires no inspection. We will know it when it happens anywhere, and by studying the dust from that explosion we can even determine what progress the other country has made.

This means that, if any country broke its pledge, we would know it and could promptly resume our own testing.

Third, these tests themselves may cause the human race unmeasured damage.

With every explosion of a superbomb huge quantities of radioactive material are pumped into the air currents of the world at all altitudes—later to fall to earth as dust or in rain. This radioactive "fallout" carries something called strontium 90, which is the most dreadful poison in the world. Only a tablespoon shared equally by all members of the human race would produce a dangerous level of radioactivity in the bones of every individual. In sufficient concentration it can cause bone cancer and dangerously affect the reproductive processes.

Prior to the atomic age, radioactive strontium was practically nonexistent in the world. Careful studies show that today all of us—all over the world —have some of it in our bones. It enters our bodies through the foodstuffs grown in soil on which the bomb dust has fallen.

I do not wish to be an alarmist and I am not asserting that the present levels of radioactivity are dangerous. Scientists do not know exactly how dangerous the threat is. But they know the threat will increase if we go on testing. And we should remember that less than half of the strontium created by past tests by Russia and the United States has as yet fallen to earth from the stratosphere.

So it seems clear to me that, if it is humanly possible, we should stop sending this dangerous material into the air just as soon as we can!

Fourth, the dangers of testing by three powers are ominous enough, but there is another reason why it is important to act now. Last May, Mr. Stassen, the President's disarmament assistant, said that within a year the "secret" of making the hydrogen bomb would spread around the world. Think what would happen if a maniac, another Hitler, had the hydrogen bomb. And imagine what the consequences would be of a dozen nations conducting hydrogen bomb tests and wantonly thrusting radioactive matter into the atmosphere.

These are the reasons why it seems to me imperative that a world policy of stopping these tests be established at the very first possible moment.

I proposed last April that the United States take the initiative toward this end by announcing our willingness to stop these tests, "calling upon other nations to follow our lead," and making it clear that, unless they *did*, we would have to resume our experiments too. That was my proposal. It was simple. It was safe. It was workable.

And since that time both Russia and Great Britain have declared their willingness to join us in trying to establish the kind of policy I have suggested.

What are we waiting for?

It seems to me that we should lose no more time in starting to make the most of what appears to be a better climate for progress in this field.

Therefore, if elected President, I would count it the first order of business to follow up on the opportunity presented now by the other atomic powers. I would do this by conference or by consultation—at whatever level—in whatever place—the circumstances might suggest would be most fruitful.

In the meantime—and frankly because bitter experience has proved that we cannot rely even on the firm agreement of one bloc of world powers— we will proceed both with the production of hydrogen weapons and with further research in the field.

Now, just a word about the opposition that has developed to this proposal from the President, Mr. Nixon and others.

It is said that it does not provide for "proper international safeguards." This misses the point, for, as the scientists have long explained and the

President has himself acknowledged, we can detect any large explosion anywhere.

It is said that other countries might get the jump on us. The President implied that we would stop our research while others would continue theirs. But I have made no such suggestion, and obviously we should not stop our research. We should prepare ourselves so that, if another country violated the agreement, we could promptly resume our testing program. And I am informed that we could be in a position to do so—if we have to—within not more than eight weeks.

The President even implied that the proposal would somehow reduce or curtail our power to defend ourselves. It would not. We would give up none of our stockpile. We would even add to it, as needed, for current production. We could continue to develop and test smaller nuclear weapons. We should continue our research and development work on guided missiles, for the defense of our cities and for use in the field.

I call your attention to the fact that many distinguished scientists, as well as other leading figures in this country and the world, share my views. On this matter the beginning and end of wisdom do not lie in the White House and its advisers.

But what I find most disturbing is the President's desire to end this discussion which so deeply concerns all mankind. He said at his press conference last week that he has said his "last word" on this subject. We cannot sweep the hydrogen bomb under the rug. But we can discuss it seriously and soberly, with mutual respect for the desire we all have for progress toward peace. This is one subject on which there cannot be, there must not be, any last word!

This is one matter on which the defeatist view that nothing can be done must be rejected. I say that something can be done, that the deadlock can be broken, that the world can make a new beginning toward peace.

And, finally, I say that America should take the initiative; that it will reassure millions all around the globe who are troubled by our rigidity, our reliance on nuclear weapons, and our concepts of massive retaliation, if mighty, magnanimous America spoke up for the rescue of man from the elemental fire which we have kindled.

As we all know, in the world in which we live only the strong can be free. Until we succeed in abolishing the institution of war itself, we must have, together with our allies, the strength to deter aggression and to defeat it if it comes. That is the first condition of peace in an armed world.

One last word.

The search for peace will not end, it will begin, with the halting of these tests.

What we will accomplish is a new beginning, and the world needs nothing so much as a new beginning.

People everywhere are waiting for the United States to take once more the leadership for peace and civilization.

We must regain the moral respect we once had and which our stubborn, self-righteous rigidity has nearly lost.

Finally, I say to you that leaders must lead; that where the issue is of such magnitude, I have no right to stand silent; I owe it to you to express my views, whatever the consequences.

I repeat: This step can be taken. We can break the deadlock. We can make a fresh start. We can put the world on a new path to peace.

May He who rules us all give us the courage and patience, the vision and the humility we will need, and grant His blessing to this work.

H-BOMB: PROGRAM PAPER

●

Several days ago President Eisenhower submitted to the public a statement on the H-bomb, containing reasons why, in his opinion, test explosions should not be discontinued.

In order to help the public get at the truth of this controversy between the President and myself, I am herewith making public a memorandum which examines in detail Mr. Eisenhower's claims and the evidence he advances to support them.

I believe this study speaks for itself, but, in summary, I would call attention to these principal points:

1. It seems to me that, after all Mr. Eisenhower's arguments are shaken down, the net effect is one of hopeless defeatism. The President is not only hostile to new constructive thinking by others on how to save the world from hydrogen devastation, but he quite clearly has no creative or hopeful ideas of his own in this critical field. As in so many other fields, the President simply offers another do-nothing solution.

2. The President presented his document to America and the world as an official statement, but it appears to be no more than a campaign pamphlet. And even as a political paper it is remarkable for misstatements and distortions.

Statement issued from Washington, October 29, 1956.

These misrepresentations are dealt with separately later in this paper, but special attention should be called to the President's effort to create the impression that my proposal would somehow weaken the defenses of the United States. He knows better, or at least should know better. Along with other Democrats, I have been doing all I can to keep the Eisenhower administration from slashing our defense establishment during the last four years. It ill becomes the President to talk about dropping our guard when his administration has consistently put dollars ahead of defense. I want to see our defenses strengthened, not weakened, and there is nothing in my H-bomb proposal inconsistent with this object.

And let me add this. My proposal for an agreement to stop the test explosion of the big H-bombs would, if accepted, strengthen the military position of the United States in relation to Russia. We are ahead of the Russians in H-bomb development, the President himself has said, and to freeze the H-bomb race at the present level would prevent the Russians from catching up with us, so long as the agreement is in force in this very important weapon.

3. The President seems insensitive to the danger of radioactive fallout from H-bomb explosions. Despite the growing doubts of eminent scientists, the President assures the people that they need not be concerned over the consequences of this dangerous fallout.

4. The President seems content to rest the future security of the United States exclusively on nuclear weapons. I call attention to the fact that only a few years ago we thought the A-bomb guaranteed us military dominance. Yet the Russians quickly overcame this advantage. Our H-bomb advantage—such as it may be—is already disappearing. In a short time Russia will have as many H-bombs as we have, or more. What then? The President has no answer. My own answer is that when we reach a point where terror cancels out terror we must turn to diplomacy and new ideas to find a way toward nonnuclear peace. That is what I seek and that is what I intend to fight for.

5. Most of the world is sitting on the sidelines as helpless spectators of this nuclear race. Let us not overlook them, for with them may lie the future peace of the world and therefore our security. ·The President's exclusive concern with a possible hot war must not be permitted to blind us to the cold war and the contest for the allegiance, or at least the independence, of those vast areas of the world in Asia, the Middle East and Africa which would like to look to the United States for leadership, for peace and security.

Finally, I would commend to Mr. Eisenhower and to all of our people what Albert Einstein is reported to have said when he was asked what kind of weapons would be used in World War III. His reply was: "I don't know what terrible weapons will be used in World War III. But I do know the weapons which will be used in World War IV—they will be sticks and stones."

The modern technology of war has put humanity on the road back to the cave.

I believe that humanity has some higher and nobler destiny.

The President issued several memoranda in support of his statement calling for the continuance of exploding large H-bombs.

I will take up the major points included in these memoranda in some detail.

The administration has attached to the President's statement a chronology of disarmament negotiations since the Second World War. In his statement, the President refers to the fact that "in the past two years alone, the Soviet Union has rejected no less than fourteen American proposals on disarmament."

The reason that the administration's efforts to obtain general disarmament have all foundered has been the Soviet rejection of a system of adequate inspection. Yet, as this record shows, the administration has repeatedly refused the opportunity to take a concrete step toward disarmament in the one area where inspection is automatic—the explosion of large nuclear weapons.

Moreover, this chronology omits the fact that on September 6, 1955, the President's Special Assistant for Disarmament informed the United Nations Disarmament Subcommittee that the United States would offer no alternative arms control program other than the so-called "open skies" formula—a plan originally proposed by the Truman administration. Thus no progress whatever has been made toward disarmament by the Eisenhower administration. Indeed, the President reported to Congress on July 15, 1955, that "no one has been able to devise a better . . . plan than the Baruch Plan of 1946."

We are thus stalled on dead center by the rigidity of the Eisenhower administration's approach to the problem of disarmament.

Nevertheless, the President "remains," as he says, "hopeful that . . . the reality of significant disarmament will come to pass." That hope is, of course, shared by all Americans.

But no one who knows the facts is very hopeful that the Soviet Union will agree to a system of adequate on-the-spot inspection within the foreseeable future. For any system of on-the-spot inspection would require a repudiation of that secrecy which is indispensable to the Communist tyranny that governs the Soviet Union.

The President, it appears, offers no solution to the disarmament stalemate. For so long as this stalemate persists, what can we expect of the future?

With no restrictions upon the testing of nuclear and thermonuclear weapons, the atomic monopoly is now possessed by three nations—the United States, the Soviet Union, and Great Britain.

Mr. Stassen, President Eisenhower's disarmament adviser, said five months ago that within a year the secret of making the hydrogen bomb would spread all around the world.

Once this occurs, once other industrialized nations—such as France, Japan, Argentina, Czechoslovakia, Eastern Germany, India, or even Communist China—begin to make and explode nuclear and thermonuclear bombs, the threat to peace will be immensely multiplied. So long as the H-bomb remains a monopoly of the three nations which now possess it, a continued military standoff may ensure a long period in which such bombs are not used as instruments of war. But once the possession of these bombs spreads to other countries, which is unlikely for technical reasons if testing is prohibited, the danger of their aggressive utilization will have increased manyfold. When that day comes, an irresponsible dictator, a maniac, another Hitler, might well detonate the world.

Once the bomb is possessed by countries in addition to the present three, the problem of its control will have become infinitely more difficult. Few nations will willingly remain "have-not" atomic nations when their neighbors possess the means to destroy them. And once the bomb is in the possession of a number of nations, all wantonly shooting poison into the atmosphere, the danger of impairing or destroying human life through bomb explosions is enormously increased.

With a sense of urgency impelled by these considerations, I proposed a halt to the tests of large hydrogen weapons. Under that proposal, the stopping of these tests would have the following results:

1. It would greatly delay if not render it impossible for any nation not now producing bombs to make such bombs. This point the President's statement wholly ignores.

2. It would end or greatly diminish the rate of cumulative pollution of the atmosphere that is a real and present danger to the health of men, women and children now living—as well as to future generations.

3. It would break the disarmament stalemate that now exists. It would be a concrete step toward ending the arms race in the one area where headway can be made because we can detect violations at once.

The administration's statement either ignores or distorts these propositions.

It completely ignores the practical certainty that, if testing is not stopped, the atomic "have-not" nations will possess the bomb within a short time. It denies categorically that H-bomb testing presents perils to the health of humanity.

It implies that for the United States to enter into an agreement for the discontinuance of H-bomb tests would jeopardize our superiority in these weapons and would endanger our national security.

To support its position, the administration marshals a confusion of omissions and misstatements, as the following point-by-point analysis of the key points of the white paper makes clear.

Analysis

President's memorandum: "Three: In the light of these facts, your government has kept enlarging its stockpile of nuclear weapons, and has continued development and testing of the most advanced nuclear weapons. The power of these weapons to deter aggression and to guard world peace could be lost if we failed to hold our superiority in these weapons."

The President's memorandum is misleading in implying that we must necessarily continue to explode nuclear weapons in order to maintain our "superiority" in those weapons. To the extent that the United States, by agreeing to stop large H-bomb explosions, would affect its progress in the development of nuclear weapons, the Soviet Union would also affect its own progress. To the extent that the Soviet Union could continue the research and development of all such weapons short of testing, the United States would also continue such research and development. To the extent that we have "superiority"—or as it is expressed elsewhere in the President's statement, a "commanding lead"—we would safeguard that superiority, that lead, by reducing the charges of a Russian technical breakthrough that might assist them to close the gap.

I repeat again that an agreement to end explosions of large H-bombs should not apply to the testing of smaller nuclear weapons; the United States, as well as other powers, would be free to go forward with such tests.

President's memorandum: "Four: The continuance of the present rate of H-bomb testing—by the most sober and responsible scientific judgment —does not imperil the health of humanity. On the amount of radioactive fallout, including strontium 90, resulting from tests, the most authoritative judgment is that of the independent National Academy of Sciences. It reported last June, following a study of 150 scientists of the first rank, that the radiation exposures from all weapons tests to date—and from continuing tests at the same rate—is, and would be, only a small fraction of the exposure that individuals receive from natural sources and from medical x-rays during their lives."

Many outstanding scientists vigorously disagree. Scientists emphasize that no one knows with certainty whether the present rate of H-bomb testing will or will not produce significant damage to millions of people alive today. This is true especially of children; as they mature, the calcium that goes into building up their bones will be contaminated with the fallout of strontium 90 from H-bomb tests.

On this subject, the National Academy of Science reported in June, 1956: ". . . How much radiation will produce a given result, how much can be done to counteract the deleterious effects, these are largely unsolved problems."

Thomas E. Murray, a member of the Atomic Energy Commission, has stated: "We know that there is a limit to the amount of this strontium that the human body can absorb without harmful effects. Beyond that limit, danger lies, and even death.

"The problem has been to fix the limit. It is still an unsolved problem."

The International Commission on Radiological Protection and the British Medical Council warn that the danger level for radioactive strontium should be set not at the level used by the Atomic Energy Commission but at one-tenth that level.

Obviously, the President's statement greatly exaggerates the degree of certainty that is possible on the basis of present scientific knowledge. In addition, in relating its comments to the present rate of H-bomb testing, it gives a wholly false picture of the danger from strontium 90 fallout. The report of the National Academy's committee on pathological effects of atomic radiation, which is the basis for the National Academy's comments on this subject, was prepared in January of this year and its findings are already out of date. Since that time the nuclear monopoly enjoyed by the United States and the Soviet Union is now shared with the United Kingdom—and, as has been earlier pointed out, there is every prospect that within a relatively short time other nations will be producing nuclear weapons.

The Federation of American Scientists Radiation Hazard Committee declared on October 25, "Certain areas of the world may have already passed the 'danger point' in strontium 90 saturation." The committee said Atomic Energy Commissioner Willard F. Libby, official AEC spokesman on fallout hazards, has been "very optimistic in his estimates of the danger to mankind from radioactive fallout."

On Thursday of last week, members of the AEC Research Project at the University of Rochester Medical Center in New York declared President Eisenhower's defense of further H-bomb tests was "confused" and represented an "oversimplification" of the facts of life on the fallout.

Nineteen scientists, including William F. Nieuman, top researcher of the AEC's project at the University Medical Center, specifically took issue with the fallout references President Eisenhower made last Tuesday night in his defense of further H-bomb tests.

The President said the National Academy of Sciences' June Radiation Report declares: ". . . That the radiation exposure from all weapons tests to date—and from continuing tests at the same rate—is, and would be, only a small fraction of the exposure that individuals receive from natural sources and from medical x-rays during their lives."

Actually, the Rochester Scientists declared: "The National Academy of Sciences' report does not say that the levels likely to be reached, if bomb testing continues, are safe . . . there is good reason to fear that they may not be safe." The FAS Radiation Hazards Committee Report, issued in Boston, declared: "It may well be true that in certain areas of the world the strontium 90 hazard has already passed the danger point, to say nothing of the additional production of this material in further tests." The report said strontium 90, which seeps into the human bone, produces blood changes and can lead to cancer, has been steadily descending upon the earth since the H-bomb tests began. The scientists said the strontium 90 concentration is greatest in the soil where calcium is scarcest and the human system, instead of absorbing calcium into the bones, then absorbs the strontium 90.

The FAS group cited Commissioner Libby's own speech in illustrating that certain areas in Wales have strontium 90 concentrations "50 times greater" than the world-wide average. It reasoned that Libby's "maximum permissible level" of strontium 90 intake, while still safer for people in other parts of the world, might be exceedingly critical for low-calcium soil areas like Wales. The scientists also criticized Dr. Libby for basing his standards for permissible dosage on "occupational exposure" as in the case of an X-ray technician, rather than the "prolonged exposure" which people suffer in having radiation in the soil all around them. The FAS group further said that fallout safety levels are being based on the "limited" experience of humans with radium poisoning and a comparison of this with the strontium 90 effects on experimental animals. The scientists pointed to a report by the British Medical Council declaring children's growing tissues are "particularly radiosensitive" and so could not tolerate the same maximum permissible dose level Libby has allotted to humans in general.

The FAS committee also said recent administration references to a National Academy of Sciences Report on Radiation have persistently referred to the Genetics Section of the report and glossed over the Pathological Section. It is the Pathological Section which warns against the strontium 90 hazard caused by H-bomb tests.

And in Pasadena, A. H. Sturtevant, California Institute of Technology geneticist and one of the scientists who had signed the National Academy of Sciences Report on Genetic Effects from Radiation, declared: "The danger from radioactive strontium in fallout is greater than the information available to the committee led us to suppose." Sturtevant recommended that his committee's conclusions on fallout dangers be "revised upward."

Under these circumstances, to issue reassuring statements on the dangers of strontium 90 on the assumption of a "continuance of the present rate of H-bomb testing" is irresponsible. It is tantamount to a public health officer saying that the population of a city need take no precautions against a smallpox epidemic since, for the moment, no more than three cases had appeared, when there was a practical certainty that, if precautions were not promptly taken, the disease would spread to many times that number. And, as a distinguished newspaper columnist pointed out the other day, it casts the United States in a suspicious light by its neighbors. It is like adding a little arsenic to your neighbor's coffee each day, but assuring him that it isn't enough to kill him.

But apart from the fact that the rate of testing will certainly increase, the administration's optimism is misleading for another reason—the supposition that strontium 90 is absorbed uniformly among human beings. This is not true. From the Atomic Energy Commission's own measurements, the people of certain areas where the soil is low in calcium are absorbing a concentration of strontium 90 that is five times above the average. Even if further tests were discontinued, people in those areas would be subjected to radiation from strontium 90 that would exceed by several times their absorption from natural sources.

I repeat that the President's memorandum fails entirely to point out that when it compares the dangers of radioactive fallout from H-bomb tests to the exposure from medical X rays or from natural sources, it is basing its assertion exclusively on a report of the National Academy's Committee on Genetic Effects of Atomic Radiation. This has nothing to do with the really serious danger—the pathological damage from strontium 90 fallout. The President's memorandum leaves out the most important point: pathological damage.

Scientists agree that the genetic damage from bomb tests is of relatively minor concern compared with the pathological damage from strontium 90, which, as has been previously pointed out, is assimilated into the bones, particularly of children, and which can produce blood changes and cause blood cancer.

In attempting to minimize the hazards of the effects of radioactive fallout by comparing them to an individual's exposure to medical X rays, the author of the report even neglects to mention that the National Academy regards the extent of X-ray exposure as itself a possible danger. In fact, in the same chapter of its report, the Committee on Genetic Effects makes specific recommendations for reducing the medical use of X rays.

President's memorandum: "Six: There is radioactive fallout, including strontium 90, from the testing of all nuclear weapons, of whatever size . . . thus, the idea that we can stop sending this dangerous material into the air—by concentrating upon small fission weapons—is based upon apparent unawareness of the facts."

This statement is completely irrelevant. It can be regarded only as a deliberate effort to mislead. The fact is that the amount of radioactive fallout from a single large explosion has been and can be as much as that from a thousand smaller bombs of the Hiroshima size. Essentially all the strontium 90 in the stratosphere comes from H-bombs.

President's memorandum: "Seven: With reference to the Soviet Union: Its sympathy with the idea of stopping H-bomb tests is indisputable. This idea merely reflects the Soviet Union's repeated insistence, ever since discussion of the Baruch Plan in 1946, that all plans for disarmament be based on simply voluntary agreements. Now, as always, this formula allows for no safeguards, no control, no inspection." As to the assertion that an agreement to stop H-bomb tests would allow for "no safeguards, no control, no inspection," the President again disregards the key fact that violations of such an agreement can no more be hidden than an earthquake.

President's memorandum: "Eight: A simple agreement to stop H-bomb tests cannot be regarded as automatically self-enforcing on the unverified assumption that such tests can instantly and surely be detected."

This statement is amplified as follows in Paragraph 22 of the memorandum that accompanies the White Paper: "While the system of long-range detection or monitoring is believed to be as effective as it can be made in the present state of scientific knowledge, it cannot insure the detection of every test irrespective of size, location or type and composition of the weapon tested."

I repeat again for the dozenth time that I have never proposed the prohibition of tests of other than large H-bombs. President Eisenhower himself stated categorically on October 5: "Tests of large weapons, by any nation, may be detected when they occur." The President repeated this statement in substance in his October 23 paper. Therefore, there is no difference of view as to the detectability of the kind of bomb included in my proposal.

We will know if the Russians explode a big H-bomb, and the world will know it too.

3

Draft, Disarmament and Peace

AN ARMED SERVICE OF PROFESSIONALS

•

The issues before the country have emerged much more clearly in these past few weeks, and so has the people's mood—clearly enough, incidentally, that the Republican managers have decided that, while they don't mind a part-time President, they can't stand a part-time candidate.

I want to talk with you tonight about what I think is in some ways a startling and surely a significant thing that has developed in this campaign. It isn't new by any means, and yet I don't believe it has come out so clearly before. We realize more and more that the political lines in this country are now sharply drawn between those who are satisfied with things exactly as they are and those who feel, on the other hand, that there is still a tremendous lot to be done in America and in the world.

And I don't need to fill in the names of the parties, either.

There are only nineteen days left until the election. And so far the Republican candidates haven't made one single new proposal or suggestion for conducting the affairs of this country.

They say, smugly, that they are running on their record. What record? Or maybe I should say: whose record? For the fact is that the Republicans' proudest boast when they return the keys of office next January will be that they left things not too much worse than they found them—thanks, I may add, to a Democratic Congress these last two years.

It isn't just that these Republicans lack new ideas. They seem to despise new ideas. When someone makes a proposal for strengthening America, the automatic Republican response is to call the proposal irresponsible, dishonest, deceitful, theatrical and even wicked. If it has to do with

From a speech at Youngstown, Ohio, October 18, 1956.

farmers, it may even be immoral! And worst of all, afraid to face a new idea, they twist and distort it—until public understanding or discussion becomes almost impossible.

This isn't accident. It is the deliberate design of a political leadership which doesn't want voters to think, which knows, I suspect, its own bankruptcy of new ideas; and knows that its one forlorn hope is to wage the biggest advertising campaign in the history of American politics.

They talk of peace—but they refuse to talk—and try to keep the rest of us from talking—about how we can win the peace.

I have repeatedly said, and I am glad that the Republican candidate now agrees, that there is no difference between the two parties on the goal of a peaceful world. America has no war party, just as it has no peace party.

But there are important differences about what real peace means and about how we can achieve it.

We are all deeply grateful that the guns are stilled and we are not now engaged in a shooting war. And, Republican folklore to the contrary, it wasn't Eisenhower's election but Stalin's death that caused the Communists to end the war in Korea and turn their attention to Indochina, and you know what happened then!

But we know, too, that the uneasy condition that prevails in the world today which we call "peace" is based on a balance of terror, and that's a dangerous foundation.

The world is divided into three camps, the Communist bloc, the free bloc and the uncommitted or neutral nations. The cold war, in its larger sense, is a struggle for the allegiance of those nations which have not yet made their choice between freedom and Communism. Nations to whom economic progress, a better standard of living, is more important than proving how anti-Communist they are to please us—nations who want to know what America is for, not just what it is against. When they do choose, it will tip the scales of the world—and surely history's greatest demand upon this generation is that we throw America's full weight into this crucial balance.

We know that the world is spending something like $100 billion a year for war and defense—several times more than is being spent by government on the health, education and welfare of all the human race put together.

America alone is spending almost $1,000 a year for every family in the United States. In the last three years we have spent three times as much money on defense as in any other three-year peacetime period in our entire history. And I'm astonished that the Eisenhower administration is so proud and pleased and content with this situation.

I am not content. And neither are you. This isn't what we mean by peace. And it calls for a people's decision as to how we are to achieve that true peace which can only come if America leads the way.

I have urged in this campaign that we face up to the great issues which are presented in the great struggle of the twentieth century. They call for strength—and this strength takes many forms. They call for new answers to new problems.

In our struggle for peace we have to think of everything we do from all points of view—our own security, the effect on others—friend, foe or neutral.

It is of our security in a less universal matter that I wanted to speak particularly tonight.

It is a serious subject and I must speak seriously.

We are living in an age of complex new weapons and new military techniques.

It was in this connection that I said earlier in this campaign, before the American Legion convention in Los Angeles, that:

"Many military thinkers believe that the armies of the future, a future now upon us, will employ mobile, technically trained and highly professional units, equipped with tactical atomic weapons. Already it has become apparent that our most urgent need is to encourage trained men to re-enlist rather than to multiply the number of partly trained men as we are currently doing."

I noted in connection with this matter of meeting the increasingly urgent need for experienced and professional military personnel that this may well mean that we will need and want in the foreseeable future to turn to a method other than the draft for procuring such personnel.

This suggestion has been taken by some—and deliberately misconstrued by others—as a proposal for weakening our armed forces. It is exactly the opposite. It is a proposal for strengthening our armed forces.

The point is simply that we already need and will need more and more a type of military personnel—experienced and professional—which our present draft system does not give us. The draft means a tremendous turnover in our military personnel, and a resultant high proportion of inexperienced personnel. There is ample evidence that this inexperienced personnel is not meeting today's needs.

The Assistant Deputy Chief of Staff of Personnel for the Army, Major

General Donald P. Booth, said this to a Congressional committee last May 31:

"The use of the Selective Service, with its short period of duty, causes a heavy turnover of personnel throughout the Army to the detriment of efficiency, unit spirit, economy, and battle worthiness . . . the two-year system is not conducive to economy nor stability."

A total of some 750,000 men will leave our armed forces this year. Simply to give basic training—nothing more—to their replacements will cost the American taxpayer $2.5 billion.

Air Force Chief of Staff, General Nathan F. Twining, testifying before a Congressional committee, condemned this needless personnel turnover in blunt terms—as to both its cost and its damage to our military effectiveness.

"If this trend continues," said General Twining, "there would be more than a 100 per cent turnover in the Air Force every five years. No industry could absorb this rate of personnel turnover. Nor can the Air Force. This rate of turnover would lead directly to an alarming decline in operational effectiveness."

It was such facts that persuaded Senator Mike Mansfield in March, 1955, to conclude:

"An armed service of professionals cannot be built by conscription. As in any profession, there must be a certain amount of incentive. The current situation in the branches of the service gives very little incentive to a young man to make a career out of the Army, Navy, Marines or Air Force."

It was such testimony that persuaded the Democratic Congress in 1955 to pass a career incentive act which resulted in base pay increases of from 7 to 17 per cent for enlisted men. It helped, but it was only a first step.

Every young man who has served in our armed forces knows the incredible waste of our present system of forced but short-term service. He knows the money that could be saved, the new efficiency that could result from a volunteer system which calls on young men not to endure two years of service because they have to, but to choose it—and for a longer period —because it offers advantages that seem to them appealing.

There seems to me every reason for searching out ways of making military service attractive enough that sufficient numbers of young men will choose such service voluntarily and will then remain in the services for longer periods.

By cutting down on turnover we can reduce the present enormous cost of training replacement after replacement. The money that is saved by this reduction in training costs can be used to pay our soldiers, sailors and airmen better salaries, to provide them with improved working conditions and perhaps to offer special bonus inducements for longer service. In this way we can develop a more effective defense, with higher morale, and I believe no higher cost.

Where there are needs for particularly highly trained men, as for example in radar, electronics and other specialties, I think we should consider offering university scholarships which will provide specialized training, in conjunction with a liberal education, to applicants, otherwise qualified, who will agree to spend a specific period in the armed forces.

No one could feel more strongly than I do the imperative necessity of keeping our armed forces at full strength. And I include the necessity of meeting our obligations on this score under the NATO agreements.

What I have proposed, I repeat, is a consideration—from the standpoint of military effectiveness, and from no other standpoint—of what is the best way of obtaining the military personnel we need.

I do add—and I think I speak for every person in America—that we will count it a better day when we find that these military needs can best be met by a system which does not mean the disruption of the lives of an entire generation of young men; which lets them plan their education, and get started more quickly along life's ordained course.

This is, I submit, a matter that should be seriously considered by the American people. The Republican candidates insist that it should not even be discussed, that this isn't the people's business, and that with a military man in the White House things like this can best be left up to him.

Well, I say just this: What is involved here is the security, perhaps the life or death, of this nation. What is involved here is the use that should be made of two years of our sons' lives. What is involved here is whether there should be new ways of more effectively meeting new problems. And I say that these are decisions that must be made not by one man—not by one general—not even by one man as president—but by the American people.

And I say beyond this that these decisions are not to be entrusted to an administration that has now built up a four-year record of rigid refusal to consider new ideas or new ways of doing things—and a four-year record of appalling indifference to human concerns.

THE DRAFT AND DEFENSE*

•

I want to talk to you tonight about the need for enthusiasm and new ideas in our national life.

Like most Americans, I've read some of what that wise New England philosopher, Ralph Waldo Emerson, wrote. I fear I've forgotten a lot of what he said, but I've remembered this: "Nothing great," Emerson said, "was ever achieved without enthusiasm." How true that is! As we look back over the centuries, we can see that nearly all the glorious achievements of mankind, nearly all the best things in our society, sprang from the uncrushable enthusiasm of those who believed in the genius of man, and who believed in the possibility of doing the seemingly impossible. To these enthusiasts, whose optimism often exposed them to scorn and ridicule, we owe so many of the good things of our civilization.

This thought of Emerson's—this tribute to the power of man's ability to master his destiny—came to me again when I heard the President's recent expression of views on war and peace—the area above all others where we need fresh and positive thinking.

I was distressed to see that the President not only had nothing new to suggest for the future, but he seemed resentful over the efforts of others —including myself—to find some more hopeful answers to the problems of life and death that now confront us.

To be more specific, I have said before and I'll say it again that I, for one, am not content to accept the idea that there can be no end to the draft, to compulsory military service.

Let me make it perfectly clear that, as long as danger confronts us, I believe we should have stronger, not weaker, defenses. Ever since Mr. Eisenhower became president we Democrats have fought hard to prevent the administration from putting dollars ahead of defense. The Democrats in Congress forced the administration to reverse itself and restore deep cuts in the Strategic Air Force even during this last session of Congress.

But my point is that the draft does not necessarily mean a strong defense. Conditions change, and no conditions have changed more in our time than the conditions of warfare. Nothing is more hazardous in military policy than rigid adherence to obsolete ideas. France crouched

From a speech at Minneapolis, September 29, 1956.
* (We have deleted discussions of economic issues and the H-bomb treated adequately elsewhere. Eds.)

behind the Maginot Line, which was designed for an earlier war, and German Panzers ran around the end. The Maginot Line gave France a false—and fatal—sense of security. We must not let selective service become our Maginot Line.

What I am suggesting is that we ought to take a fresh and open-minded look at the weapons revolution in connection with the whole problem of recruiting and training military manpower. We may very well find that in the not-far-distant future we not only can but should abolish the draft in order to have a stronger defense and at lower cost. Defense is now so complex, its demand for highly skilled and specialized manpower so great, that the old-fashioned conscript army, in which many men serve short terms of duty, is becoming less and less suited to the skilled needs of modern arms. And it is becoming more and more expensive.

Let me say right here in all frankness that I have no special pride, no conceit, in the suggestions that I have tried to advance. No one will be happier than I if others find better solutions.

Once we start exploring this possibility seriously, new ideas will be forthcoming; that is always the case when men turn their creative energies full time upon a problem. Right now I had hoped to do no more than get this kind of creative thinking started.

And I am distressed that President Eisenhower should dismiss this objective out of hand. If anyone had proposed the abolition of the draft right now, today, the President's attitude would be understandable; indeed, I would share it. But I don't see how we can ever get anywhere against the rigid, negative view that we cannot even discuss the matter, or even look forward to a time when we can do away with compulsory military service. I say it's time we stopped frowning at new ideas and started *thinking* about them!

Peace is not a partisan issue. Every American, Democrat and Republican alike, wants peace. There is no war party in this country; there is no peace party.

And the way to get started on the difficult road to disarmament and peace is not, I repeat, to scorn new ideas.

This negative, defeatist attitude among Republican leaders comes in an unbroken line from the League of Nations fight down to the present. And the fact is that the Republican party has been so divided since the first war and the League of Nations fight that even to this day it cannot conduct a coherent, consistent foreign policy.

But this is not to suggest that the Republican party is any less dedicated to peace than the Democratic party. I'll leave such charges to them. The question is of means, not ends, for both parties are dedicated to peace, however they may differ on how to realize this great objective. I think it is fair to say that, generally speaking, the Republican way has been the narrow, nationalistic one of the low, limited horizon, while the Democratic way has been that of the wide horizon, dotted with the ships and sails of beckoning hope.

One way, of course, is just as patriotic as the other. But in my opinion the Democratic way has been more attuned to the changes, the challenge and surprise, of this ever-changing world and this revolutionary century. And I think this is just as true today as it has ever been.

PEACE

•

I have come here today particularly because I heard about the new World Arms Control Center you have set up here at the university. The people who can build a college are the kind of people who can build the peace. And surely that is the most important building job in the world today.

Your stated purpose at the World Arms Control Center is, as it is reported to me, "to stimulate practical thinking about peace." I want to talk briefly on this point in the few minutes we have here this afternoon.

First may I speak, not presumptuously or ungraciously I hope, a word of warning. I always think, when someone speaks of being "practical" or "realistic," about what seem to me two dangers: One is that in trying to be "practical" we will set our sights too low. We'll never win the peace unless we set our sights mighty high.

The other danger is that we think of our own ideas as "practical" and everybody else's as less practical, or impractical. That, too, would be a blind alley in anybody's search for the path to peace.

There is obviously not the opportunity here this afternoon to explore very deeply into the baffling and imperative subject of peace and disarmament. Let me only, for what little they may be worth, offer you a few of what seem to me the starting points in a practical approach to peace.

The beginning of practical thought about peace, I think, is the complete conviction that war is no longer a practical means of adjusting differences between nations.

From a speech at Fairleigh Dickinson University, Teaneck, New Jersey, October 2, 1956.

War holds no more promise for men of ill will than for men of good will. The mushroom cloud is impartial, falling on just and unjust alike.

And may I say that I consider this not by any means a wholly gloomy fact. It may be the single most hopeful fact of international life today. For when men of ill will see no chance of profit, the threat of war has been greatly reduced.

A second starting point, I think, is the realization that peace is more than the absence of war. Peace is more than an uneasy truce during which armed forces peer anxiously over insecure frontiers, as in Korea today. The peace we want—the peace the world needs—must be far more than this.

The first necessity for peace is the ability to deter possible foes from aggression. We must have enough military force to convince any potential aggressor that what he might possibly gain cannot equal what he will surely lose. So we need a powerful national defense—a strong strategic Air Force, ground forces capable of meeting the complex technical requirements of modern war, a great Navy, etc. And for our defense to be strong it must be geared to preventing the next war, not to the last one.

But I sometimes think that as a nation we become preoccupied with the machinery of defense as an end in itself—or at least we have succeeded in giving that impression to too much of the world outside. We have talked so much about atom bombs and our skill in devising ever more terrible weapons, we have lately put our dealings with other nations so largely on a military basis, that the world has gotten the idea that we think all the problems of our turbulent and revolutionary age are to be solved by the weight of military force.

With a strong, modern defense, we can move on to the real job—the job of organizing the peace. We can't expect to do this overnight. Peace is the building of a community—the slow growth of just and orderly ways of settling disputes—the growing realization that there are no victories in war and that what is common to us all is more advantageous to us all than the excitements over what divides us.

International law is growing, and therefore a just and orderly and peaceful world is growing, a step at a time. Korea was a lesson to would-be aggressors everywhere that international crime does not pay. The Marshall Plan and Point Four were a lesson that international co-operation does pay, that there is a powerful sense of justice and decency at work in international society.

It is because I see the building of a just and peaceful world as an organic process that I attach so much importance to the halting of large-scale nuclear tests by the great powers.

I regret that this administration has not pressed forward along this path to peace as so many have urged—Catholic and Protestant religious leaders, distinguished scientists, prominent educators, yes, and serious politicians!

I regret, also, that it seems to have ignored what appears to be an increasing desire to close the gap between East and West on such subjects as mutual inspection and limitation of armed forces. Surely we should carefully explore these proposals to see whether they were made in good faith and whether they will meet our security requirements. This administration has even withdrawn its own proposals when others indicated a willingness to accept these proposals.

I think it is one of the starting points in a practical approach to peace to recognize the danger of insistence on perfect, foolproof answers. We must always press toward those answers and not be content until we get them. But we cannot afford to reject small gains. But if desire for perfection is one potential enemy of improvement, defeatism is another. That the world has never yet achieved a system of universal and enforcible disarmament surely does not prove that it never will. After all, until a few years ago, the world had never achieved an atomic bomb. As nuclear fission broke the pattern of science, so atomic explosion may break the pattern of history. For in the hydrogen age disarmament becomes not a matter of convenience, but a matter of necessity.

That is why I am so pleased to learn of your work here at Fairleigh Dickinson. As we consider the impossible price of another big war, we may begin to wonder whether the softheaded dreamers are not those who think that disarmament is impractical, and whether the hardheaded realists are not those who demand that we give the search for the means of world disarmament top priority in our conduct of foreign affairs.

We must not deceive ourselves about the implications of enforced disarmament. The price will be high. I do not mean the cost in money. I mean the cost in the readjustment of old habits, of old ways of thought, of national attitudes, and such readjustment would involve an even more tremendous wrench in a totalitarian society like the Soviet Union—perhaps a far greater wrench than there is reason to suppose the Communists are likely to make.

I do not know how as a nation we will answer these questions. I do know that it is not too soon to begin facing them. I can assure you that I can conceive no matter of higher urgency or deserving more sustained and personal executive attention than the search for the abolition of the institution of war.

If peace could be won by rhetoric, it would have been ours long ago. Few commencement speeches in the last decade and probably fewer political speeches have failed to pay tribute to the importance of peace. But unfortunately peace will not be won by wishing for it or by reciting the word. It will be won by men who have the vision to see, and the courage to act.

If I have sounded like a professor, I hope you will remember that I'm really a politician.

But, of course, this is New Jersey, the home of Woodrow Wilson. And so you perhaps know that most professors have a bit of the politician in them, and vice versa. It is said that if you can, do, and if you can't, teach. But I think that if a politician could, he'd teach, and since he can't, he runs for office.

At any rate, I'm running hard—and I hope you'll help me. I'd like to see New Jersey in the Democratic column again this fall. And I think you'd like it, too.

4

Foreign Aid

FOREIGN AID: PROGRAM PAPER*

•

The problem of foreign aid deserves special treatment, for in no area has the leadership of the Eisenhower administration been more confused and ineffective—and in very few areas will our failure so imperil the whole future of freedom in the world.

One-third of the world is today in ferment. Millions of people, long denied the elementary decencies of life, are on the march, seeking to make up in a generation the lost time of centuries. Their goals are the goals of us all—clothing, food and shelter, a chance to earn security in life, an ambition to stand erect and hold their heads high, a hope of giving their children better opportunities than they had themselves, an inarticulate, urgent aspiration for a world squarely based on a recognition of the equal dignity of all human beings.

The question remains whether the peoples on the march will move toward these goals along the road of democracy or whether, in their zeal to make up for lost time, they will rush into new forms of authoritarianism. The answer to this question will greatly influence the outcome of the contest between the free world and Communism.

The Eisenhower administration has stood baffled and helpless before this challenge. It has had no serious policy for the underdeveloped world. It has not taken the lead in bringing about co-operation and understanding between the older nations of Europe and North America and the new nations of Asia, Africa and Latin America. Its so-called aid programs have been largely misconceived. It has expended its energies in brittle military pacts and self-righteous preachments—while Communism and

* Governor Stevenson completed this paper during the last days of the campaign, but because events crowded so fast at that stage, it was never made public. Eds.

neutralism have spread. If we continue the present confused and half-hearted policy, we risk the loss of a third of the world by default.

More than this, such a policy is contrary to our whole genius as a nation. We ourselves were born in revolt against colonialism. We transformed a wilderness of forests and deserts into a land of limitless abundance. Our history and our experience equip us uniquely to be the friend and leader of other countries who share our historic passion for national and social fulfillment. The American Revolution has far more to offer the peoples of the underdeveloped world than the repressive revolution of Communism.

In this spirit we have a great and inspiring role to play in helping younger nations to tackle their problems. Our programs of economic aid are an indispensable—though by no means an exclusive—element in our approach to the uncommitted world. The story of foreign aid under the Eisenhower administration shows in brief compass the bankruptcy of our present policy.

The Importance of Foreign Aid

Over the past four years, we have been spending $4-5 billion a year in one form or another for foreign aid. Though this is but a tenth of what we spend each year for security purposes—and 1 per cent of our annual output of goods and services—it is still big money.

There is good reason for spending this money on foreign aid—if it is spent wisely. Foreign aid should be a major instrument for deterring war and for laying the foundation of peace. It should be a major instrument for maintaining the unity of the Free World, and especially for building constructive links between the underdeveloped areas of Asia, Africa and Latin America and the industrialized nations of the Atlantic Community. It should be a means of keeping essential raw materials available for the American economy. It should be a means of checking the Soviet effort to isolate the United States from Asia, Africa and Latin America. It should do these things; and it can.

The cost of an adequate foreign aid program would be large but not excessive. We are primarily interested in the underdeveloped countries. The best estimates suggest that they cannot absorb more than $3 billion yearly. This cost would of course be shared with other countries. Should we allow for this and the wastes of our military aid program, it is doubtful that at the outset the additional costs for the American taxpayer would exceed $1 billion yearly, and it would be hoped that a substantial part of this would be repaid.

But over the past four years these very heavy expenditures have been so misdirected and so mismanaged that they have failed to fulfill the nation's interests in these directions. It is the purpose of this statement to make clear how this major failure in our foreign policy has come about and to indicate how, if elected, I propose to go about handling the foreign aid problem.

THE GREAT WORLD REVOLUTION

The heart of the matter lies in the extraordinary revolution which is taking place in Asia, the Middle East, Africa and Latin America. The peoples of these areas have shaken off their traditional fatalism and apathy. They are now clear in their minds that they can shape their own destinies.

They intend, in particular, to achieve two objectives, and they will not be denied: first, they seek effective national independence and a status of equality in the world's councils; second, they seek to modernize their societies, and to increase economic welfare and achieve human dignity for themselves and for their children.

Both of these great objectives—effective independence and improvement in human welfare and dignity—require that they transform their economies from a state of relative stagnation to regular growth. The nations and dependent areas of Asia, the Middle East, Africa and Latin America are at different points on this road to modernization; but they share a passion to achieve it.

More than half the human beings of the non-Communist world are caught up in this great revolutionary process. The lands in which they live represent the balance of the world's power: that is why Moscow and the Chinese Communists are now concentrating their efforts in these areas.

Further, the trade which exists and could develop between the underdeveloped areas and the industrialized portions of the Free World could represent the difference between continued prosperity, on the one hand, and stagnation and unemployment on the other, for Western Europe, Japan, and in the long run, even the United States.

Finally, and most important, whether the revolution of the underdeveloped areas will produce democratic or totalitarian states in Asia and Africa may largely determine whether or not democracy can continue to exist as we know it in America and Europe.

Every element in the national security problem—immediate and long run—depends, in one way or another, on our meeting successfully the challenge of this great revolution which is now under way.

The Eisenhower administration has demonstrated that it does not understand this challenge and cannot cope with it. This is why the Communist offensive has gathered momentum and made serious inroads into the Free World in the past four years.

THE COMMUNIST OFFENSIVE

To understand the present Communist offensive one must go back to two great defensive victories of the Free World. In 1949 we brought Stalin's postwar offensive in Europe to a virtual end with the Berlin Airlift. In April and May, 1951, the reorganized Eighth Army, under General Ridgway and General Van Fleet, inflicted a tremendous defeat on the Chinese Communists in Korea.

Stalin and Mao Tse-tung had hoped to engulf Western Europe and Free Asia. This effort had clearly failed by the summer of 1951. NATO was building rapidly in a Western Europe, strengthened in heart by the Truman Doctrine, in its economic sinews by the Marshall Plan; and, while the Communists were being fought to a standstill in Korea, the governments and peoples in the Philippines, Taiwan, Indonesia, Burma, India and Pakistan were finding their feet. It was clearly time for a new Communist strategy.

Months before Stalin's death, the new Communist strategy was written down for all to read at the Nineteenth Party Congress in Moscow in October of 1952. The strategy was to split the United States and Western Europe from the underdeveloped areas by associating Communism with the aspirations of the people of Asia and Africa for peace, independence and rapid economic development. And, meanwhile, Soviet military strength in atomic weapons would grow, and Moscow would be able to mix its blandishments with a new threat.

After Stalin died, this policy was pursued with increasing vigor and flexibility. As early as May, 1953, my friend Chester Bowles, who had been observing the evolution of Soviet policy as ambassador to India, wrote:

> There are already disturbing signs that Moscow's indifference to the political possibilities of economic assistance to the non-Communist nations of Asia may be changing and that a new period of "ruble diplomacy" lies ahead. . . . A devastatingly effective Soviet version of Point Four could be put together for less than one-fourth of the present $8 billion annual increase in Russia's annual income. . . . If we continue to put our exclusive faith in military negation we will lose our big chance.

Mr. Bowles proved to be an excellent prophet; but the Eisenhower administration ignored his warning.

In recent years the Communist Bloc has developed a line of credits to underdeveloped countries of the Free World totaling nearly $1 billion; and it has substantially expanded its trade with these countries. Moscow has picked its spots carefully, in order to maximize the disruption of the Free World's position.

It is in itself a condemnation of the Eisenhower foreign aid program that the Russian effort should have been more effective as a loan program than the vastly larger American program made up mainly of grants. For example, the U.S.S.R. has put more than $100 million in economic assistance into Afghanistan, the classic Russian invasion route into the Indian peninsula, and has now sent a military mission to modernize the Afghan army. It has made major economic arrangements with India, Burma and Indonesia, key areas which were largely ignored in the Eisenhower administration's concentration on military pacts of doubtful military value.

In the Middle East, Moscow leaped the so-called northern tier Baghdad Pact by the arms deal with Egypt, thereby achieving in a few weeks, with the aid of Mr. Dulles, what the czars had sought for centuries.

In its relations with Afghanistan and Egypt, the Soviet Union has laid the basis for what could prove to be major breakthroughs in the Free World's strategic position.

Elsewhere, the Communist offensive, mixing threat and economic inducement, threatens to undermine our structure of Strategic Air Command bases: in Iceland, North Africa, the Middle East, and Japan.

In another direction Moscow has converted a major Russian weakness into an asset, while the Eisenhower administration has been converting a major American strength into a liability. Communist agricultural policy has resulted in inadequate output of food and raw materials. Thus Moscow and Peking have been happy to accept agricultural imports from the underdeveloped areas.

Meanwhile, the Eisenhower administration was crudely dumping American surpluses in ways which damaged the interests of some of the underdeveloped nations and some of our best friends, leaving them no alternative except to become increasingly enmeshed in trade with the Communist Bloc. In the last two years, the program of dumping has been greatly accelerated.

As I shall indicate below, this was wholly unnecessary. Our food and fiber surpluses, rightly used, are one of our major national assets.

The Communist offensive looks formidable; and it is formidable, given the misdirection of American policy.

But it has a fundamental weakness.

In the end Moscow and Peking, for all their professions, do not want independent national states in the underdeveloped areas; they want Communist states.

In the end Moscow and Peking do not want these societies to modernize themselves successfully by the democratic methods of political freedom and individual consent; they want their present governments to fail and to give way to Communist governments.

The Communist offensive could have been rendered relatively harmless, if the Eisenhower administration had not failed to take the initiative.

THE FOREIGN AID POLICY OF THE EISENHOWER ADMINISTRATION

What kind of foreign aid policy do we have?

This year the Eisenhower administration presented a foreign aid bill to the Congress. This bill was virtually identical in purpose and scale with that of 1955 and 1954. Its purpose is mainly to supply military aid and support to a limited group of our allies. In Asia, for example, more than 80 per cent of these funds are scheduled to go to South Korea, Indochina and Taiwan.

There is certainly a case for military support of allies when they wish to receive it and when it can be demonstrated that American military expenditures abroad yield a greater return in Free World security than similar expenditures on our own military establishment.

There is certainly a case for regional and bilateral military pacts, when they fulfill a clear strategic purpose and when a well-balanced American policy gives the participants a sense that the United States is concerned not merely in stopping Communist military aggression, but also in helping them build progressive societies.

In Turkey, for example, we have demonstrated since 1947 that such balanced programs were possible. But these essential conditions for a successful military aid program have not been fulfilled in the past four years.

It was evident to the Congress during this past spring and summer that the administration—three years after Stalin's death, with the Communist economic offensive fully developed—had failed to make a fresh reappraisal of the Free World's military position, had failed to take into account the revolutionary forces at work in the underdeveloped areas, had failed to take account of the offensive being mounted with increasing success against the Free World by the Communist Bloc.

Like old generals, the administration leaders were still fighting the last war against Stalin—an essentially military struggle—rather than the new war against Bulganin and Khrushchev. In fact, while the aims of the Kremlin have remained the same, the tactics have radically altered. Old formulas do not work; but all the administration could lay before the Congress were the old, threadbare programs.

While these large sums were being requested from the Congress and the taxpayer, the President and the Secretary of State made statements indicating that even they were beginning to think that the military approach to foreign aid was overdone. But they did nothing to reshape the legislative proposals.

Congress was asked, in short, to put through a bill in which the administration no longer had confidence and which it could not defend.

The Congressional opposition to the 1956 foreign aid bill indicated no reluctance to face up to the nation's responsibilities. It did reflect a well-grounded belief that the administration had failed in its fundamental responsibilities. Indeed, it speaks well of the patriotism and good sense of the Congress that, despite every incentive to cut down expenditures on foreign aid, it maintained our economic programs on a stopgap basis; and it has taken steps on its own initiative to seek a new economic foreign policy.

For the past three and a half years, the major problem of the nation's foreign policy has been clear: shall the United States in quest of peace positively associate itself with the great popular movements in Asia, the Middle East, Africa and Latin America, or shall it stand aside and let the Communist offensive succeed?

The Eisenhower administration has been unable to make up its mind. It has mixed pious platitudes with expensive military aid programs, of dubious military value. It has left the initiative to Moscow and Peking. And in so doing it has endangered the security of the nation.

Now, in his fourth year of office, and at the prodding of the Democratic majority in the Senate, President Eisenhower is at last asking that the problem be studied by a committee largely composed of big businessmen without experience or qualification in this complex field.

The Eisenhower administration's record on foreign aid is a record of weak and indecisive leadership, feeble and misdirected effort, costly to the taxpayer and, above all, damaging to the nation's interests.

A Democratic Approach to Foreign Aid

What kind of foreign economic policy should we have?

Where military assistance abroad can positively deter Communist aggression, where such assistance is wanted, and where we judge such expenditures contribute more to the common security than like expenditures on American strength, or on economic aid, then, but only then, should we continue military aid. Military aid should be judged on military standards and be part of the military budget.

But the decisive opportunities in foreign aid lie elsewhere.

We need an expanded program of world economic development based on the following four principles:

First, aid should take the form mainly of loans rather than grants. Neither we nor our friends like handouts. We wish to join them in genuinely productive enterprises; and productive enterprises can be supported by loans. Where aid is required for schools, health, highways and other overhead there is a case for grants.

Second, the program should be shared with others. It will be far more effective if the industrialized nations of Europe contribute to the venture along with the United States. They stand to benefit in every way from assuming responsibility with us in this joint enterprise.

Third, the program should be planned some years ahead. Investment takes time. Many of the newer nations are working toward goals laid down in five-year plans. They must know firmly on what loans and technical assistance they can count. It is wrong in every respect to wait until crises arise and then to throw in large sums, or to stagger along, planning uncertainly from year to year, reacting to Communist initiatives rather than acting steadily on American principles and interests. The four-year Marshall Plan is suggestive of the procedure. A plan, a commitment subject to some revision with experience.

Fourth, the program should include all the underdeveloped nations of the non-Communist world prepared to participate, whether or not they are joined to us in military alliance.

There are many forms such a program might take. And before deciding finally on details—should that be my responsibility—I would wish to consult the distinguished committees of the Senate and the House of Representatives on the problem as well as our friends abroad who might participate as lenders or borrowers. But those are the principles on which I would act and the direction in which I would lead.

I would like to comment a bit further on some special aspects of such a program.

There is now good reason to believe that something like a quarter of the American contribution to such a program could take the form of food and fiber surpluses. If we casually dump these surpluses on the world market, they will hurt rather than help the national interest. But if we weave them carefully into an international development program, they can be converted into a major national and Free World asset.

I have repeatedly proposed a world food and fiber bank. Such an enterprise could not merely help use our surpluses, it could make a major contribution to a Free World economic development program.

I reject President Eisenhower's pessimism and defeatism about American farm surpluses. Our farmers need not feel that they have done wrong when they have grown too much. In the framework of the effort I propose, our farmers could once again know that their arduous and devoted labors were contributing to the nation's security and to the welfare of humanity.

A second aspect of this program would be an expansion and redirection of technical assistance. President Eisenhower's atoms-for-peace program is sound; but it is incomplete and it has been implemented with typical Republican sluggishness. We need to bring the best scientific brains of the Free World to focus on the application of science to the needs of the underdeveloped areas, not merely in the field of atomic energy, but also in solar energy, new sources of food, new sources of water supply, and in many other fields.

In a quite different direction we have opportunities to develop technical assistance in the form of management contracts, where American private firms set up new factories, manage them for a time and, for a reasonable fee, train up their successors. Here, to mutual advantage, American private enterprise can be put at the disposal of underdeveloped areas, without any fear that their sovereignty will be impaired. The contribution of universities to technical assistance should also be expanded.

In general, it is clear that at the present time the normal flows of private capital cannot alone do the job that needs to be done in the underdeveloped areas. Governments must take the initiative and work out a basic program. On the other hand, against the background of an intergovernmental program, private enterprise could do a larger part of the job than at present, and it could increasingly take over the task of accelerating economic development in foreign areas, as time goes on. I am pleased at the increased contribution of private finance revealed even as I now consider this problem.

It would be my purpose to use the possibilities of private enterprise to the limit in such a program, without shirking the need for prompt, adequate intergovernmental action.

What would be the cost of a program adequate to meet the challenge we face? Would it be more or less than our present expenditures?

Frankly, I cannot say, but I believe it can be handled within our present foreign assistance budget. If we examine present programs on a country-by-country basis, we will find that important savings could be made. These savings might well cover what was needed for additional loans and technical assistance in new directions; and there should be, in addition, a shift from military to development assistance.

The Russian success stems in part from their willingness to accept in payment the exports of the borrowing nations. Could we not make similar arrangements, for example, to build up our stockpiles? In this way the underdeveloped countries can pay us in local currencies and ultimately in goods, and thus not be forced to seek dollars in a market short of dollars. The borrowing country is allowed to pay in domestic currencies, to be used in purchases within the country in so far as this is the only practical method of payment.

What I can promise is that, if elected, I will present to the Congress and the American people a balanced program founded on the principles laid out in this statement: a program mainly of productive loans, rather than outright grants, capable of putting our food and fiber surpluses to work, based not on a negative response to the Kremlin's maneuvers, but on a constructive and positive American effort to promote economic growth and national independence.

AMERICAN OBJECTIVES AND FOREIGN AID

What can we, the people of the United States, expect from a world economic partnership built on these principles?

Would such a program increase the military strength of the Free World? To a degree it would. It would render the underdeveloped areas less subject to Communist infiltration, less vulnerable to "brushfire wars." And it would make it easier for them to support the military programs they believe necessary for their security. But this is not its primary purpose.

Would such a program win us friends, make people like us more? To a degree it might. When men work side by side in common enterprises, real and deep associations develop, and common understanding. This was an important by-product of the Marshall Plan. But this is not the primary purpose of the program I propose.

Would such a program lead to the spread of private enterprise and the kind of capitalism in which we believe? Over a period of time I believe it would. As democratic societies successfully develop their economies and develop men capable in industrial management, they are likely to permit that diffusion of political and economic power which is the essence of democracy and capitalism.

The lesson of the world's experience in recent years is that nationalization of industry is a clumsy way to do business. One after another democratic socialist party is dropping nationalization from its program. But this is for them to decide. Our economic foreign policy should not be used as a device for exporting our own economic institutions.

Would such a program be of direct economic advantage to the United States? Indeed it would. Properly designed, such a program would, as I have indicated, permit the orderly, constructive use of our agricultural surpluses. It would help ensure for the long run the raw materials we shall increasingly have to import. It would raise world income, the basis of world trade. It would lay an indispensable foundation for a return to convertible currencies in the Free World. But our primary purpose is not national economic advantage.

Would such a program stop the spread of Communism? It is, of course, the proper response to the present Communist economic and political offensive in the underdeveloped areas; and, properly carried out, it should render that offensive harmless to our interests.

But the purpose of such a program is not negative. It is not a reaction to the Kremlin's latest tactics. It is constructive and positive. We must end this undignified and ineffective business of chasing around the world with blank checks, trying to outbid the offers of Soviet diplomats, a tactic that puts pressure on our best friends to blackmail us.

What is it, then, that we seek? To see the societies of the under-developed nations develop along stable, constructive, democratic lines. The peoples in these areas seek increased dignity for their nations and for individual men and women within them. They impatiently seek economic progress as the necessary basis for these large national and human purposes.

It is Moscow's interest to have this impatience lead them to embrace Communism. It is our interest that they achieve economic progress by democratic means.

It is Moscow's interest that the powerful national sentiments which now move these peoples disrupt the peace and unity of the Free World. It is our interest that this new nationalism be turned not outward in disruptive adventures, but to constructive efforts within their own societies.

In short, the United States has a major and persistent interest in doing what it can to assure that the billion men and women who now live in the underdeveloped parts of the Free World pass through the great revolutionary process now under way and emerge as citizens of growing nations, dedicated to peace and to the proposition that the state is the servant of the individual.

The fate of ourselves, our children, and our grandchildren, the security of our nation and its future place in the world, hinge on whether or not this comes to pass.

What We Must Do

What I have written here is not new in American thought or conviction. The American people have supported our Point Four effort and other measures to assist the underdeveloped nations on precisely these grounds. Labor leaders, businessmen, teachers, churchmen and informed citizens throughout the country have been arguing along these lines for some years. As far back as the spring of 1953, I made this theme the subject of the Godkin Lectures I delivered at Harvard. I am convinced that a consensus exists among our people capable of sustaining the kind of program I have outlined.

Why, then, has the administration not moved? Why, with the new Soviet social offensive gaining ground every day, has the President not launched a program of this kind over the past four years?

The answer lies in the character of the Eisenhower team and in President Eisenhower's concept of leadership. That team is split down the middle. It is dominated by big businessmen who simply cannot comprehend the nature and complexity of the revolutionary thrust of an age and the human longings which animate it. Men who have spent their lives fighting social change at home are not likely to welcome it in other countries.

These men hold powerful positions in the government. And in a tragic failure of leadership, President Eisenhower has been unwilling to override them. He has made a typical compromise: power has been left in the hands of the Republican right-wing businessmen who oppose such a program; speech-writing has been turned over to the liberal Republicans who would support it.

Let us be clear. This is not a clear-cut issue between the two parties.

There are Republicans who understand this matter as well as Democrats. The Republican party has, in part of its being, a great international tradition: the tradition of Theodore Roosevelt, of Elihu Root, of Charles Evans Hughes, of Wendell Willkie, of Henry Stimson.

That tradition is still alive in many distinguished Americans. In a new Democratic administration its representatives will find posts of honor and operating responsibility, as they have in previous Democratic administrations—a status ironically denied many of these responsible Republicans over the past four years.

How, then, are we going to get the kind of foreign policy we need?

The record of the Eisenhower administration indicates that, if the nation is to maintain its leadership in the Free World, the nation must be led by a Democratic administration. Only then can the nation get its first team in charge of our foreign affairs, only then can the idealism, energy and wisdom of the American people be made effective.

I am confident that in January, 1957, a first team will be on the field. And it will turn to this problem of foreign aid—and to others—in good heart. For the challenge we face in making an effective world program for economic development is one that fits the nation's talent and genius and deepest tradition, as well as its interest.

This challenge requires that we work side by side in mutual tolerance with other peoples.

It requires that we apply our technical skills and know-how under new circumstances.

It requires that we learn as well as teach.

It requires that we associate ourselves with men's hopes, rather than solely with their fears.

It requires, in short, the best that is in us.

Only in that spirit can America rise to the challenge of the mid-century and help the world along the road to a lasting peace.

III

PROGRAM FOR A NEW AMERICA

1. The Economy

2. Education

3. Health

4. Older Citizens

5. Resources and Power

6. Agriculture

7. Depressed Areas

8. Civil Liberties and Civil Rights

I

The Economy

WHERE IS THE MONEY COMING FROM?:
PROGRAM PAPER

•

I am trying in this series of papers on the New America to broaden our vision of the humane and creative future that lies within our grasp.

I have proposed programs to ensure us all against the high cost of medicine, to combat the crippling and killing diseases that cast a shadow over our life; to build the schools and train the teachers to give our children the education they deserve; and to give new security and meaning to the life of older citizens. I have spoken often of the need for a full development of our great bounty of natural resources, for the rebuilding and renewing of our cities, and most important of all, for the building of peace.

I believe that a rich, energetic, and compassionate America can do all this and more if its leaders have the will and if our idealism is aroused. I am heartened by the response of the American people to the programs that I have thus far set forth.

There is one question, however, that I want to ask and to answer myself, and that the American people often and rightly ask, too. That plain and realistic question is this: Where is the money coming from?

The answer to this is that the money for our programs of welfare will come from our own economic growth as a nation. As our national product increases, our tax revenues will rise. Indeed, at present tax rates, the revenues can be expected to increase much more than the cost of the programs I have proposed.

Moreover, this can and must be done without the silent robbery that goes by the name of inflation. The Republican party has tried to portray

Release dated October 29, 1956.

85

itself as the party of sound money. This is ironic, when one recalls the fierce Republican opposition to the measures which kept inflation under control in the difficult conditions of the war and postwar years.

Excluding war and demobilization years, I find that the average rise of the cost of living under the Democrats has been 0.2 per cent per year. The rise per year under the Republicans has been twice as great, and they have now managed—in peacetime—to bring our cost of living to the highest point in history. In short, the Democratic record of controlling inflation is good, and better than the Republican.

Our record of sober and responsible management of the economy also is good.

The old cynical joke about politicians is that they vote for every spending bill, and against every taxing bill.

Perhaps there have been a few of that breed who have almost managed to fit that picture of pure and unadulterated irresponsibility, but if they exist, they have not shown themselves around my camp. I have been the Governor of a large and complex state, and that experience added to my respect for the ancient canons of public thrift, of fiscal responsibility, of dutiful stewardship of public funds.

I am proud to say that in my years as Governor of Illinois we managed not only to increase needed expenditures on roads and schools and other state services, but at the same time to keep the state budget in balance, and avoid any increase in general revenue taxation, and also leave a substantial part of the wartime surplus intact. Illinois was one of few states that did not need any new general purpose taxes in this period. One year I had to veto fifty-seven bills because the Republican-controlled legislature authorized many millions in spending for which they provided no funds.

I submit my record as Governor of Illinois as evidence of fiscal responsibility and economy in government.

But by economy in government I meant then, and I mean now, true economy. It is economical to avoid waste and to examine every proposal with a careful, realistic eye as to its real merit and its financing. It is not economical to let needed public services deteriorate, to skimp on needed programs of general welfare, to be niggardly with the needs of future generations. For what, after all, is economy? It is not simply the accumulation of great unused storehouses of wealth. It is the wise use of that wealth, without waste, and with careful attention to the future's needs; it is the use of what we have to serve human living in the wisest way.

It is not true economy to neglect our educational system, which not only provides the trained manpower essential to our progress in technology, but also is itself a chief source of the knowledge and skill and character that are among the great ends of living. It is not economical to fail to provide adequate medical care and medical research, and to let men be ill and children die when they need not. It is not economical to let older citizens eke out a bare existence, and find the twilight of their days insecure and bereft of meaning. It is not economical to allow our cities to deteriorate, juvenile delinquency to grow, and slums to increase, when wise action by government could help to prevent these evils. It is not economical to let the years pass when we could be creatively building for the full development of our natural resources for all the people. It is not true economy, where wealth accumulates and men decay.

As the size and complexity of our society increase, the role of government activity must not be allowed to decline—as it has, up to the election year, under President Eisenhower. It is not economical to neglect our public needs, to postpone confronting them, or to try to buy the needed public services in a bargain basement.

We cannot evade the choices of our time by absurd and contradictory formulae like "conservative with money and liberal with human beings"; for it's exactly our responsibility to decide how best our money can be used to serve human beings. The fundamental decision of the Democratic party is to face that responsibility in a spirit of dedication to human values. I urge the readers of this paper to read it in that spirit and to see behind the statistics and the cold economic prose the warm and living vision of the happier families and fuller lives of the New America.

My purpose in this paper is to confront fully and frankly and responsibly the economic underpinning of that New America.

I. CAN WE AFFORD THE NEW AMERICA?

The question, Where is the money coming from? can be asked from two points of view. The first and fundamental question is: Where will the American people find the productive capacity—the labor, land, plant, and equipment, and natural resources—needed for these programs? The second question is: How will the federal government raise the revenues these programs require? If we can find a satisfactory answer to the first question, we can also answer the second.

And the answer to the first question is found in the great and constantly increasing productive capacity of the United States.

If full employment is maintained—and we are committed by the Employment Act of 1946 to maintain it—then our national production should grow at the rate of at least 3 per cent a year and our national product should now increase by at least $15 billion a year. That anticipated rise is based on the average growth over the years, an average that we have every reason to believe can be continued. This, in fact, is a minimum rate. Dr. Arthur Burns, the President's Economic Adviser, has just held out the prospect of an increase of $200 billion in ten years, or $20 billion per year.

The greatest resource for maintaining that rate of growth, of course, is the energy of human beings, and we're going to have more and more of that. The population of our country is growing at a rate that only a few years ago seemed impossible. This means a great and continuing increase in our labor force, and therefore in our product. Indeed, with the coming of these millions of new American workers, it could be said that we had better maintain our rate of growth or else unemployment will steadily rise. The increased population means new human needs that must be met; but it also means a still greater increase in the product from which to meet them.

The new plant and machinery made possible by our savings, and the steady advance in our efficiency and our technology, also will contribute to the continuing growth of our national product. We now have a national product of over $400 billion. By 1960, we should have a product of $450-500 billion. In another decade—measuring in dollars of the same purchasing power—we can expect our annual production to reach $550-600 billion. This means we will have $150-200 billion worth of additional goods and services.

I do not mean to imply that such an increase will come automatically. Continued growth requires the co-operation, effort and intelligence of all of us, and wise action by the government. But, on the basis of past performance, we can work for this increase in solid confidence; I am confident we can achieve it, and more, because I am not a "prophet of doom and gloom."

To make the most of the opportunity this new bounty will provide, we must divide it wisely between what we use as private consumers, what we reserve for private investment, and what we devote to governmental services.

On this score, the Eisenhower administration has made an unwise division; it has made the wrong choice. It curtailed our federal programs in the vital fields of education, natural resources, and technical and economic aid. Not until the 1956 election stared them in the face did the Republicans begin to restore some of the programs to meet pressing human needs.

Yet, in 1955, they were moved to propose a $100 billion highway program. One is tempted to contrast their eagerness to spend excessive sums on highways and their reluctance to spend on schools. I also favor a substantial road program, but there must be balance.

While private consumption was rising by $40 billion, the Republicans were cutting expenditures for important government services. The long-range result of such a policy is to increase the disproportion between private opulence and public need. In a rich land and a time of abundance there is no justification for such a policy.

It is false economy.

We can see the shortsightedness of such a policy when we consider that in the long run the outlays for services such as health, education, and slum clearance raise our national income far more than they cost. Where, for example, would our vaunted productivity be if it were not for the nine or ten years that our population has averaged in schools? It is surely foolish to fail, as we have been failing, to stimulate that great investment in the future. The high level of education, probably more than any other factor, accounts for the high productivity out of which we are now denying that same education an adequate share.

Similarly, public health and other programs of government have contributed much to cutting mortality rates by 50 per cent since the beginning of the century, extending the average life by twenty years and the working life by five years. This last factor alone adds $25 billion to labor income per year.

The New America programs that I have proposed would increase the working potential of the older citizens, reduce the time lost because of illness, increase the adequacy of our educational system, provide for the full development of natural resources, and they will far more than pay for themselves in the long run. Even those that do not have so tangible a return—like the preservation of parks and wildlife—are nevertheless a worthy part of an economy that understands what is truly valuable.

The programs which I propose might cost about $3 billion in two or three years and rise to three times that amount in a decade, a period in which our national product is expected to rise by $150-200 billion. In other words, I am suggesting that we devote roughly 5 per cent of our prospective gains in national output to these essential national programs. We shall also want to reserve a generous share of our total fiscal capacity for the states and localities to enable them to meet their rapidly growing responsibilities.

We can afford to do this and at the same time spend what we must for our military security, for the defense of the free world, and for contributions to the economic health and progress of the underdeveloped countries of the world. If we succeed in achieving the increase in national product of which we have shown we are capable, we can do all that I have proposed and still enjoy most of the fruits of our economic growth in the form of increased private consumption.

The answer to the question, Can we afford the New America? is: we can.

Where Will the Taxes Come From?

Our second question is, How will the government finance this program?

Seen in the perspective of an expanding economy, the answer is clear: our existing taxes will yield all the revenue needed and leave an ample margin for tax reduction.

The anticipated increases in national output will increase the tax revenues of the federal government without changes in tax rates or structure. As what we all earn increases, what the government receives increases. If tax rates are kept at present levels, federal tax revenues should increase from their present level of over $70 billion to $100-110 billion by 1965-66. This increase of $30-40 billions in federal taxes would be three to four times what is needed to finance the national investments that I have proposed.

Moreover, some of the new programs will be financed on a contributory basis and will, thus, provide for additional revenue. For example, cost of higher benefits under old-age insurance would be met in part at least through a small rise in payroll taxes, paid by workers and employers.

Of course, we cannot count on all the increased revenue for new programs; some of it will be absorbed by the added cost of existing programs of federal, state and local governments. Also we cannot anticipate how much we will need to spe_ d on the most important programs of all, those for military security and forei n aid.

But, nevertheless, in the absence of a major war, there is every reason to believe that we not only can meet the claims of these programs out of increased tax revenues that respond automatically to higher incomes, but even reduce tax rates. The total amount of money the government will receive in taxes, of course, will rise; but there is every reason to believe that it will be possible to lower tax rates. Indeed, if security expenditures could be lowered substantially, then even the total amount of taxes might fall. Of the gains of output, the American people should be able to appropriate most for private use.

President Eisenhower and the Republican prophets of doom and gloom ridicule our ideas for a better America and say that we could not balance the budget, cut taxes, and increase expenditures, too. But if we look at the picture as a whole, in the light of our expanding economy, we should be able to do just that.

Tax Policy for Stabilization

Our budget policy for the future, however, must not be looked at in isolation from general economic conditions. We have to use the government's power to tax as a balance wheel to help keep a stable economy.

When economic activity is high and resources are fully employed, the budget of the government should be balanced, and a surplus may even be called for. Unless we have such a policy, we will have inflation.

But when capacity to produce goods rises faster than the market can absorb them, the opposite government policy is called for. A reduction in taxes can offset the adverse effects of inadequate buying, and head off threatened declines of output.

The reduction of taxes would put life-giving dollars back into the bloodstream of the private economy, and help it to recover strength. In a period of threatened recession, we should cut taxes, even though this course may involve temporary budget deficits. When private spending declines, in order to keep people employed, we may need not only tax cuts but also an increase in our programs for schools, hospitals, roads and the like. Government can never again allow the human waste of a depression.

President Truman recognized and applied these principles. In the interests of fighting inflation and reducing the national debt, he rejected the easy road of political expediency by vetoing, in 1947 and 1948, the tax cuts enacted by a Republican Congress. He did this in the interests of preserving the stability of the dollar for all of us, and it took more courage and responsibility than anything the Republicans have done, despite their many words about the stable dollar.

During the Truman administration, the federal government fought inflation by achieving surpluses in the cash budget in five out of seven years. The total net surplus during that period amounted to more than $12 billion; and the national debt held outside of government trust shrank accordingly.

The Eisenhower administration has not shared these views. Obsessed with the idea that the budget must be balanced at all cost, and at all times, and eager for political tax reductions, it has made the attempt to reduce the budget the center of government policy. This has been largely at the expense of our national security and other necessary government services, and has also made us fail to weave government tax and spending policy into the fabric of the private economy.

The same ideas have led the Secretary of the Treasury to suggest that, if a boom develops and there is a surplus, he will recommend a tax cut. In other words, in a time of rising inflationary pressure, the administration would add to the pressure through tax cuts. This, I say, is upside-down economics. The government's responsibility is to stabilize the economy, not to accentuate dangerous trends.

The worst time to reduce taxes is in a boom. This is particularly true when high priority government programs for defense and other purposes must be continued, and sometimes even increased. In such a situation, we should welcome a surplus, for it removes money that would otherwise be spent, and thus it helps to dampen inflationary pressure and to retain the value of the dollar.

The time to cut taxes is when we are not able to buy all that we can produce. Then we need the additional buying power that a tax reduction provides.

Before leaving the matter of budget balancing, I must note that the present administration has been more concerned to make the budget *look* balanced than actually to balance it.

To illustrate: in 1955, the administration proposed a road program of $100 billion, to be financed by borrowing. Yet this program, if enacted, would not have increased the apparent budget deficit, because it was to be handled outside the budget through a corporation created for the purpose. The inflationary consequences of this proposal were real, but they were kept hidden.

There is more of this sleight of hand in the redefining of many federal credit programs as guarantees, instead of as loans. Though the real cost remains the same, this makes the apparent cost lower, and looks better in the budget. Also, government assets, such as commodities, industrial plants and mortgages, have been sold by the government, and the proceeds recorded as current receipts, thereby also improving the appearance of the budget. But the apparent improvement is not real any more than the factory owner confronted with large current bills makes himself solvent by selling his machinery.

A policy was adopted of leasing governmental post offices instead of constructing them, which avoided current construction costs. But it added to our future outlays, and will increase the taxpayer's total bill.

I can understand the President's anxiety to give an appearance of modest federal expenditures. He must be embarrassed by his 1952 promise of a $60 billion budget, when today the budget is $70 billion, and his cash outlays are a record for a peacetime year. But if deception in the budget is understandable, it is not admirable.

MONETARY AND BUDGET POLICY

Our budget policy must be aimed at avoiding the extremes of unemployment and inflation, and our monetary and debt policies must serve this same purpose. The Eisenhower administration has placed a heavy reliance on monetary policy as a means of stabilizing the economy. The objections to their scarce-money policy are two: first, it hasn't worked well; second, it has resulted in many difficulties and inequities.

I am all for using monetary policy, but as one weapon in an armory of economic weapons. Some flexibility in money rates is welcome. But I am concerned over the clumsy manner in which monetary policy has been used. In 1953, the Treasury almost without warning imposed a dear money policy, and the result was so shocking that the administration quickly reversed itself. In 1956, the Federal Reserve embarked on a tight money, high interest rate policy, but took no measures to soften the blow for the weak who were especially vulnerable.

The high interest rate policy of the Republican administration has played havoc with residential mortgage credit. It has created great difficulties for small businessmen and farmers and others dependent on bank credit. It has had no noticeable effect on large corporations, which finance their expansion largely by their own funds and have access to credit even in a tight money market. Thus, by hurting the small operator, the scarce-money policy has contributed further to the dangerous and rapid concentration of industry. Also the benefits of high interest have not been spread fairly among the various groups of lenders.

Injustices are also evident in government debt policy. For example, the three-month Treasury bill now yields a return that is 70 per cent above the 1952 rate; the 3-5-year bond yields about 60 per cent above that rate. The rich investors buy these securities. Even high-grade corporate and municipal bonds now yield 40 and 20 per cent, respectively, more than in 1952. But the E Bonds, purchased by the small investor, yield no more than in 1952. This is discrimination in favor of the big against the small investor.

But let us consider another aspect of debt policy. Sound government credit depends on a sound tax base, and this base is provided by a growing economy. The weight of our still large national debt, primarily the result of war, will shrink as the economy expands. By 1966, at present price levels, the interest costs of our present debt should be only about one-third of the 1945 cost relative to output.

We should try to reduce the debt when we can, but debt reduction, as such, must not be made the major objective of fiscal policy. It must be undertaken when, but only when, it fits the requirement of a healthy and expanding economy.

I believe that the American people insist on national security, and that they realize it depends on how we discharge our responsibilities. I believe that the people want to provide public services in step with the requirements of a growing country and that they are ready to pay for these services and so accept smaller cuts in tax rates than they might otherwise receive. Finally, I believe that the American people want a budget policy that is devoted to the requirements of an expanding and stable economy and to the welfare of all the peple.

II. The Cost of the New America

I now turn to a closer look at the cost of the programs I have proposed. We must not allow enthusiasm for such programs to cloud our realization that they will be costly. At the same time, we should beware of inflated estimates of their cost, put forward by people who don't believe in them anyway. These are the people who have always derided new ideas as "pie in the sky." And we should remember that the growth of the economy should enable us to finance my program for a New America and still reduce tax *rates* significantly.

It should be remembered, too, that these investments will make a contribution to greater productivity and higher income out of which eventually they will more than pay for themselves. And it is well to try to see what these cold figures really can mean in millions of happier, fuller lives.

1. OLDER CITIZENS

In my policy statement on providing for the needs of older Americans I proposed as an objective that a citizen, after retiring from the active labor force, should be in a position to maintain his accustomed standard of living. At present there are 5.4 million families in which the head of the family is over sixty-five years of age. The average income of these families is about $2,300, only 55 per cent of the national average of about $4,200. Since the aged do not have some of the financial responsibilities a family has in its more active years, my goal could be achieved if the income of the family units of older persons is raised to about 75 per cent of the national average. The needed help in meeting the heavy burden of illness among the old will be one of the primary objectives of our health program, and therefore comes under that heading.

The ultimate costs of raising the incomes of 5.4 million families to three-fourths of the national average income—that is, of providing an addition of about $800 per family—would amount to $4.3 billion. If measures are taken to make it easier for older workers to get a job, surely one-third of this desired increase in income can be obtained through improved job opportunities, leaving about $3 billion to government finance. Of this $3 billion, $2.4 billion should be obtained through Old-Age and Survivors Insurance, since approximately 80 per cent of the aged are included in this program. The remaining $600 million should be obtained through Old-Age Assistance, about two-fifths of which would be provided by the states.

Thus, total federal expenditure of some $2.7 billion will be necessary. This amount may be financed in part from general revenue and in part from increased rates of payroll tax. This goal should be obtainable by 1965-66. As the program is developed gradually, the estimated increased cost for 1960 will be about $900 million. Since the reserves in the Old-Age and Survivors Insurance Fund have reached $22 billion and are growing at the rate of $1.5 billion per year, there is something to be said for financing half this rise out of reserves. The remainder, for the time being, would come out of a payroll tax. But in order to be certain that we do not underestimate costs, I assume that the total charge will be on current taxes.

2. HEALTH

I have recommended that a comprehensive private health insurance program be established. I have emphasized that this program should be voluntary and that it should be administered on a state basis. But federal support appears to be essential to an adequate program. Also, I have recommended increased appropriations for medical research and for hospitals.

The estimated federal contribution to a comprehensive private health insurance program is about $1 billion by 1965. This amount is about 25 per cent of the estimated total cost of the program at that time. Under one reasonable plan, the insured and their employers would contribute about one-third and one-quarter, respectively, and the balance would be financed by state governments. I want to make it absolutely clear that the private contributions are voluntary and are not in any sense a tax. A comprehensive private plan of this sort takes time to develop. The estimated federal cost by 1960 would reach about $300 million.

My recommended program for hospital construction provides for additional federal outlays of $100 million by 1960, and $300 million by 1965, with contributions by state governments. The additional cost of the program for medical research is estimated at $250 million for 1960 and $400 million for 1965.

In all, this leaves us with an estimated additional federal cost of about $650 million for 1960 and of $1.7 billion for 1965.

3. EDUCATION

In my statement on education I have suggested federal aid for school construction as well as aid to increase teachers' salaries. By 1960 a minimum program for education would involve a cost of $700 million, and by 1965, I suspect, at least $2 billion will be needed to meet even the most basic requirements. Then the federal government would be paying 13 per cent of the school bill of $15 billion at present standards. At the same time, the total costs of public school education should rise substantially above $15 billion by 1965 if we are to have a school system commensurate with our economic capacity and standard of living.

In addition, I have recommended that we should each year provide scholarships for 100,000 able students who cannot otherwise afford college education, and 2,500 graduate fellowships. If it were possible to get these programs started promptly by 1960, the cost would be $140 million, and by 1965 perhaps $420 million.

4. OTHER PROGRAMS

I have dealt with the major programs above, but there are other requirements which must not be overlooked. These include:

A program for low-rent housing which allows for an increase of, say, 100,000 units per year over current programs, and outlays for financing experimental programs for farm housing and middle-income housing;

A program for urban redevelopment, including slum clearance (our present program would require two hundred years to deal with current slums);

A program of vocational rehabilitation;

A program for development and conservation of our natural resources. I assume a rise in such expenditures at least in proportion to that in national income. Some of these expenditures will be self-liquidating.

Assistance programs, other than those for older citizens, cost the federal government $500-600 million. The least we can expect here is a rise of 50 per cent by 1965-66. This rise would match an expected increase of at least 30 per cent in per capita income and would raise average benefits to some extent above their current low level relative to per capita income. Surely assistance of $59 per month to the blind and half that amount to a dependent child is not adequate.

I have not included in these totals any rise for outlays of state and local governments; nor any increase for security or foreign aid.

Clearly state and local expenditures, especially those for schools, must and will rise. Fortunately, their revenues will also expand through economic growth. But additions to state and local taxes will also be necessary.

Outlays for security and foreign aid are to be determined, I hope, by the requirements of security. If the crisis is great enough, we shall have to forgo not only any expected improvement in our standard of living, but even accept a cut.

I make no allowance for highways nor for permanent disability, since Congress has already provided for their financing.

I have declared that improvement in agricultural income is imperative, but with expenditures of an estimated $5.7 billion for fiscal year 1957, more than $4 billion per year in excess of average Democratic outlays in fiscal years 1951-1953, I believe we can assure farmers a fair income without greater expense.

What, then, does all this add up to? When we put these figures for new programs all together, we get a total of $3.2 billion by 1960, and $9.7 billion by 1965-66, which is about 4.5 to 6 per cent of the expected rise of the national product in both cases. These amounts are only about 25 to 30 per cent of the increase in federal tax receipts we can expect from that rise in the national product. In other words, what we need to do, we can do.

III. THE TAX STRUCTURE OF THE NEW AMERICA

One question remains: How will the tax burden be distributed? My answer is that citizens should contribute according to their ability to pay.

PERSONAL INCOME TAX

Since income is the best index of ability to pay, the personal income tax should be the sheet anchor of the federal tax structure. In its earlier stages the primary function of the personal income tax was to siphon off part of the incomes of the wealthy.

But the tremendous increase in tax requirements in the course of World War II made it inevitable that the people in the middle and lower income groups should bear a heavier tax burden. Exemptions were sharply reduced and the number of taxpayers rose from about 8 million to over 50 million. The personal income tax thus changed its dinner jacket for overalls.

Not only was the personal income tax vastly changed, but its weight in the tax structure was heavily increased. This development was a good one, because the alternative would have been heavy reliance on sales taxation.

Sales taxes are regressive—that is, they take a larger share of the income of the poor. As we look to the future development of the peacetime tax structure, we must guard against too much reliance on sales taxes.

The recent book, *Eisenhower: The Inside Story*, reveals that the Secretary of the Treasury wanted a sales tax but was advised not to suggest it to Congress. And the former Eisenhower Commissioner of Internal Revenue, Mr. Coleman Andrews, whose job it was to collect the income tax, is now leading a crusade against it. In his view it is the worst thing that has ever happened to this country. These ominous signs suggest what many Republicans secretly think about progressive taxation.

This is not to say that all is perfect with our present income tax. When the time for tax reduction comes, the first move should be toward relieving taxpayers in the lowest income groups. One way to do it is to increase exemptions. Another way to go at it is to lower tax rates at the bottom of the scale.

At the present time there is a tax of 20 per cent on the first $2,000 of taxable income. We may split this lowest bracket in two and adopt a substantial reduction in the tax rate for the first $1,000 of taxable income. Much is to be said for this method as a first step in the process of giving tax relief to taxpayers with the lowest incomes, because it does not narrow the coverage of the income tax.

The income tax problem over the middle and higher income brackets is a different matter. We have built up in this area what appears on paper to be a highly progressive surtax rate. But over a period of years we have added special provisions to our tax laws under which an increasing proportion of the income of middle and upper bracket taxpayers is taxed at much lower rates, or even escapes tax entirely.

Very few high-income-bracket taxpayers actually pay tax at the rates of tax set forth in the Internal Revenue Code. The actual effective rates of income tax for all taxpayers with incomes of $100,000 a year or more is well below 45 per cent, when we take into account various types of income which are not subject to tax, such as income from tax-exempt state and municipal bonds, and certain deductions which exceed actual cost. This 45 per cent rate is in striking contrast to the Internal Revenue Code rate of 67 per cent and more on these high-income taxpayers.

Some of these provisions were the result of sincere efforts to deal with difficult technical aspects of taxation. Others were the result of palpable attempts to create tax privileges for special groups. This eroding or nibbling away of the income tax has been in process for a good many years. It continued with renewed vigor in the 1954 legislation sponsored by President Eisenhower and Secretary Humphrey.

The benefits of the Revenue Code of 1954 went almost entirely to tax-payers in the high-income brackets.

Even on the basis of administration figures, only $90 million in tax relief could be considered as benefiting the average wage or salary earner. This was due to the allowance of deductions for interest charges on in-stallment contracts and liberalized deductions for medical and dental ex-penses.

Further reductions amounting to $310 million went to selected categories of taxpayers, including some low-income and some high-income taxpayers. There were changes in the rules on annuity and retirement income, on dependents and on heads of families, and on child care expenses.

The balance of the $778 million went principally to high-income groups. At best, only one-quarter of the total relief in 1954 went to the two-thirds of families with incomes of $5,000 or less. At least three-quarters of that relief went to taxpayers with higher incomes. Some estimates put the figure at over 90 per cent.

I suggest a halt on further erosion of the income tax base. Tax re-adjustment should include the cutting down of very high surtax rates to more moderate levels, in exchange for the elimination of loopholes. There must be more effective collection, such as a broadening of the withhold-ing provisions of the income tax so that they will apply to dividends and interest in the same way they do to salaries and wages. Also, we must find a more satisfactory way of dealing with capital gains and other special provisions. In this way, more moderate rates could be applied honestly to all incomes, not just to some.

CORPORATE INCOME TAX

The corporation income tax is our second largest revenue producer. While excessive taxation of corporate income could damage incentives for investment, the necessary rates of corporate income during the last twenty years have not prevented the greatest period of corporate growth in the history of the American economy.

When conditions permit, some reduction in the size of corporation tax will be in order, but even then it is destined to remain a major part of our tax structure. Also, when there is room for revenue reduction, we could improve the fairness of the tax by correlating it more closely with the personal income tax on dividends.

But more is lost than gained by a method such as the administration proposed in 1954. Their plan would have done much toward reducing the double taxation for stockholders in high-income brackets but little to improve the position of shareholders in the lower income brackets. Also the pensions and other welfare funds which invest in stock would not have received any benefits from their proposal. Congress refused to accept their plan. So the administration settled for a plan which reduced the inequities of the administration proposal to smaller proportions, but did not eliminate them entirely. When revenue reduction becomes possible, I would prefer a method which will not benefit one class of taxpayers over another, and which will have better economic effects. This method would give a partial credit to corporations for dividend payments.

It would be possible also to improve the effect of the present tax on small business concerns. This can be done through readjustments of rates, or through new methods of accelerating depreciation aimed primarily at small business firms.

As in the case of the personal income tax, there remains the job of improving the tax base by eliminating special privileges. A good illustration is the treatment of capital gains on the sale of depreciable assets, a loophole that was broadened by the accelerated depreciation provision of the 1954 Revenue Act.

STATE AND LOCAL FINANCES

This statement has concerned itself so far with federal financial problems. Of no less importance are those of our state and local governments. State and local expenditures, taxes and indebtedness have more than doubled since the war. In the first three years of the present administration their expenditures rose by 30 per cent, in contrast to a decline of 5 per cent for the federal government. Their debt increased by 40 per cent, in contrast to a rise of 5 per cent for the federal government. Thus, the great burden of meeting our surging civilian needs has fallen largely upon our hard-pressed states and localities.

This calls not only for federal concern, but also for firmer support of state and local efforts in school construction, urban redevelopment, hospitals and health, road building, and the like. It calls for a policy of constructive co-operation on the part of the federal government.

The federal government must accept as one basic test of proposals for tax revisions this question: Do they contribute to state and local fiscal capacity? To be sure, all federal tax cuts give states and localities more elbow room in taxation. But some taxes are more adaptable to local and state use than others. A national government which truly respects the steadily rising pressures on state and local governments will, therefore, set aside revenues in those specific fields—for example, amusement taxes—which lend themselves to local initiative and use.

Unfortunately, we do not hear, as we did in 1952, of the intention of the federal government to turn taxes over to state governments. We hear only of transferring responsibilities to these governments, not the means of financing them. In the President's view, spending in excess of receipts leads to bankruptcy. But this standard apparently is applied only to the federal government!

We should adjust federal fiscal policies to take account of the needs of states and localities. A responsible national government can enlarge the capacity of state and local governments to meet the needs imposed on them by co-operation in government borrowing, co-operation in tax enforcement, and above all, co-operation in financing basic services.

CONCLUSION

The Democratic party has demonstrated that it can act to meet the large and life-destroying dangers of depression. The Republicans at best meet recession with action that is too little and too late.

But we are determined that there shall be not depression, but growing abundance in the years ahead. That is the context in which this program is presented. And, given that assumption, our program is realistic.

In the expanding economy of the next ten years, I propose, therefore, that we spend by 1965 on the order of $10 billion per year additional on our program for the New America. It amounts to but one-third to one-fourth of the rise in federal government tax revenues from our growing prosperity, and is only about 50 yer cent of the gains in the national product that both Republicans and Democrats expect. I suggest that this is little enough for a great, rich land to spend on needed public services.

These economic questions, at first, are matters of cold, hard material fact: the amount of iron, the number of kilowatt-hours, the condition of the soil, the number of men in the labor force. But that is not the whole story. At the last, the question of what we can do and will do depends upon what we really value. The way we deal with the material goods we have depends upon, and reveals, the true nature of our spirit. The means are at hand for us to build a nation that is as much devoted to the promotion of the general public welfare as it is to the pursuit of private happiness. I believe we can have much more to spend as citizens, and we can also have the public services that are indispensable for our growth. All we need now is the intelligence and the will.

2

Education

EDUCATION: PROGRAM PAPER

•

The dream of a New America begins in a classroom.

This is as true today as in the days of the little red schoolhouse. The giant steps our nation has taken toward the goal of universal educational opportunity has, more than anything else, given us the technical and economic progress we enjoy today. Public education in America has been the great lever by which we have lifted a whole society by lifting each person toward his own full potential.

These educational achievements of the past have put us now on the threshold of a New America. But whether we can cross this threshold and seize the brilliant opportunities that lie beyond depends heavily upon what we now do to advance American education ever further. The passport to a better society is better education—for one and all.

Better education for all American youth is thus an imperative for a New America, but it is also an extremely difficult assignment. Our schools and colleges are today up against severe obstacles and handicaps. We must work hard just to keep from losing ground in education; we must work doubly hard to gain new ground.

We must identify our most critical problems in education and come directly to grips with them. If we make one set of decisions, we can look with confidence to a future in which our children and grandchildren will have a chance to realize their talents and fulfill their promise.

If we make another set of decisions—or if we make no decisions at all and let drift take over the superintendency of our schools—then we can anticipate only the growing misuse and waste of our human resources, only the frustration of the American promise.

Statement issued October 1, 1956.

Unless we are prepared to do something about the crisis of our schools, there is simply no use even of talking about a New America.

CRISIS AND SUCCESS

When the Founding Fathers wrote the Constitution, education was an aristocratic privilege. But the logic of American history has meant a steady widening of educational opportunity. "If a people expects to be both ignorant and free," said Jefferson, "it expects what never was and never will be." Today there are 36 million young people from every walk and station of life in our schools. Truly now education belongs to all of us.

This triumph of the educational idea in America, coupled with the sharp rise in births during and since World War II, has filled our schools so full that they are today bursting at the seams.

And the great rush has only begun. Five years from now our already overcrowded elementary schools will have to serve two extra children for every ten now in school. By 1970 our high schools will have six-seven extra students for every ten now in school. College and university enrollments will double during the next ten to fifteen years.

These are not speculations; these figures come from counting the noses of children already born.

CRISIS AND QUALITY

The crisis in education is not just a problem of overcrowding. The kind of world we live in has compounded the crisis.

At home, we are entering a period of rapid technological and social change—a period which will test our ideas, our knowledge, and our creativity. And abroad we confront a world in ferment, where the aspirations of long-submerged peoples, as well as the dogmatic fanaticism of the Communists, have created tensions that the rising generation must know and master. "Human history," H. G. Wells wrote, "becomes more and more a race between education and catastrophe." The faster trouble runs in the world the better the job our schools must do if we are just to keep ahead of disaster.

But keeping ahead of disaster is not enough. The problem is more than one of giving desks and primers to the boys and girls flooding into our schools. We look to education not just to keep us out of trouble; we look to education to keep advancing us toward a fuller and more fruitful life.

SUMMARY

This is our educational crisis in broad outline. It would be irresponsible to promise quick and rapid solutions. We cannot produce overnight an abundance of modern, well-lighted school buildings with plenty of capable and devoted teachers, where every child is free to realize his best self. The short-run task of rehabilitating our schools is one for a generation. The whole task of education will never be finished.

But what I do consider possible—what I believe to be long overdue and now imperative—is that we stake out the generation-long task and start doing something about it at once.

I want to emphasize at the outset that education is primarily the responsibility of the community, of the local and state government. And full credit must be given for the encouraging developments in our communities. Most local governments have been enlarging their support of education; citizens' groups are working valiantly to improve our schools; private foundations are providing aid and leadership in the fight for improved teacher training and for better salaries.

When the local community can improve conditions no further, however, and there is still much to be done, we are right to look to the federal government for assistance.

But, in the end, success or failure in meeting the educational challenge will rest largely in the community. It must make the maximum financial contribution within the limits of its resources. It must provide efficient and economic operation of the schools. All the federal government can do is to make it possible for the community to discharge its responsibilities.

But to do this, the federal government must take a number of steps as swiftly as possible:

Proposal Number One: the establishment of a national policy of federal aid to education where local and individual resources cannot meet the need.

Proposal Number Two: assumption immediately by the federal government of a share in meeting the present urgent financial requirements of our educational system, particularly those for more classrooms and for more, qualified teachers.

Proposal Number Three: a program designed to help ensure against able students being denied a chance to have a college education because they can't afford it, and to encourage such students to enter teaching or other lines of work where there are serious personnel shortages.

Proposal Number Four: expansion of the exchange programs which in the last seven years have sent thousands of American students and teachers overseas and have brought foreign scholars to this country.

Proposal Number Five: development of new approaches to the challenging opportunities in vocational and adult education.

SPECIFIC PROBLEMS

There are six great problem areas in American education today.

1. THE SHORTAGE OF BUILDINGS

Many of you know from your experience with your own children the shortage of school buildings which has led to such grave overcrowding of existing facilities—to classes too large for effective teaching, to children attending schools in shifts, even to the use of unsafe buildings.

A careful Congressional study showed that in 1952 we needed new classrooms equivalent in size to a one-story building, 50 feet wide, stretching from New York to San Francisco! And the deficit now is vastly greater.

We should be building 100,000 new classrooms each year.

Actually we have been building little more than half that many.

In other words, we are losing ground at the rate of about 40,000 classrooms a year. And we are losing ground precisely where we can least afford it—in the poorer districts of the country.

2. THE SHORTAGE OF TEACHERS

Today's ominous shortage of qualified teachers had its beginnings in a great national mistake—our failure to give teaching as a profession sufficient reward and honor. Now, as the wave of children born during the war begin to grow up, we are paying the price for neglect of our teachers. We do not have enough good teachers—we do not have enough teachers at all. This teacher shortage may reach proportions of disaster for our culture and our economy.

Today young men and women—many who would like to serve their fellow men as teachers—are taking jobs in industry and in other professions. Why? Because they earn more in the vital five to ten years when they are hoping to get married and to establish families of their own; because there is a ceiling, and a rather low one, on what they would earn, in both money and prestige, even after many years as teachers; and because their initiative might not be fully challenged in education, where responsibility does not increase with experience and ability and promotion often results less from superior performance than from length of service and the earning of various credits.

Unless we do something to improve the status of our teachers, fewer and fewer of our able and ambitious young people will go into the teaching profession. This can result only in a gradual downward drift of the level of teaching and hence of our whole level of education. It is not just that we need more teachers. It is that we need more *good* teachers—that we need, indeed, the best teachers in the world. Our children deserve nothing less.

How well equipped are we to meet the needs of the next few years?

We know that enrollments will increase at a predictable rate.

Although I find a baffling confusion in the statistics in this field, it is clear that we are falling tens of thousands of teachers short every year. The most reliable figures indicate that right now we are short about 75,000 to 90,000 teachers in the total teaching force.

We know, too, that we will need about 40,000 more school teachers every year to take care of the new children coming to school. And we know that we need perhaps three times that many new teachers every year to replace experienced teachers who drop out of schools—to get married, to raise children, to go to higher-paid jobs in business, or to retire.

When the schools opened this September, they had to hire some 90,000 (another source reports 78,000 to 80,000) "emergency" teachers—that is, inadequately trained teachers. The rest of the slack was taken up by crowding more children into already overcrowded classrooms.

And this year our colleges turned out only 2,600 qualified new mathematics teachers and about 2,000 new science teachers qualified to teach physics. At that rate of supply, how can we expect our 80,000 high schools to turn out children equipped to live in the world of modern science?

In the colleges and universities, the situation is even more serious. In the next ten or fifteen years, enrollment will probably rise by 100 per cent. For every teacher now employed, two-three new ones will have to be found in the next fifteen years.

It will not be easy to meet this shortage. It has developed because we have failed to give teaching the dignity and status this vital function deserves. To be blunt about it, we have not paid teachers enough.

We have all heard it said, perhaps said it ourselves, that money isn't everything to a teacher; that teaching is a life of service. But who can doubt that a truly professional standing based on a truly professional salary would make all the difference in the world in attracting fully qualified people into teaching.

"The teachers of this country," said William James, "have its future in their hands." The national neglect of the teaching profession may do incalculable harm to us all.

3. THE SHORTAGE OF TALENT

We can already see the consequences of our educational shortages. Recent studies by the Commission on Human Resources and Advanced

Training have demonstrated that our schools and colleges are not meeting the growing demands of our country for specialists, men and women trained to do the important jobs of our society. Business and government, society as a whole, need more scientists, engineers, doctors, social scientists, technical experts, psychologists; above all, we need more good school and college teachers.

It is too bad that it takes a divided world to bring these shortages home. In the first five years after 1950, the number of young people who earned engineering degrees in this country dropped from 52,000 to 23,000, while in the same period in the Soviet Union the number of graduates from technical schools offering courses equivalent to those of our engineering schools grew from 28,000 to 63,000. Russia's gain practically equaled our drop, and Russia is now producing two engineers for each one we turn out.

I do not suggest that we should set our sights or determine our needs by comparison with the Soviet Union. But I do suggest that the growth of Communist power may be explained as much by Communist investments in education as by any other one thing. And I think we might well ask ourselves whether a free people by free decision will also be prepared to make this best of all investments—investments in the education of its youth. The answer must be "Yes."

The shortage of trained technicians is by no means our only, or perhaps even our greatest, want. In a free society, where the will of the citizen is determining, we need, above all, citizens with a good liberal arts education. We need businessmen and workingmen and women who know our history and our literature and the values of our civilization; we need specialists and experts, to be sure, but specialists who know far more than their specialties, who are, first of all, educated people. We need poets as well as public servants—yes, and we need politicians! A group of scientists at the California Institute of Technology recently concluded that the most critical bottleneck to future national growth would be not natural resources, but "brain power."

And I want to say that I see these shortages as causes for concern, but surely not for dismay. They reflect the fact that our dynamic society has an insatiable appetite for capable, well-educated people. As we feed that appetite, we move toward the New America.

4. THE SHORTAGE OF FACTS

What the Office of Education can tell us about our schools and colleges is shockingly little compared to the facts that other federal agencies can give us about agriculture, banking and industry. Your congressman can send you more information about hoof-and-mouth disease than he can about the challenges confronting our educational system and the terrible wastage of human resources that an inadequate educational system inflicts. We simply do not have clear, accurate and up-to-date facts to answer some basic questions about our schools. This is highly unsatisfactory.

5. THE SHORTAGE OF POLICY

The fact is that the Eisenhower administration has utterly failed to develop a comprehensive national policy for education. It has not set up the administrative machinery to produce such a policy. It has not probed or put into perspective the facts of the educational crisis. It has failed to offer strong leadership in the cause of our most valuable resource—our children.

In 1955, President Eisenhower convened a White House Conference on Education. For nearly two years, the prospect of this conference had been used as an excuse for inaction.

The conference had been billed as an effort to define the relationship of the federal government to education, but it did not do so. Its report supported limited federal grants for school construction, but left open other questions. In short, our schools were asked to wait through three years of gathering crisis for a definition of the federal role, only to emerge with no definition.

Not until after the conference did the Eisenhower administration act. The action then was to put forth a weak bill for federal aid limited to school construction alone.

When the House of Representatives took up the 1956 School Aid Bill, the President sat by while 96 Republican congressmen first supported an antisegregation rider to the bill and then voted against the bill itself. Indeed, in the midst of the debate, a Republican congressman read a letter from Mr. Eisenhower in which he wrote: "In short, unless we are careful, even the great and necessary educational processes in our country will become yet another vehicle by which the believers in paternalism, if not outright socialism, will gain still additional power for the Central Government." A majority of Democrats supported the school bill; a majority of Republicans opposed it. It was defeated.

The record of the Eisenhower administration is a record, so far as education is concerned, of words and of conferences—but of little action, and no results.

The failure in conception, the failure in action, is a symptom of a deeper failure. It is a symptom of incapacity or unwillingness to see the problem of education in human terms—in terms of boys and girls with abilities and aspirations, children who may either be held down and defeated by a poor educational system or be given new possibilities and new goals by a good one. Who can watch a child go off on his first day at school without wishing him everything he needs to equip him best for life and assure the most complete personal fulfillment?

I cannot believe that the American people hold anything superior to the future of their children. I know that the nation which can afford the best automobiles, the brightest television sets, and the biggest aircraft carriers in the world can also afford the best schools. The need is for leadership—leadership which is interested, determined and imaginative; leadership which cares about our children; leadership which cares about the kind of world they will build; leadership which understands that, in the end, all human achievement begins and ends with people.

A NEW ROLE FOR THE FEDERAL GOVERNMENT IN EDUCATION

Together, these shortages have produced the educational crisis. The problem now is how to meet the crisis—and how to meet it in a way consistent with our traditions and our ideals.

It is essential that we be absolutely clear in our minds about two things: how we decide what our children shall learn and how we pay for their learning.

From the start, we have thought it best to let the citizens of local communities decide what kind of education they wanted for their own children. In time, the state governments began to work with the local authorities, insisting that the communities meet certain standards and encouraging local initiative to improve the schools. But operation and policy have remained essentially in local hands—and this is the way it should be. A healthy educational system can grow only from local roots.

THE FEDERAL GOVERNMENT AND EDUCATION

But let us also be clear about one other thing: this tradition has not prevented the federal government from taking an interest in education and from supporting our educational system in a variety of ways—ever since the Army, under General Washington, began to provide "general instruction" in 1779. In 1862, when President Lincoln signed the bill establishing the land-grant colleges, the federal government laid down the basis for our state colleges and universities. In 1867, Congress set up the bureau now known as the Office of Education. Beginning in 1917, federal funds were made available for vocational education in local school districts. In the past twenty years, largely under Democratic leadership, the federal government has provided moneys to initiate and support a considerable number of school activities—the school-lunch program for pupils and the GI Education program being perhaps the best known.

In short, the federal government has for a long time been giving money for educational purposes without dictating what the schools should teach.

A NEW SITUATION

Two great social changes make it imperative that we look now to the federal government for a much larger part of the support of our schools.

One change is the fantastic expansion of our school population. This has led to an enormous increase in the school bill.

We are now spending more than three times what we spent in 1938 and about 40 times what we spent in 1900.

Annual public school expenditures by state and local governments stand at near the $10 billion mark in 1956. Estimates indicate that during the decade ahead the education bill will rise to $15 billion just to meet our minimum needs, and to perhaps as much as $20 billion if educational standards are raised to what it is generally agreed they ought to be. And this does not take into account the cost of private education or higher education.

The second great change is that for various reasons the local communities have been less and less able to foot this bill.

In the past, local communities have relied mainly on property taxes to pay for schools—taxes on land and personal possessions.

In recent years the local communities have been having a very hard time realizing enough money for schools from property taxes.

There are several reasons for this. For one thing, assessments have rarely reflected the true value of the property. More importantly, property values have not gone up proportionately with the rise in national income and production, so that property taxes have not yielded nearly so much, for instance, as income taxes. In relation to the national product, the general property tax yields only one quarter as much as it did twenty-five years ago.

It will thus be necessary in the years ahead to depend more and more on the taxing power of the state and federal governments for the money for our schools.

Some state governments are in a position to contribute more than they have in recent years. Some are not. In any case, state revenues are reaching their limits, especially in so far as they are not directly affected by an enlargement of income. So it has become increasingly up to the federal government to provide the money to set our school system on a solid basis.

We should face this problem squarely and promptly.

As I have said, the best information available indicates that it will cost us, as a nation, from $500 million to $1 billion *more* each year for the next ten years to build the schools, hire the teachers and pay them enough to attract able teachers to take care of our rapidly growing school-age population.

We have three choices:

1. We can do without the new schools and new teachers we need, or

2. We can leave it to the states to do the best they can to match the means to the needs, or

3. We can raise part (at least of the added requirements) through federal taxes, primarily the income tax.

These choices are *not* going to be easy ones. To me, the first one is out of the question. The second one, for the reasons discussed above, appears in most cases to be almost impossible; there just isn't this much more "give" in the local property tax and the state revenue sources.

The prospect of increased federal expenditures—for anything—is one that any holder of national office or any candidate for such office must face with stern anxiety.

But I say this: Any opposition to increased federal expenditure for education is honest, under today's circumstances, only if it includes a clean-cut decision that we do not need more schools and more teachers, and especially teachers of quality, than local sources are providing. I don't believe any responsible person thinks this is true.

I hope, as part of this series of papers, to make bluntly clear the economic and fiscal consequences of any enlarged federal "welfare" programs. I am setting forth here only what I think are the goals America has in mind. We always want and need more than we can have at any given time. And we shall have to decide which of these things we feel we can afford and which ones we can't.

PROPOSALS FOR EDUCATION

Proposal Number One:
A Policy

A Democratic administration will set the highest priority on the establishment of a clear-cut national policy for the improvement of educational facilities.

The goal of our national policy should be to permit the fullest possible development of each individual's capacities and talents through strong and equal educational opportunities. It should aim, not just at getting more

children into more classrooms for more years, but at making each child's
education a richer and more challenging experience than ever before.

A necessary step toward the development of such a policy is to remove
the United States Office of Education from its present hiding place and to
give it higher status.

At the present time the Office of Education is a stepchild of our government. A survey not long ago revealed that less than 1 per cent of the
federal funds actually spent on education was channeled through the
Office of Education. The chief of this office has less importance than
second- and third-rank officers in other departments.

It has been frequently proposed that there should be a separate Department of Education in the President's Cabinet. I think this should be given
consideration, but I think we should be sure that it would not aggravate
the administrative problem in our federal government. And I think we
would also want to be careful that such action would not introduce a
political element which would be undesirable and shift the center of gravity
in this field from the local to the national governmental level. In any event,
however, a fundamental reorganization of the federal government's administrative machinery for the handling of the problems of education
seems imperative.

Proposal Number Two:
Federal Aid to the States

There is substantial agreement today that some form of federal financial
assistance to the states for educational purposes is required. The real
issue now is not where there should be federal assistance, but rather what
form it should take and how much it should be.

This program should include aid for school construction. The Kelley
Bill, which was before the House of Representatives this year, represented
a substantial step toward this end.

But I do not think that the federal aid program can advisedly be limited
to grants for school construction. The building shortage is the most obvious one, but the hidden crisis—the shortage of teachers—is surely as
important.

The priority needs differ from community to community and from state
to state, and the federal government is not in the best position to judge
those individual needs. Some communities desperately need new classrooms, but others are more immediately in need of more and better teachers, more books, or a richer curriculum. It seems to me we should consider a program of general aid, leaving the states and communities free

to assign their own priorities in using supplemental funds from the federal government.

There will be the question of whether the federal grants should be made outright or on a matching basis. There are advantages and disadvantages to both forms. The matching grants offer certain safeguards. Yet they may also mean a disruption of broader state and local fiscal programs. Although such a decision would have to be worked out on the basis of full explanation and discussion, and ultimately by Congress, my own present thinking is that at least a part of the federal aid program should be on a nonmatching basis.

There would, of course, have to be means of positive insurance that federal funds would not be used to reduce or supplant state or local support for education.

I would think that federal grants would take into account both the number of school-age children and the element of economic need in the various states.

Many states already follow an equalization principle in distributing state aid among their communities; a federal program embodying the same principles would give further encouragement in this practice. The federal and state governments alike should be concerned with reducing the severe educational handicaps presently suffered by youngsters who, through no fault of their own, happen to live in economically underprivileged communities.

I would feel that Congress should adopt legislation that leaves little room for administrative discretion in the fixing of the amount or terms of the federal grants; thus any attempt to inject federal control would have to be thrashed out in the open on the floor of Congress and could not be tucked away in the fine print of some administrative regulation.

It must be recognized that this program will be costly.

President Eisenhower proposed a school construction program of $250 million a year, totaling $1.25 billion over five years. The Democratic-sponsored Kelley Bill would have authorized $400 million of construction grants annually, for a total of $1.6 billion over four years.*

We must expect that, as the school population keeps on rising and as we turn to meeting not only the school construction need but also the teacher shortage, these figures will have to be raised. I have already referred to the estimates which have been made indicating the inevitable increase during the next ten years in the total amount of educational costs in this

---

* (The current Eisenhower bill proposes $325 million per year for seven years, the Kelley bill $600 million per year. Eds.)

country. We must decide how much of this should be borne by the state and local governments (as 97 per cent of it is now), and how much we should shift to the federal government.

It is impossible to fix a price tag on a federal aid program without having first made a determination as to how much of this added burden the states and local communities can and will bear, whether federal participation should go beyond school construction costs (as I think it should), whether the federal grants should be on an outright grant or a matching grant basis, and so forth.

But I do want to suggest that just as a business matter every dollar we spend on educating American boys and girls will be returned—with interest —in terms of their increased productivity; and further, that if we decide to skimp on education, every dollar we save will probably be lost twice over in terms of things like the costs of juvenile delinquency, boys unable to meet the standards for military service, the unavailability of scientists and engineers, and increased relief rolls.

Proposal Number Three:
Grants for Higher Education

It is estimated that each year at least 100,000 of our ablest high school students stop their formal education for primarily economic reasons. The record is also clear that there is today a serious shortage of young men and women adequately trained in certain fields, such as teaching, science and engineering.

I think we should seriously consider, and probably explore at least on an experimental basis, some of the proposals that have been made to meet these problems.

One of these proposals which seems to me to commend itself is for the establishment of a limited number of federally supported undergraduate scholarships or loans to students who want to go to college, are qualified to make good use of a college education, and will otherwise be denied this opportunity.

I think we should also consider the granting of fellowships, on a basis of merit and need, to specially qualified students who are prepared to commit themselves to service in teaching or in other fields of particularly acute shortage.

I realize that these proposals present many problems and implications which must be carefully and fully explored.

One of these is the desirability of so administering this program as not to affect the balance between public and private institutions. It has been urged, in this connection, that any program of scholarship or fellowship grants which may work more to the benefit of private than of public colleges and universities should be balanced by grants to states for aid to higher education in public institutions. The point is an important one and, whether in the suggested form or some other, should be taken into account.

If a loan, rather than a scholarship and fellowship, program appears advisable, then I should think that arrangements would be worked out for making these loans through local banks, with appropriate government protection.

The problems of determining need and qualification would have to be met.

Any scholarship program of this kind would have to be carefully drawn and restricted to prevent abuses by the unworthy and also to prevent any displacement of the private philanthropy which has been and will continue to be indispensable to the development of our colleges and universities.

To avoid the political and administrative complications that such a program might entail, it might be well to place its administration in the hands of an impartial, competent organization, just as has been done with the eminently successful Fulbright program of awards to scholars for study abroad.

Both to avoid excessive costs and to permit adequate tryout of the operation of such a system I would recommend, as I have indicated, that it be undertaken originally on an experimental basis. But I cannot urge too strongly that something of this perhaps bold character will be required if we are going to meet the problem of high costs of higher education on the one hand and serious shortages of adequately trained young men and women on the other.

Proposal Number Four:
Expansion of Exchange Programs

I think we should continue and expand the exchange programs under which, in the last seven years, over 42,000 grants have been made to enable Americans to study abroad and foreign students and scholars to visit the United States. At a time when this country has had to assume leadership of the free world, these programs have been of great value in giving our citizens fresh understanding of conditions abroad. They have also helped dispel myths and misunderstandings about this country overseas.

Proposal Number Five:
Expansion of Vocational and Adult Education

The federal program of assistance for vocational education should be expanded. The present administration has sought on two occasions to cut the program, by 25 per cent one year and by an additional 6 per cent the next. Yet vocational education is given to only about one-half the students below the college level who need and want it; more than 5,000 high schools serving farm children lack programs of vocational agriculture.

The rapid pace of change in the world and the prospect of increased technical development and a shorter work week are driving home to us the important fact that a person's education should not and must not end with a school diploma or a college degree; it only begins there.

Opportunities for continuing education, all through life, must be an important ingredient of the New America. Already there are some 50 million Americans engaged in one form or another of adult education—more than the total enrollment of our elementary and secondary schools. The need and the demand will mount rapidly. What should we be doing to meet this important need? Obviously there are no easy answers. We must seek them out, try them out, apply them on an adequate scale.

A strong system of adult education will do many things for us as a nation. Not least of all it can liberate us from old passions and prejudices, it can help us as citizens find wiser answers to new and pressing public problems, and it can make us impervious to artificial answers in the form of hucksters' slogans.

This is another major educational challenge to which we must turn our attention; another national challenge calling for leadership at the highest level.

"In proportion as a Government gives forth to public opinion," said George Washington, "it is essential that public opinion shall be enlightened." Education is one of the pillars on which our freedom rests. When we neglect education, we weaken the whole foundation of free society. And when we neglect education in an age of global conflict, we risk the very safety of our nation and the future of freedom in the world.

But, more than this, education is one means by which the individual can realize his own highest capacity.

It is essential, therefore, that education be available equally to all, without distinction or discrimination based on race or creed or color or economic condition.

The crisis in our schools is not only a challenge to democracy and to national security. Above all, it is a challenge to conscience—to our moral conviction of the worth of individual human beings, to our love and hopes for our children, and to our faith in America.

Thus far we have responded to the challenge by pious words, by conferences, by token gestures, by promise and postponement.

The time has now come to respond by deeds, courageous, decisive and strong, in the tradition of our nation and in the spirit of our democracy.

SCHOOLS

•

You people were told, two or three minutes ago, that this is a paid political program.

And I have been told that this means that by now a large number of you are turning the television knobs to something more exciting than a political speech.

I'm going to ask you to wait just a minute.

I am a strong believer in the right not to listen. And when you make as many speeches as I do you soon become an authority on how boring they can be—especially to the fellow making them!

But what I want to talk about tonight lies so very close to my heart, and I think to yours, that I am going to urge a little that it is very much worth some of our time.

If you are a boy or girl in grade school, or a teen-ager, or if you're in college now—then my subject this evening is you.

And if you are the mother or the father of a child in school or of a youngster heading that way—then I think you will agree with me that the matter of education in America today—and tomorrow—is about as important a question as there is. I guess, for myself, with three boys of my own—all in school, but all pretty well along—I count the importance of education second only to peace on earth. It won't help to educate them, of course, if there isn't a tomorrow for them to enjoy and, I hope, improve.

And if you are not a student or a parent, you are an American citizen and you know the value of education to the earning of a livelihood and, even more important, you know the value of education to the growth, development and security of this country and its freedom.

Telecast at Milwaukee, September 28, 1956.

School started again this month. And in hundreds and thousands of communities this opening of school brings new realization that things on this front just aren't right; they aren't what they should be.

For some of you the problem is that your child can go to school only half a day because the schools in your town are so overcrowded, or the new school isn't finished. You are wondering whether a part-time scholar can learn the fundamentals properly.

Or perhaps you have a child in a classroom that has thirty-five or forty pupils in it. You know this means that, if your child doesn't catch onto his reading lesson on the first go-round, it's just too bad. The teacher isn't going to have much time to give him special attention.

We are short, in America, classrooms for 5 million children.

Or maybe your child has a teacher who is on an emergency certificate. This means, in plain words, that she isn't fully trained and qualified as a teacher, according to the minimum standards of your state.

In 90,000 schoolrooms in America class was called to order this morning by an "emergency teacher."

Or, even if your child's teacher is fully qualified, you're probably aware that she is in all likelihood underpaid. In fact, maybe she's doing baby-sitting or other jobs nights and weekends to make ends meet.

The average earnings of teachers in America's schools are today less than the average earnings of workers in America's factories.

Or perhaps you are more concerned about the over-all quality of the education your child is getting. You are wondering if he is learning the skills of mind and hand he will need to live in this world that is so much more complicated than the one you and I grew up in—and whether he's getting enough of what a good teacher can tell him of democracy's meaning, and of how to tell what is good from what is bad or just mediocre, and of the difference between truth and untruth.

It all adds up to a crisis for our schools that presents, in my judgment, a great danger for our country.

First, but only because it is most obvious, we are terribly short of classrooms. The figures show that with the tremendous increase in the number of school-age children, and even with an all-out local school building effort in thousands of local communities, we are losing ground, falling behind, at the rate of 40,000 classrooms a year.

And I should warn you that just five years from now there will be twelve children in our elementary schools for every ten there now.

Second, although the school building shortage is bad enough, the teacher shortage is far worse.

Schools are not really made of stone and wood; they are made of teaching. Wherever the great teacher Socrates was, there was a school—in the open streets of Athens, at a dinner table, or in a prison facing death. Jesus, speaking parables, made a school of the barren shore of a lake.

It is teaching, far more than buildings, that determines the quality of education.

And the worst of it is that we cannot see what is happening to the teaching in our schools.

We do know though that just in numbers we are hundreds of thousands of trained teachers short right now, and this situation too is getting worse —the shortage is increasing at the rate of at least 50,000 teachers a year.

Here is the most staggering fact of all: If we want college-trained teachers for our children, one-half of all our college graduates during the next ten years will have to go into teaching. This is a far larger proportion than is going into teaching now. And classes will get bigger and teaching standards lower.

The third problem is that many young men and women who want and who deserve a college education cannot get it today.

One hundred thousand of our ablest high school students today stop their education short, primarily for economic reasons.

I can't be indifferent, nor can you, to the fact that this crisis in education has arisen in this age of abundance in this richest of all nations in the history of man. It does us a grave injustice.

And I think we are wakening now to a full realization of what we have been doing to the future of America. It isn't the figures I have mentioned that shock us. What does drive this failure of ours home is its now all-too-familiar symbols: the roaring hot-rod car, teen-agers' beer cans along the roadsides, juke box blues dishing up love and religion in identical groaning tones, the rural mailbox ripped off just for laughs, a switchblade in the hands of a city teen-age gang boy.

Most of our children, who are sound and sensible, can take all this and leave it alone.

But among a minority—and this minority has grown bigger in recent years—there is emerging a frightening spirit of cynicism, arrogance, wanton destructiveness, a toying with violence; and, underlying all this, a sense of disrespect for the standards of the past and a carelessness about the future.

Another measure of this failure is emerging in the statistics which show that our schools and colleges are not meeting the growing demands of our country for specialists, for young men and women trained to do the important jobs of our society: to be scientists, engineers, doctors, nurses, social scientists, technical experts—above all, teachers!

It has taken a divided and competitive world to bring these shortages home. We are worried when we hear that Russia is producing two engineers for each one we turn out. But even if the Soviet Union disappeared from the face of the earth in a clap of thunder, even if cold wars and hot wars were suddenly to become things of the past, we would still have the problem of developing enough talents to man the posts of the New America and to help make the world a better place to live.

How can these things be? How can the wealthiest nation on earth, which for a decade has been boasting about its ever-expanding economy, fail to keep producing that most humble but most important of things: yeast for its bread?

The biggest material problem we have, of course, is money: money to build schools and to pay teachers a salary that will attract the teaching force we need. We are spending about $10 billion a year now on public school education—about 2.5 per cent of our gross national income. The costs of doing the job we need to do will be much higher still.

We have wanted and we have tried to meet our educational needs at the local level. And we are going to insist that the control of education stay in our local communities, particularly in our county and city and village school boards.

This is the crowning feature of our democracy at work—that the citizens of a town should determine what their own children should be given in their own town's schools. Here, surely, in this way of doing things, is the seat and safeguard of our individual liberties. The central power has no control over our separate minds.

But two great changes make it plain now that we are going to have to draw on federal tax funds for part of the money to pay our educational bill.

One change is the fantastic expansion of our schools. In early days our schools were for the privileged few. Today they are truly for all, and this autumn we have enrolled 36 million children!

The other change is the serious inadequacy of the property tax. And that is the tax from which we have traditionally financed our schools. It is about the only source of our local revenue. In relationship to the national product, the property tax yields only one-quarter as much as it did twenty-five years ago.

This means that we really have no choice now except to use federal funds to bolster up our educational program. In fact this has now been agreed upon at least in principle.

Now, what are we doing to meet this problem?

While we were falling behind at an alarming rate on school building and on the recruitment of teachers, the President first proposed an elaborate scheme that might have been of aid to bankers but not to our schools. Next, when the White House Conference on Education was finally held and, of course, gave the idea of federal aid for school construction a firm mandate, the President, now three years after his inauguration, finally proposed another bill that seemed to me sound in principle but inadequate.

But when a similar proposal introduced by Democratic Congressman Kelley came on for a vote in the House, a large majority of Republicans voted against it, while the majority of Democrats voted for it.

It must be said, in fairness—and leaning far over backwards, in fact—that the situation on that vote was complicated by other factors which crossed party lines.

But I say, I am sure in equal fairness, that with strong leadership from the White House, many Republicans would have supported that bill. As it was, in the midst of the debate this spring, a Republican congressman read a letter from President Eisenhower, which was hardly helpful, in which he said "unless we are careful, even the great and necessary educational processes in our country will become yet another vehicle by which the believers in paternalism, if not outright socialism, will gain still additional power for the Central Government."

I do not know whether this letter accurately reflects the President's view on this vital matter. But I would not expect much leadership on behalf of our schools from anyone who does entertain these philosophical misgivings about federal aid.

To sum up, we have had, during these four years, fine words, conferences, and lofty, high-sounding proposals about education. We have had no action and no results.

Now, what of the future?

Because there are so many facets to this problem, and because their full discussion would take a good deal more time than we have tonight, I am preparing and will issue within the next few days a written statement outlining the course it seems to me we should follow.

But I want to indicate briefly how it seems to me we should help our local governments do what we all want to do for our children and for our country's future:

First, we need a national educational policy, and we need it just as urgently as we need a coherent foreign policy and defense policy.

The goal of this educational policy must be nothing less than the achievement of the fullest possible development of each individual's capacities and talents. It should aim, not just at getting more children into more classrooms for more years, but at making each child's education a richer and more challenging experience than ever before.

Second, we have reached, indeed we have passed, the time for action in the commitment of federal funds to aid the states in their educational programs.

This federal aid program must include aid for school construction. The bill which was before the Congress this year should go far toward meeting this need.

But the federal aid program must also, in my judgment, be broadened to help meet the hidden crisis in education today—the teacher shortage.

Perhaps we should leave to each individual state the determination of whether its share of federal funds should be used to increase teacher salaries or to build new buildings.

We will have to face and resolve the questions of whether these federal funds should be granted outright or on a matching basis, and whether they should be distributed on the basis of the number of school-age children in each state or on the basis of other criteria of need.

I want to mention here, regarding these details, only that it seems to me imperative that we ensure against federal funds being used to reduce or supplant state or local support for education, and that we ensure also against these grants ever being a means of transferring to the federal government any degree of control over the content of the educational process.

Third, I think we should investigate thoroughly, and adopt, unless serious difficulties are disclosed, a national program of college loans or scholarships.

Such a program could be devised to meet two acute problems.

One is the unfairness and waste, as I see it, of any competent, ambitious young American's being denied, for economic reasons, the college education most boys and girls in this fortunate country are now able to get. I don't think 100,000 boys and girls who want to go on with their schooling and have the stuff to use it should be denied that chance.

Such a loan or scholarship program could also, particularly in connection with grants or loans for graduate work, be used to attract able young men and women into the fields of expert and professional training—like teaching and science and engineering—where we are today so dangerously short of adequate manpower.

Here, again, these are obvious problems of detail: whether these grants should be in the form of loans or scholarships; how the individual's economic need should be measured, and so forth. Perhaps the handling of such a program should be turned over to an independent organization, outside the government, as has been done with the eminently successful Fulbright scholarship program. I don't think these details present any insuperable difficulties.

Through these programs of federal aid to the states and federal scholarships or loans to qualified young men and women, I think we could go a long way toward giving our children a chance to realize their talents and fulfill their promise.

Now, I realize that programs such as these I have suggested cost money. Experience as Governor of one of our largest states has given me a healthy respect for the price tag on any program of this kind.

But I would say this: First, the costs of these programs are not nearly so large as their opponents will try to pretend. Second, I think every dollar invested in a child's education will be repaid—with interest—in his increased productivity as a member of the American society and economy.

And third: I think the American people hold nothing superior to the future of their children. And I am convinced that the nation which can afford the best automobiles, the brightest television sets, and the biggest aircraft carriers in the world can also afford the best schools.

Indeed we cannot afford to be penny-wise, and people-foolish.

Having said all this, I hardly need add that it is for me a basic assumption of any program for the better education of our children that we mean they should all be treated as completely equal, regardless of race or creed or color or economic condition.

And now this final word. I have said this is a task for leadership. But leadership in a democracy can be no more than the capturing of a people's will and the channeling of a people's power to realize their own ideals.

I believe so strongly in what I have said here tonight that it makes me uncomfortable that there is nothing any one man can do about it alone.

And so I appeal to you for your help if you think about these things as I do.

But my appeal tonight goes surely beyond any partisan line. And if this business of our children's training does perhaps bear in more sharply on the consciousness of America's women than of its men, I want, nevertheless, to issue tonight's challenge to all of us as Americans.

It's a marvelous thing to be an American. And it isn't just a lucky break. It's an unresolved responsibility, a responsibility to make this country a sounding board for new ideas, a welcomer of everything free and hopeful, a generous nation, the eternal home of liberty, and the temple of truth—a responsibility, in short, to make America what we started out to be—and what the whole free world expects us to be.

This is the spirit I have been trying to describe as the New America. And because you and I can only approach the future, and find our fullest satisfactions in what we can hope our children will do, I say that for me the dream of the New America begins in the classroom.

3

Health

THE NATION'S HEALTH: PROGRAM PAPER
•

The New America means to me an America in which we use to the full our almost unbelievably great resources for the enrichment and the fulfillment of human life.

The greatest resource is, of course, life itself. It is people, our bodies, our minds, our spirit.

The worst loss we can suffer is death. The worst waste we can commit is illness. The saddest thing in life is human suffering in mind or body.

Some of the facts about the nation's health are shocking. As things now stand, and unless and until we do something about it:

One out of every twelve American children born this year will have to spend some time in a mental institution;

Ten million Americans are suffering from arthritis;

One out of every seven Americans will die of cancer;

Our hospitals are jammed to the doors and in many hospitals even the corridors are being used as space for beds;

Doctors and nurses are critically scarce in many parts of the country and are working too hard for their own health and well-being almost everywhere;

Almost a quarter of a million people die each year whom medical science knows how to save;

The cost of medical care is beyond the reach of millions of American families;

The annual loss to the nation from illness is approximately $30 billion a year, a sum roughly equivalent to the total individual income tax revenue of the federal government.

Statement issued October 9, 1956.

There is another side to this picture: On the whole, Americans clearly are living longer and healthier lives than ever before and are fortunate in comparison with other peoples. Because doctors and medical researchers have made great progress in the diagnosis and treatment of the diseases of childhood and youth, the average age of Americans is increasing. This is, of course, part of the reason we are more vulnerable than we need to be to diseases of middle and old age, such as cancer, heart disease and arthritis, to name only three.

But, granting that we have reason to be grateful, the facts about the nation's health clearly reveal that much remains to be done and that we need to make a significant improvement in the nation's health a national goal.

Evidence comes in from every side that the pace of medical advance is accelerating. Breakthroughs on many fronts in the war against disease, like the development of a safe and effective vaccine against poliomyelitis, are probable—provided we act boldly and constructively to support research and to assure all our people good medical care. New knowledge is being won every day about cancer, heart disease, arthritis, rheumatic fever and other diseases, knowledge that can lengthen and lighten our lives if we will use it.

PRINCIPLE OF A NATIONAL HEALTH PROGRAM

Probably nothing contributes more to an individual's sense of well-being, once his basic needs for food, clothing and shelter are met, than good health. I believe that in developing a national health program, we should and will accept the following principles:

1. Access to good medical care is a basic human right in a civilization founded, as ours is, on the dignity and worth of the individual human being.

2. The federal government should do, toward promoting health in America, only what cannot be done—or as a practical matter will not be done—privately or through any other agency.

3. The pursuit of knowledge, in medicine as in all other fields, must be free and the practice of medicine must rest upon a private relationship between patient and doctor.

GOALS OF A NATIONAL HEALTH PROGRAM

The fundamental purpose of a national health program is quite simply to improve the health of all our people. To do this requires, in addition to such accepted and ongoing programs as those to assure the purity of our food and drugs, the safety of our water supplies, protection against epidemics, and so on, progress toward four major goals.

First, we must make sure that medical research, which underlies all medical progress, is not held back by lack of funds.

Second, we must train enough doctors, dentists, specialists, nurses and other medical personnel so that all genuine needs for medical care can be met.

Third, we must build enough hospitals and other facilities so that all genuine needs for institutional care can be satisfied.

Fourth, we must assure against anyone's being denied good medical care for financial reasons.

These goals are set high, as they ought to be, for we must aim high if we are to make the most of our opportunities. They will not be accomplished in a day or a year or perhaps in a decade, but they should guide and inspire our actions. We should make progress toward them as rapidly as possible.

The concern of the Democratic party with the nation's health is not an election-year phenomenon; it is a long-standing concern, which has found tangible expression in countless good works.

The National Cancer Institute was founded under Franklin D. Roosevelt's leadership in 1937. This was the inspiration for the creation in succeeding years of six additional National Institutes of Health. These institutes are advancing the frontiers of human knowledge about the major killing and crippling diseases, such as heart disease, arthritis, neurological disorders and mental illness.

In 1946, the Congress passed the Hill-Burton Act to help local communities build hospitals. Under this program, which has recently been extended and expanded, more than 100,000 hospital beds have been provided, mostly in rural areas which had lacked hospital facilities.

More recently, the Democratic Eighty-fourth Congress won distinction as the "health" Congress. It deserves credit for the broadest health program in our country's history. It acted to make the Salk polio vaccine available equally to all our children. It acted to improve the care of the mentally ill. It acted to expand private medical research facilities by grants for laboratory construction. It made the largest appropriation in our history for medical research; extended the life of the Hill-Burton program, which is bringing locally controlled hospital and health facilities to communities throughout the nation; supported advanced training of nurses and public health personnel and the education of thousands of practical nurses; established a permanent "survey of sickness" to locate the existence, incidence and toll of disease as an aid in determining where and when specific threats to our health can best be attacked; greatly expanded the National Institute of Dental Research to strengthen the devoted efforts of America's doctors of dentistry, and established a National Library of Medicine to assist doctors and medical researchers.

This is a record of which the Democratic party is proud. It is the best security for our pledge to expand and improve our health programs.

I am glad to say that most of the measures adopted by the Democratic Congress last year were recommended by President Eisenhower and enjoyed bipartisan support, though it is fair to add that the President and his administration had opposed needed actions on several important fronts for three years, reversing themselves only in this election year.

A Program for the Nation's Health

I. RESEARCH

Men have long and rightly been fascinated by the great stories of medical research and have reserved a special place in their affections for the great figures of medical history. Men everywhere instantly and instinctively recognize them as universal benefactors, selfless men inspired by reverence for life and dedicated to the good of humanity.

One by one, ancient scourges like smallpox have been conquered. Childbirth once took the lives of many, many mothers; it no longer does, and what this has meant in terms of human happiness is beyond measurement. The terrible killers of children—scarlet fever, diphtheria, typhoid fever, respiratory ailments and others—have been eradicated or brought under quite effective control, and now we have all been thrilled to learn that poliomyelitis, a disease that darkened every summer and struck fear into the hearts of all parents, is being conquered.

In the last four years, I dare say, no one has done more than Dr. Jonas Salk, who, true to the great traditions of medicine, sought not honor for himself but a healthier, happier life for his fellow man.

The list of other diseases that have been successfully attacked or controlled is long.

The value of these achievements cannot be reckoned. They have meant life itself for millions. And on a strictly economic calculation, if one could be made, the reduction of the costs of medical and hospital care and the extra production of those whose lives have been lengthened and of those who have been spared costly work-absences on account of sickness, have repaid manyfold all the sums spent on research. Perhaps no other field of human endeavor has returned such rich dividends, both in human happiness and in dollars.

There remain today, however, broad frontiers still to be crossed in the world of medical research.

The most basic need is for more young men and women trained for medical research.

No amount of money spent on research and no multiplication of modern laboratories will produce results unless there are good researchers to use them. Only a few young men and women have the special qualities of mind and character that are needed. It is all the more important, therefore, to make sure that those who have research potentialities are enabled to develop them.

Those who do have the ability and the interest will be found, certainly in the typical case, among those who are training themselves for careers in medicine. The educational aid program, which I want to discuss a little later here, should be designed and managed with a view to encouraging young men and women with research potentialities to enter research as a career. Account will also have to be taken of the need to reward researchers with incomes at least somewhat competitive with those that can be earned in the practice of medicine and in industrial research. There has been, I think, too much tendency to rely on the dedication and sacrifice of research people to attract and hold them to lives of service.

There is a large and growing need for modern laboratories and other facilities, especially facilities independent of the federal government and located at hospitals and other institutions around the country. Congressional investigations have revealed that many worth-while research projects are being held back by lack of adequate facilities. According to a report of the Senate Labor and Public Welfare Committee, admirably qualified researchers are sometimes "unable to make their services available to the people of America simply because they do not have the laboratories, facilities and equipment with which to do the work the Nation and the Congress very much want to have done."

Dr. Cornelius Rhoads, director of the Sloan-Kettering Institute for Cancer Research, has said, in endorsing the Hill-Bridges Bill for grants for research laboratory facilities on a matching basis, that "it is an absolute necessity that these facilities be made available if hundreds of thousands of lives are not to be needlessly lost."

Fortunately, the Hill-Bridges Bill originally opposed by Secretary Hobby [Mrs. Oveta Culp Hobby, former Secretary of Health, Education and

Welfare], was subsequently passed by the Congress and will make $90 million available over a three-year period in matching grants to build medical research laboratories. This bill is a good start. But, while it is obviously desirable to synchronize the expansion of research facilities with the expansion of the number of qualified researchers, the program will have to be extended and enlarged to meet the full need for modern facilities.

The third need is for research funds. The report of the Hoover Commission on research and development in May, 1955, indicated that several hundred research projects which had already been approved could not be undertaken in the fiscal year 1956 because the Department of Health, Education and Welfare had not even requested the necessary funds.

Last year the government spent more money for eradication of hoof-and-mouth disease than for research on mental illness, which afflicts some 9 million people.

It spends three times as much money on animal and plant disease research as on cancer research. Indeed, medical research receives less than 5 cents of each federal research dollar.

This year the Eisenhower administration asked for $127,000,000 for the National Institute of Health, including research programs. This was raised to $184 million by the Congress over the strong opposition of the administration. In all four years of this administration the Democratic leadership in Congress, aided by a minority of Republicans, has raised the inadequate sums proposed by President Eisenhower.

A good example is the field of mental health. The Democratic Eighty-fourth Congress launched a vigorous attack on mental illness. Rejecting inadequate proposals by the administration, it voted to triple the size of the psychiatric research program and to double the program for training desperately needed psychiatrists. It also greatly increased support for community health clinics and other preventive measures. Aware that mental illness costs state and federal government hospitals alone more than $1 billion a year and fills more than half of our hospital beds, the Congress also contributed to a searching three-year nongovernmental study of the entire human and economic impact of mental illness.

The fundamental research needs are for more qualified researchers and more research facilities. We must continue to rely heavily on private philanthropy in this area. The splendid work of some of the great foundations is well known and accounts for much of the progress we have made. But there remain large needs which experience shows cannot be met by existing means. There are few federal activities which so directly promote the general welfare of all the people.

2. AID TO MEDICAL EDUCATION

The United States needs more doctors. We have fewer doctors today, relative to our population, than a century ago. In February, 1955, Dr. Howard Rusk, chairman of the Health Resources Advisory Committee, reported to the President that "we have a tight supply situation in the three major health professions—medicine, dentistry and nursing." Responsible estimates indicate that we need 25,000 more doctors right now. Because our population is rising rapidly, the need will become larger and more critical in the years ahead.

There are two major reasons for the growing shortages.

First, our medical schools are overcrowded and understaffed. The National Fund for Medical Education has estimated that the nation's medical schools need new buildings which will cost from $250 million to $300 million, and an additional income of $15 million a year to meet present operating deficits. The financial pinch restricts both the number of students the medical schools are able to admit and the amount of research they are able to undertake.

To help meet one of these needs Senator Lister Hill proposed in 1955 that the federal government give $250 million over a five-year period in matching grants to medical schools for construction only. Although this proposed legislation was supported by the American Medical Association and the deans of most of our medical schools, it was opposed by Secretary Hobby on the familiar ground that it "required more study."

In 1956, an election year, the administration at last recognized—at least in principle—the crisis in medical education. This year Congress appropriated $90 million for construction of laboratory research facilities. What is needed now is a larger appropriation for general medical school construction.

The second reason for the doctor shortage is the high cost of medical education. We must do more than build new buildings; we must enable promising young men and women to enter them. With the present high costs, medical education is beyond the financial reach of many qualified young people.

I therefore favor a federal loan and scholarship program for medical education along the lines indicated in the program for education which I recently presented. If such a loan and scholarship program is adopted, I would hope that it would be administered in such a manner as to serve particularly the special need for doctors in depressed and underprivileged areas. Perhaps priority consideration could be given to applicants for loans or scholarships from these areas, upon their commitment to serve in these areas for a period following their education.

It will take time, of course, to make up for the time that has been lost in training the doctors we need. But the problem can be solved, and in solving it, we will make a large, direct contribution to the nation's health, for the lack of prompt and good medical care is now a more serious obstacle to the improvement of the nation's health than the lack of research facilities and funds.

3. AID TO CONSTRUCTION OF HOSPITALS AND OTHER MEDICAL FACILITIES

My remarks on this subject can be brief for, under Democratic leadership, a real attack is being made on this need. The Hill-Burton program has made possible the building of many hospitals and has made hospital care available in many communities which had been without it before.

Nevertheless, it is obvious, as anyone knows who has recently visited a hospital, that most hospitals are overcrowded. In many hospitals, patients are quartered in the corridors for lack of enough rooms. Many hospitals are old and not well equipped to provide modern medical care.

There is a need, too, for modern institutions for the care of the mentally ill, for the care of those with chronic diseases, and, as I pointed out in my program for the older citizens, for the care of the aged, and I think we may find there is both economy and mercy in a large expansion of our program for preventive community health clinics, which have done so much to curb juvenile delinquency, help families with other problems and to prevent uncounted people from disappearing into mental institutions.

We need to continue and expand the Hill-Burton program.

4. INSURANCE

As I said earlier, our American society has reached the point where we should recognize that access to good medical care is a basic human right. Yet we know all too well that millions of our fellow citizens today receive wholly inadequate medical care, despite the donation of much time by America's doctors—because these people cannot afford that care. We know that this is particularly true of preventive medicine. We know, too, that in hundreds of thousands of American homes, serious illness has wiped out a lifetime's savings and replaced it with discouraging debt.

This is expensive social wastefulness. It inflicts needless suffering, even death, on many individuals. It denies to many the equal opportunity for useful, happy lives.

And we know from experience that there are ways and means at hand for meeting these problems.

We learned long ago that where natural tragedies and disaster often strike in a haphazard, unpredictable way, it is to the advantage of all to share by the insurance principle the cost of the misfortunes which befall a few. The American people have gone further than the people of any other country in applying this saving principle to such misfortunes as fire and flood and storm. Nothing is more American than this co-operative way of dealing with misfortune.

For a vast number of our fellow citizens comprehensive private health insurance is now wholly beyond financial reach. The vast majority of our older citizens cannot afford it and these are the people who need this protection most. Careful studies show, too, that such insurance is characteristically unavailable, as a matter of practical economics, to families with a more than average number of children, particularly when the children are young and when medical care is most needed for them. I strongly suspect, although I find no specific data to prove it, that there is a high correlation between inadequate medical care and delinquency—although I recognize that other factors may explain this.

Let's get several facts clear:

Health insurance works. We have had enough experience with private health insurance to establish this beyond a doubt.

Health insurance need not, and our present health insurance system does not, interfere in any way with the private relationship between patient and doctor, which is a fundamental of good medical practice. It is a way of spreading the cost of medical care with fairness and justice; it has nothing whatever to do with the relation between patient and doctor beyond the payment of the bill.

More than 100 million Americans now have some form of health insurance. It should be pointed out at once, however, that most of the policies do not provide comprehensive protection. They cover, in the usual case, only hospitalization—and by no means even all the hospital costs. Indeed, only 3 per cent of the American people, it has been reported, have comprehensive health insurance covering house and office calls, surgery, hospitalization, rehabilitation services and so forth.

It is clear to me that what is good for millions of Americans would be good for all.

I am opposed to socialized medicine.

I am equally strongly in favor of a program to make comprehensive private health insurance available on a voluntary basis to all Americans, so that no American will be denied good medical care for financial reasons.

There are many ways in which this could be accomplished. I would, as president, urge upon Congress the immediate consideration of the various proposals which have been made to achieve this end. And I would urge full consideration of the views of all concerned—the medical profession, insurance experts, representatives of the groups which would benefit from the program.

But I would insist that it is a practicable and an essential objective: to make comprehensive health insurance available and attainable to everyone.

It is clear that some form of federal aid will be required to achieve this goal. This might take the form of long-term interest-bearing loans, as proposed by Senator Hubert Humphrey, to co-operative, labor and other groups desirous of getting started on group health insurance programs. This approach would help to meet the needs of groups who are not now covered and who only need capital to get their programs under way.

Some of the federal aid might take the form of matching grants to the states to pay part of the costs of voluntary health insurance for low-income families and individuals. The principle which should guide us in developing this program is, I believe, the historic principle embedded in our medical practice and our humanitarian philosophy of government, that those who can pay their own way should, that those who can pay a major part should pay that part, and that those who can pay little or nothing should pay what they can and should be assisted with the rest.

The administration of the program should rest with the states. The federal government would assure itself, before making grants available, that the insurance policies meet certain standards, that they provide, in short, truly comprehensive protection.

No one would be compelled to obtain this protection, but I am confident that most people would wish to take advantage of it.

There would be no restriction on the individual's freedom to choose his own doctor.

This program involves federal aid. In the course of our history many of our great social advances have come in this way. We have subsidized homesteaders, thus building and strengthening a free agriculture; we have subsidized education, thus building and strengthening a free society; we have as a people contributed to our own economic growth by subsidies to railroads, shipping lines, air transport, the development of power, thus building and strengthening free enterprise.

There is nothing more basic than the health of the American people, nothing more important to their future welfare and happiness and equality of opportunity.

It is time now to take this next step forward and to use the resources of the government of the people for the people's health. We shall discover that this, too, will strengthen the foundation of freedom and be another demonstration to the world of the marvelous ability of a free people to adapt its institutions to humanitarian purposes.

HEALTH SECURITY
●

Tonight I want to outline a new Democratic program to protect ourselves from another kind of disaster—the disaster of disease—physical disaster—let's call it a program for health security.

In my opinion we are not doing enough to win the battle against cancer, and against the other crippling and killing diseases. Our government is doing very little to bring the best medical care within the reach of all the people, not just some of them.

We are the richest nation on earth.

We are being told these days that all is well in America, that we are prosperous, that everything is fine.

And surely we share a great thankfulness for all the blessings of this heaven-favored land.

But we must look at both sides of our ledger: as things stand now, one out of every seven Americans will die someday of cancer—a disease whose terrible secret we know we can someday discover; one out of every twelve American children born this year will have to spend some time during his life in a mental institution; ten million Americans are suffering from crippling arthritis; millions more from agonizing bursitis.

In every state and nearly every city sick people are sleeping tonight in the corridors of overcrowded hospitals. The cost of adequate medical care has skyrocketed out of the reach of millions of Americans. We are woefully short of doctors and dentists and nurses, and of the schools where these professions can be taught.

These are shocking facts.

Telecast from San Francisco, October 11, 1956.

It is time we did something about them. There is a great deal we can do. And I think we want to do it.

I propose that we attack this problem on two fronts.

The first front is the one that most Americans today know only too well: the cost of sickness and of healing.

The second front is one that the ordinary citizen sees little of but it is there that the crucial struggle must be waged and won: and that is the front of science.

First, about the high cost of health. We know that doctors, hospitals and charities have given generously of their services and money and facilities to the sick. But in spite of all their heroic contributions, medical care is still costly. Ordinary doctor and hospital bills are a heavy burden on every family budget. Serious illness can wipe out a life's savings in a few weeks. About three million American families are today in debt for medical care.

Now, it is true that roughly two-thirds of the people in this country are covered by private health insurance of some kind. But the trouble is that this coverage is usually so incomplete that you have to get sick enough to have to go to the hospital before you are covered at all; and the insurance as a rule doesn't cover house calls by the doctor, office calls, preventive services, diagnosis, treatment, or the cost of recovery after you leave the hospital. Yet these are the very things that eat up the family cash.

Most insurance covers only the cost of the hospital bed, or of surgery, and that only within limits. If you have a long sickness, your insurance runs out when you need it most. It is like being insured for a little fire but not if the house burns down.

And some insurance, I'm sorry to say, covers very little—when the time comes, you find too many exceptions in the fine print.

The fact is that present insurance covers only about a fourth of the total medical bill of the American people. And many citizens—farm people, old people, people who live alone, the handicapped, the very poor—are generally not covered at all.

And so, every night—yes, tonight—men and women lie suffering, without care, because savings are gone and pride forbids or postpones asking for charity.

And every day children don't get the care they need—and are crippled or their health is impaired for life.

Well, what can we do about it?

The answer lies, plainly, in an extension of the insurance principle—

so that everyone can be covered by it if he wants to be. And it is plain that this is going to require more help from somewhere.

I have said many times, and I repeat, that I am against any form of socialized medicine.

I am equally opposed to those who resist all progress by calling it socialistic.

The present administration in Washington pretends to accept the idea of government aid to private health insurance programs. But what did it do? It did nothing but propose a so-called reinsurance plan which, after exhaustive hearings, was rejected by everybody—including the insurance industry—as being utterly useless.

There are various ways in which a Democratic administration would propose to work out effective federal aid for health. But all of these would look for the answer in an expansion of the voluntary private health insurance programs that are already going concerns—like Blue Cross and Blue Shield or HIP in New York or the Permanente and Ross-Loos plans here in California.

Federal aid might take the form of long-term loans to groups of citizens who want to get started in group health insurance programs. Senator Humphrey has proposed such a plan, and in it lies an inherently sound American principle: private citizens banding together for their mutual welfare.

And some federal aid might take the form of matching grants to the states to help low-income families and individuals buy, if they want to, voluntary health insurance in private group programs.

The family, the state and often the employer would divide the cost of the premium on the insurance; the family's share would vary, depending upon income and the size of the family. The family that can pay its own way should pay, the family that can pay a part of its way should pay that part, and the family that can pay nothing should not be deprived of medical care.

These private group insurance programs would, of course, have to be bona fide programs, measuring up to standards fixed by the state or federal government. They would cover preventive medicine, diagnosis, office or home treatment, drugs, probably all hospital costs, and so forth.

Let me make it plain that only those who wanted to would buy this insurance or become members of these prepayment groups.

A few years ago a Southern editor who became a member of the Presidential Health Commission wrote: "... Our democracy will never be complete until every person, rich or poor, high or low, urban or rural, white or black, has an equal right to adequate hospital and medical care whenever and wherever he makes the same grim battle against ever-menacing death which sooner or later we must all make."

It is this right, this chance for life, that I propose. We must, we simply must, bring the cost of medical care down within the reach of all our people. The insurance principle seems to offer a solution both practical and consistent with our experience.

And now of the second front in this battle for health: the front of science. We have long been fascinated by the great stories of medical research. One by one, ancient scourges like smallpox have been conquered. Childbirth once took the lives of many mothers; it no longer does, and what this has meant in terms of human happiness is beyond measurement. The terrible killers of children—scarlet fever, diphtheria, typhoid fever, respiratory ailments, and others—have been eradicated or brought under quite effective control.

And now we have all been thrilled to learn that poliomyelitis, a disease that darkened every summer, is being conquered.

The list of other diseases that have been successfully attacked or controlled is long.

For this spectacular progress we are in large measure indebted to private philanthropy. The splendid work of the great foundations is well known, but there remain large needs which cannot be met by existing means, and broad frontiers to be crossed in the world of medical research.

There is grim irony in the fact that last year we spent less on medical research in this country than on monuments and tombstones.

What is more startling and to the point is that last year the government spent more money for eradication of hoof-and-mouth disease in cattle than for research on mental illness—which afflicts 9 million people. The government spends as much on 25 or 30 miles of highway as on cancer research—and yet 25 million people now alive in the United States are doomed to die someday of cancer.

For three years the Eisenhower administration dragged its feet on programs to aid health research and medical education.

This year—an election year—it offered some constructive proposals, and some progress was made. And it would be utterly absurd to suggest that one party is for better health in America and the other party is against it.

Yet the fact is that in four years of this administration no real breakthrough in the battle for the people's health has been proposed. A family struggling with illness and medical bills has not had much sympathy.

I say it's time to get up and start fighting in this battle against disease.

We badly need new research laboratories. Work on vitally important research projects is being held up. Able research men are unable to join the fight against disease because they have no place to work. As a Democrat, I am proud that the Democratic Congress this year appropriated $90 million to build medical research laboratories. Yet even this will not do the job.

We need right now something like 25,000 more doctors—in your neighborhood and mine, in the hospitals, and in the research centers, where a handful of overworked men and women are fighting the great fights against cancer, heart disease, and the other major killers that still afflict us.

We will get more doctors only by educating more doctors. But our medical schools are overcrowded, understaffed, and underfinanced. And to make matters worse, a medical education today costs far more than most qualified young people can afford.

We need federal aid to the medical schools. We must build more buildings. And we must make it possible for young men and women to enter them.

I favor a federal program of loans and national merit scholarships for promising and deserving young people who want to become doctors. Let's give the gifted boy from a poorer home a chance to become a doctor. And let's give the American people the doctors they need. And we must train far more nurses, too.

In addition to all this, we must press forward with our hospital building program. We must improve our health facilities for the aged and we must learn more about the health problems of older people. We must expand greatly our community mental health clinics, which have done much to curb juvenile delinquency, solve family problems, and keep people from being consigned to overcrowded state mental hospitals.

These measures taken together are a broad outline of the Democratic program for national health security.

Disease will not vanish from the land, no matter who is elected. Mortality cannot be voted away. But inaction can be voted away; complacency can be voted away. And we can throw our hearts and will power and the resources of our government as reinforcements into an all-out attack upon disease.

Health, next to character, is a man's most precious asset. We are proud of our great free education system. And our spiritual needs and the character of our young are the constant concerns not only of family, but of our churches and our great organizations like the Boy Scouts and YMCA.

But what are we doing about our health? Well, we've tried to indicate in a few minutes what we Democrats would do about it.

Today medicine is on the threshold of great discoveries. New drugs, new therapies, new techniques, offer new hope to the American people. We have made progress, the fight is far from hopeless. All over the country tuberculosis hospitals are closing down because new drugs have sent their patients home.

It is time for an all-out drive for national health security.

Great America amazed the world with the atomic bomb. We can do the same—we can conquer the crippling and killing diseases that afflict mankind.

We are rich and we are strong; we can do what we want with our strength and our riches. Let us attack human pain as we attack human poverty.

Let us attack disease as we attack discrimination.

Let us strive for health as we strive for peace.

Let us build for ourselves and for our children a healthier and so a happier life in the New America.

4

Older Citizens

OLDER CITIZENS: PROGRAM PAPER

•

In accepting the Democratic party's nomination for the Presidency, I pledged myself to work, through the instrument of the party, toward the achievement of a New America.

In the New America, the traditional ideals of our nation—the ideals of freedom, of justice and abundance for all, "life, liberty and the pursuit of happiness"—will at last find their destined fulfillment.

We stand today on the edge of the New America. But to move ahead and realize its full promise is no easy task; for it means making freedom, justice and abundance meaningful, not for just a part of our people, but for all Americans.

Yet for the first time in the history of the world we have the means to attain our goals. We are entering an age of abundance unprecedented in history. In the new age, our abundance must be the servant, not just of some of us, but of us all. We will be false to our ideals unless our abundance serves to enrich the life of every American family.

I believe that a good place to start on the New America program is the welfare of our older citizens.

It is they who have contributed most to making America the land it is today. Yet they benefit least from its enrichment.

We are doing more to meet our obligations to our older citizens today than we were a generation ago. The New Deal greatly bettered the plight of the old, as it bettered the plight of every other group in the population. The goal of the New Deal years for older people was the achievement of "security." The Social Security program, a landmark in our nation's

Statement issued September 24, 1956.

progress toward social responsibility, was a substantial, though still incomplete, stride toward that goal.

But "security" has meant only the minimum necessary to keep life in a body. The goals of the New America must go far beyond the guarantee of subsistence. The New America thinks in terms, not just of life's preservation, but of its purpose. It looks, not just to man's survival, but to his triumph.

The New America aims at more than social security. It seeks the greater objective—the guarantee of human dignity.

GOALS FOR OUR OLDER CITIZENS

Our parents and grandparents deserve more than the privilege of eking out their last years in anxiety and privation. They deserve the comfort and gratitude which our abundant society is at last in a position to render them. I believe that the New America's program for our older citizens must accept these three objectives:

1. To enable a person to maintain his accustomed standard of living after the days of his regular employment have ended.*

2. To make available the facilities and services which are required to meet the special needs of older people.

3. To give purpose and significance to the evening of people's lives.

And now, let's look more closely at the facts which underlie these objectives, and at the ways by which we can move toward our goals.

THE GIFT OF YEARS

It will not do, as we think about the problems of growing old, to shrug our shoulders and say to ourselves that they have always been part of life's inscrutable pattern.

The fact is that within our own generation science and medical skill have presented us with a tremendous enlargement of life's experience. We are challenged today to use a *new* opportunity—or to let it waste.

Today there are in America 14 million men and women 65 years old or older. This is five times as many as there were fifty years ago.

Put it another way: When those of us who are my age started to school, fifty years ago this month, only one person in 25 in the communities we lived in was 65 years old or older. Today the proportion is more than double this, or one in 12.

Today, a man 65 years old may expect, taking the average, 13 more

* (See "Where Is the Money Coming From?" for a more precise statement of the accustomed standard of living. Eds.)

years of life; a woman, nearly 16 more years.

We have truly received a gift of years—a gift richer in what it can mean to us than any other gift there is.

But are these in fact years of reward? Or are they years of burden and anxiety?

Many older people have serious personal and economic problems, as I shall indicate in the pages to follow. Because of this, some people have been inclined to look upon the older people in our society as themselves constituting a problem. Of course, in one sense this is true, just as children constitute a problem when we think of the needs of education, training and guidance. But we are in error if we think of the older people in our society only as a problem. Older people as a group must be looked upon as one of our great human resources. Their presence among us in greater number is an opportunity.

There are some more figures which say all too plainly that by our scientific knowledge we have learned how to lengthen our lives before we have learned how to meet either the needs or the opportunities this gift of years creates.

With few exceptions, the incomes of older people are desperately inadequate. Of every ten people in America today who are 65 or older two have *no* personal income from any source; four have an income of less than $1,000 a year; only three have an income of more than that.

Although there is a common impression to the contrary, careful studies show that most men and women want to keep on working after 65. Only one in eight stops work voluntarily and to enjoy leisure. Some of the others are compelled by reason of health to cease full-time activity. But for millions, able to work and wanting to do so but denied opportunity, age means—more than anything else—frustration.

Low income is reflected in low living standards. In general, older people have poor housing. Much of it is dilapidated and lacks private bath, toilet, and running water. Little new housing suited to the needs of older citizens is being built. Those over 65 are at a disadvantage in either renting or buying the kind of housing they need.

Millions of older people suffer from poor health, many of them needlessly. Studies show that older people in the lowest income brackets have far more days of disability per year from chronic diseases than those whose incomes permit them to obtain early diagnosis and treatment. Patients over 65 who are admitted to hospitals remain twice as long as the typical patient. Many older citizens who are hospitalized could be better cared for and would be happier in more homelike surroundings, such as nursing and boarding homes or attractive and well-run homes for the aged. But there are not enough such institutions and many of the existing ones are substandard.

The problem of mental health is especially serious. Between 1900 and 1950, while our population was doubling, the number of patients in mental hospitals tripled. The number of patients who were 65 and older increased tenfold! Now, one out of every four patients in our mental hospitals is 65 or more—three times their proportion of the population. The average state mental institution is poorly prepared to receive these patients and does not have nearly enough psychiatrists, graduate nurses, and other trained personnel to provide good care. There is sickening irony in the knowledge that many older persons who are now in mental institutions probably should not be there at all; many could be rehabilitated. They could be better cared for in other ways—at home, in nursing or boarding homes, in homes for the aged, or in special geriatric centers. What these older patients want is just what every patient wants. They want to get well rather than to have more care. They want to get back to a normal, active, useful life. This is what we mean by rehabilitation.

One man in four who is 65 or older is widowed. But because wives tend to outlive their husbands, more than half of the women over 65 know this terrible loneliness. Nearly 4 million older citizens live away from any relative. Many of them feel unwanted; and they are driven by the pressures of modern life into a kind of social isolation. Our social service agencies are inadequately staffed to assist these people. And, although some promising beginnings have been made, our communities have not developed the facilities and programs which would assist older people in using their leisure time and drawing on the knowledge and experience and companionship of other older people in ways useful to themselves and the community as a whole.

A Program of Action

The difficulties I have just described are, happily, only one side of this picture. There are also opportunities. And, although some of the problems are difficult, on others we can do much. I think the vast majority of Americans want progress—for ourselves, for we will all be old someday, and for those who gave us the supreme gift of birth.

We have already made some headway. But there is much more to be done.

Let me repeat that it seems to me essential that we set our goals high, that we measure them not by what we *have* to do as a minimum, not by what we think may salve our consciences, but by what we *want* to do, by what we know is right.

1. As I have already suggested, I propose that we assert it boldly, as a basic article of belief, that in this age of abundance in this land of plenty, a person should be enabled to maintain, when life's regular duties are completed, his or her accustomed standard of living.

We long ago accepted this principle so far as the week is concerned. We earn seven days' living in five. We have more recently established it—in terms of "paid vacations" and "paid holidays"—so far as the year is concerned. Putting a lifetime's work on this basis is harder and in some ways different. But the principle is the same, and so is the goal.

Until we achieve this objective, life's evening will be dark, an anticlimax to the whole experience of living.

The individual must of course be expected to make, and will want to make, through savings, insurance, pension plans, and other arrangements available in a free economy, as large a contribution as possible to the achievement of this objective.

I think we can and should do a good deal more to enlarge the earning opportunities of older people. There is increasing evidence that in certain types of jobs older men and women can earn their way fully.

We should promote extension of the principle, already enacted into law in at least one state, that there should be no discrimination on account of age in employing people between 45 and 65. A man or woman in this age range who loses his or her job today frequently finds it almost impossible to get re-employment.

Congress, under Democratic leadership, recently eliminated age as a factor in employment of the federal government. It seems to me appropriate for the government to at least encourage federal contractors to develop employment opportunities for older people.

Recognizing that certain kinds of work can be better done than others by older people, we should develop much more extensively the training programs for older men and women which are now in operation in some states and local communities.

To stimulate development of such programs and to give attention to the problems of older persons generally, I recommend action on the proposal already made by Democrats in Congress for the establishment of an Office of Older Persons' Welfare in the Department of Health, Education and Welfare.

When the President recently announced, with much fanfare, that he was setting up a Federal Council on Aging "to review existing programs within the Government" as he said, and to "make recommendations," I couldn't help thinking how consistently the corporations have got action from this administration, while the people have got conferences, councils, commissions and confabs.

What this council will find is that right now there are just *nine* people on the Secretary's staff in the Department of Health, Education and Welfare who are working on this matter of enlarging the opportunities of America's 14 million senior citizens. This compares with 40,000 government employees working on the problems of the nation's business concerns!

An Office of Older Persons' Welfare will encourage and promote activity in numerous important fields. It will study the special social needs of older people; the ways in which these needs are being met in our states and communities; and it will develop new approaches. It will stimulate the training of research workers and social service personnel. In co-operation with other agencies, it will promote research in the problems of aging and help to spread our growing knowledge of geriatrics. In brief, its task will be to develop a comprehensive attack on the problems of older people. It will have at its disposal the resources of all other agencies in the government which can be of help—including the Federal Housing Administration, the offices responsible for job finding and job placement in the Department of Labor, the Public Health Service, and the Social Security Administration, among others. The Department of Agriculture, the Department of Labor, the Children's Bureau have served well the interests of the groups they were established to help. Our older citizens surely deserve similar attention to their needs.

Another step toward increasing the incomes and therefore the standard of living of our older people will be the revision of our retirement programs and policies to take account of the increasing work life of many individuals.

Both in public and in private employment experimentation is now going on with more flexible retirement policies. A highly interesting semiretirement plan, established in at least one instance by collective bargaining, enables an older employee to work part-time and thus to raise his income above Old-Age and Survivors Insurance levels by the maximum amount.

Democrats have introduced in the Congress legislation to permit retired persons to earn up to $2,000 a year without loss of OASI benefits, instead of $1,200 as at present. Upward revision of this limitation appears desirable as a way to encourage older persons to seek work and to obtain decent living standards through self-help and individual initiative. However, if this were done without taking other actions, particularly measures to maintain wage standards, it might fail to accomplish its social objective. For example, as we have already discovered, some employers try to exploit the present law by hiring retired people at substandard wages. Action to protect the wage structure against such competition would therefore be necessary, and further study will be needed to determine whether this and other problems can be met.

I think it is time for a comprehensive review and redetermination of the adequacy of existing OASI and Old-Age Assistance benefits. It would be irresponsible politics to assert categorically that these benefits should be increased to a certain figure. However, we all know that the cost of living is steadily rising and that benefits have failed to keep pace with these increased costs. Moreover, we are not thinking just of mere subsistence; we must think in terms of maintaining the improved standards of living that come with our constantly increasing productivity and rising wages. It is therefore high time that we take a good look at the Social Security benefit levels and work out whatever adjustments are found, on careful study, to be justified in the light of the needs of retired people—taking also into account, of course, the needs of other groups in our society. Such an examination I would urge upon the Congress.

I want, however, to note in connection with some of the recommendations I make here the necessity of keeping in mind two important and related factors. One is the fact that proposals for increasing the supply of work for older people must be considered in terms of the amount of work available for the entire work force. We gain nothing if the result of putting an older man to work is that a younger man becomes unemployed. So, when we talk of enlarging work opportunities for older people, the problem must be faced squarely as one of enlargement of the nation's work force. We would only compound the problem if we were to force the older people into competition for jobs with the younger folk who are now bearing the costs of starting their homes and raising their children.

The other factor is reflected in the action taken at the last session of Congress to reduce the age at which women are eligible for retirement benefits from 65 to 62. That people are able now to work longer, in terms of years, than they used to be is one side of the matter. The other is that an advancing technology may eventually mean that the nation's work can be done in fewer years of each person's life.

These considerations in no sense detract from the desirability, indeed the necessity, of making fuller provision than we now do for earnings or at least income opportunities for older people. But what they do is to suggest another whole dimension of this problem, a dimension that the advent of automation and atomic energy is even today opening up. One of tomorrow's great challenges will be to make good use of what will be very possibly be a greatly increased leisure.

To face, in the spirit of the New America, the challenge of maintaining the standard of living and the work opportunities of older people is necessarily to face at the same time the challenge of increased leisure.

2. Our second objective must be to make available the facilities and services which are required to meet the special needs of older people.

There is a very great unmet need today for more housing designed and reserved for older people. We are past the point where "living with the children" is always a satisfactory way of later life—from the standpoint of either the young folks or the old. It may be for some in some circumstances. But it is clearly not the best solution for all families. What we want is a chance for each family to make a free choice, so that where the mother and father do live with the children, it is a decision that is not forced on them and where they, themselves, are not forced on each other. And the plain fact, well and poignantly known to tens of thousands of American families, is that there is a cruel shortage today of places where an older couple, or more particularly an older man or woman, can go when "keeping house" is no longer practicable.

Careful studies show the need for federal financing of special housing for older people. Some of this must be public housing. I think we should explore, too, the possibilities of federal underwriting of housing projects of this kind financed primarily, or at least sponsored, by fraternal organizations, private charitable groups, and labor unions.

The other great need is for action, drastic action, on the health front.

Under the Hill-Burton Survey and Construction Act, the federal government has begun to provide hospitals for the chronically ill, nonprofit nursing homes, geriatric clinics, and rehabilitation services. This program is moving far more slowly, however, than it should. The Republican administration has used only a small part of the funds voted by the Congress for these purposes. This situation must be remedied at once.

A further grave need is for insurance to meet the costs of medical and hospital care. Older people most need such protection, and they are the least able to afford it. Only 26 per cent of those over 65 years of age have hospital insurance, as compared with almost 60 per cent in all age groups.

I shall urge a thorough investigation by Congress of the possibility of adding a program of hospital insurance for the old to the present Old-Age and Survivors Insurance system. I think we must consider carefully, too, the various suggestions which have been made for the encouragement, possibly the underwriting in one way or another, of private programs of comprehensive health insurance which preserve the private patient-doctor relationship. It is particularly important, so far as older people are concerned, to take action in this area because most private plans are now closed to older people. We do not want compulsory insurance—but neither do we want older people to be involuntarily excluded from voluntary plans.

Finally, in this area, I urge the immediate and substantial expansion of our programs for research into the causes and cures of the diseases which are the accompaniment of so many people's later years.

Last year, with 10 million American men and women suffering from heart disease, the federal government spent only $14.1 million on heart disease research—or about $1.40 for each person presently afflicted.

As things now stand, one out of seven of us will die of cancer. Last year the government spent $18 million on cancer research, or approximately 10 cents for each person in the country.

I have already spoken of the terrible ravages of mental illness and its heavy incidence among older people. The government is spending only $15 million a year on research in this field—or 1 or 2 per cent of the more than $1 billion the states and federal government spend on mental illness.

Last year the government invested about a penny a person for research in arthritis and rheumatic diseases, two more heavy afflictions of our senior citizens.

How foolish such false economy is! Let me put the matter in an exceedingly hardheaded way. Suppose we could cure cancer or heart disease. The productive efforts of those who, as a result, would survive would return to the economy in a few days all that has ever been spent on research. There is no investment like an investment in productive human beings.

3. Our third objective must be to give purpose and significance, in broad terms, to life's later years.

Let us think of this as the framework of our broader purpose within which the action of government is taken. For I expect that a great many older people, asked what they want most, would answer to this effect: "That life seem worth while, that it continue to offer a chance to grow in one way or another and to be part of things." Or, as an older lady said to me this spring: "We just want to be wanted."

It does seem to me that part of the idea of the New America is a climate in which these intangible, even indefinable, needs and wants of individuals will be recognized, respected, even anticipated.

I suspect, for example, that fifty years from now—and perhaps much sooner—we will look at the "problem" of old age less as one of preserving earning opportunities than as one of using leisure purposively and satisfyingly. This will probably affect not only our employment and retirement policies, nor even just our housing and health programs, but our educational policies as well.

Conclusion

The New America is not made up of small decisions. None of the specific recommendations or suggestions I have made here would, taken alone, open its gates—even in this one area of a program for our older age.

I think of the path to our infinitely greater future as one we must pursue by setting our sights above the small decisions, by accepting our ideals as *attainable* goals, and by making the small decisions then in terms of moving toward these goals.

If the issues are narrowly conceived—as being, for example, whether we want to spend more on public housing for older people or whether to add a few dollars to the monthly assistance check—then we can argue endlessly, and we will.

But if the specific issues are all approached in terms of whether we think a person's standard of living should or should not drop off abruptly when he reaches the age of 65, or whether an older person should or should not have an opportunity to contribute to society if he wants to, then the answers to such questions as these become plain.

The two key facts are, for me, that we *want* to do these things and that we *can* do them.

I am mindful of the price tags on some of these proposals. Four years as Governor of Illinois made me acutely aware of the expense of any public program, for it always affects so many people.

One reason the present administration in Washington likes conferences and study groups is that they don't cost anything to speak of.

But I am completely convinced that an adequate program for older people will be, in the fullest sense of the term, sound economy. The costs of present programs for older persons—mental hospitals, old-age assistance programs and all the others—are tremendous; and they will continue to rise unless we make greater progress in providing employment to those older people who are able to work and who want to work and unless we can reduce the costs of medical and institutional care by improving the health of older persons. Programs which enable our older citizens to stay in good health and which keep them participating to their full satisfaction in productive effort are, in a real sense, financially self-liquidating.

But there is more than economy involved here.

We want to make our dollars the tools of our hearts. We want to make the years after 65 years to look forward to, years of dignity and self-respect, years not of frustration, but of fulfillment.

PROBLEMS OF THE OLD

•

There is a theory among politicians, you know, that people vote their fears rather than their hopes. Sometimes, as I listen to myself and some of my fellow candidates, it seems to me we sound more than anything else like fire engine sirens clamoring that if we don't get to the fire the house and everybody in it are going to be lost.

I think we overdo it. We have never yet in this country met a problem we couldn't lick, and we have come through every crisis stronger than we went in. And so tonight I propose to talk with you not about our problems and our dangers, but about some opportunities.

The Secretary of the Treasury announced on Thursday that we are going to wind up our accounts this year—the federal government's book-keeping year, which ends next month—with about $1,828 billion savings for the year in the national treasury.

This is good news.

And my respect for this accomplishment is not diminished by the fact that it is a somewhat belated fulfillment of the Republican boast of 1952 about balancing the budget, nor even by the fact that during President Truman's administration we paid off $12 billion on the national debt, and under President Eisenhower we had by the early months of 1956 gone $13 billion more into debt.

But I *am* concerned by the fact that it is an open secret in Washington that defense appropriations were kept down this year in order to balance the budget in an election year, on the understanding that it would have to be increased by at least $1.5 billion next year.* If this is the case, I can find little fiscal satisfaction in such perilous politics.

Yet for the moment at least we face the pleasant question of what we want to do about a surplus of about $2 billion.

In the answers to this question, I suggest, there will probably be reflected some of the basic differences between the two political parties.

On the basis of what they have done during the past three years, it is

From a speech at St. Petersburg, Florida, May 19, 1956.
* (The Governor was generous. The 1958 Budget proposes a rise of $2.3 billion in national security outlays, a rise of $3.1 billion expenditures and $4.7 billion in cash payments; and on the basis of the experience of the last few years, expenditures will exceed budget outlays by $3 billion. Eds.)

certain that only an election year will spare us pressure from many administration leaders to use this $2 billion surplus to cut taxes primarily for the benefit of the large taxpayers. One of the few affirmative fiscal acts of this administration has been to cut taxes, and to distribute most of the benefits to the big corporations and the well-to-do.

And indeed Congressman Daniel Reed of New York, the chief Republican spokesman on taxes in Congress, has already proposed cuts to relieve the largest taxpayers—the $200,000-a-year boys. He says they are today suffering "severe individual hardship."

Let me make it perfectly clear that, as far as I am concerned, if anybody doesn't hate high taxes, well, he just hasn't paid his taxes. April 15 is the unhappiest day of my year—even if I am unemployed just now! And as a candidate for the office I seek nothing would please me more than to be able to promise, in good conscience, that I would as president support a general tax cut—and especially in the lowest brackets. I keep hoping frankly that this may be possible. But I am sure that there are a number of other things to be considered first.

Business is booming right now. If it slacks off, we will want and *need* to reduce taxes in order to stimulate private spending. But we cannot be for tax reduction in *bad* times in order to stimulate spending and also for tax reductions in *good* times because there is the prospect of a budget surplus. The latter tax reductions would help bring inflation.

If in our family budget-keeping at home we find that at the end of the year we have a little something left over, we sit down and decide what we want to do with it; whether to put some money in the bank, to pay off some debts, or whether there are some things we ought to buy because they're badly needed.

In a democracy like ours, we handle our affairs as a nation the same way. And, frankly, I think there are some things we need today so badly as a national family that we ought to take care of them before we start talking about cutting the taxes of our highest-income taxpayers.

I am thinking about our welfare programs, and particularly the problems of our older citizens. If we have money in the bank—about $2 billion —this year, I suggest that this is the time to work out a decent program to meet not only the needs but the *rights* of our 14 million senior citizens.

Here we are, the most prosperous nation in the world—but the hard fact is that the men and women who contributed the *most* to this prosperity are not sharing in it. It is mighty hard for me, frankly, to understand how the party of the administration, how the Republican leaders, can boast about the prosperity they have brought this country when the fact is that the average income of couples 65 years of age or older in

America today is only $2,300. This may be security—if all you mean by that is something to eat and wear and someplace to sleep; but it surely isn't dignity or meaningfulness. And it certainly · isn't the way we all want it to be.

Let me be very clear about this. I'm not talking about a matter of charity. I'm talking about a matter of *right*. I'm talking about the *fact* that almost 14 million people in this country today are 65 years old or older, that every one of us is hoping to enter upon these tranquil, golden years, and that the way we have things set up now they aren't golden years at all for literally millions of people, nor tranquil years, but years instead of fear, of frustration and of futility. I am talking about fairness, and decency and good sense—and about what we propose to do, not for others, but for ourselves.

So I want to go over with you here tonight the outline of what I think our approach to this situation—this *opportunity,* if you will—ought to be. I don't believe in making an emotional appeal on something like this or in playing politics with people's lives—and it's people's lives that we're talking about here. I am asking your support for my candidacy for the most responsible and influential office on earth. But you are entitled to know not only *how* I feel about something like this, but *what* I would do about it—yes, and what *I have* done about it.

I think we would all want to start with the agreement, indeed the insistence, that the primary responsibility for making the evening of our lives what we want it to be rests upon us as individuals.

I think we would agree, next, that it will be in the *local* communities, through private organizations, and city and county agencies that we will want to concentrate our group efforts to meet these problems. I know about the Day Centers, the Hobby Shows and Fairs, the Senior Citizen Divisions of the County Welfare Planning Councils, the Golden Age Clubs, which represent some of the approaches being made in various Florida communities.

I know from my experience as Governor of Illinois how essential these local community programs are. So many of these tragic problems came to us at the state level only when an elderly person was brought to the doors of our overcrowded hospitals. And we knew that in many cases this pitiful chapter could have been prevented if there had been proper and sufficient development in the local communities of those work and recreational programs which keep the poison of loneliness and futility out of people's minds.

Yet there is a large responsibility here, too, on the part of the state governments. One of my greatest satisfactions as Governor of Illinois was the beginning of local clinics in a number of towns to deal preventively with psychological disturbances, largely among older people. And it seemed to me, and I said in my inaugural address as governor in 1949, that "Public welfare is perhaps our most moving and urgent problem." So I recommended to the Illinois legislature that as a first step the old-age assistance payments be increased and that "pension payments for the aged and the blind [be provided] solely on the basis of need and without arbitrary maximum."

Within four months we amended the Old-Age Pension and Blind Assistance Acts so as to increase the maximum monthly grants by 18 per cent. And we removed the administrative limit on old-age pensions and blind assistance grants, making it possible for any amount of medical expense to be included in the grant in any month.

I set up, in 1950, a State Committee on Problems of the Aging—one of the first in the nation—and it became an active service agency. As governor, I am proud to say, I turned over $350,000 from my contingency funds to the Director of Public Welfare to pay for the board and lodging in private homes of older people who would otherwise have been forced to stay in inadequate institutions. And, most significant of all, I established either the first or second Geriatrics Research Hospital in the country at Galesburg, Illinois.

I want you to know, frankly, that when I talk about these things I am talking from the depths of personal conviction, confirmed by a record of action, and I think that conviction and performance constitute the human heart of government in today's democracy—when words are so easy.

Yet we have learned in more than twenty years since Franklin D. Roosevelt and the Democrats lifted this country out of the slough of despondency and misery that there is much to be done at the national level, too!

It is over twenty years now since we took the momentous step marked by the passage of the Social Security Act. I suspect that history may well record that as the most important of the New Deal's accomplishments.

In these last two decades we have made some improvements in the original Social Security program. But these improvements have not been fundamental. And today the Social Security program continues primarily as a guarantee against the extremities of want and insecurity.

This is, in America's age of abundance, too little, and major changes are called for in the Social Security program.

The present retirement benefits are too low, and should be substantially increased.

I think the present provisions reducing benefits under the federal old-age insurance plan when a person goes out and earns some money should be thoroughly reviewed and that these provisions should be changed, although I realize the problems which are involved here and which must be taken into account. I hate—hate—to see activity, enterprise, self-help, initiative penalized. These are the great human virtues; these are the qualities Americans have preached and applauded.

The eligibility age for women employees and for the wives and widows of covered employees should be reduced to 62, as the House of Representatives decided last year.

I would favor strongly, too, the present proposal that retirement benefits should be paid where a person 50 years old or older becomes totally and permanently disabled.

On Tuesday of this week President Eisenhower's opposition to these last two proposals resulted in their defeat in the Senate committee. I hope the Senate will reverse the committee report, and I think it will. But we have been put on notice that this single-interest Republican administration is *opposed* to the enlargement of the Social Security program to meet the needs we face.*

Nor is the expansion of Social Security enough.

I commend to you the bill introduced in the House of Representatives last March by Congressman Yates of Illinois. It is the most comprehensive program I have seen, and Congressman Yates's statement on the floor of the House when he introduced this bill (H.R. 8863) will stand, I predict, as an enduring human testament of our times.

He proposes, among other things, the establishment of a Bureau of Older Persons in the Department of Health, Education and Welfare. It is a revealing reflection on the sense of values of the present administration that it has had a staff of 40,000 people working on the problems of the nation's business concerns and exactly nine people (with a budget of $65,000) working on the Secretary's staff on the problems of our 14 million senior citizens.

And when the President announced a few weeks ago, with much fanfare and fine words, that he was setting up a Federal Council on Aging "to review existing programs within the Government," as he said, and "to make recommendations," I couldn't help thinking how consistently the corporations have had action from this administration, while the people get conferences, councils, commissions and confabs.

I don't believe it takes much study to know that we need, and need now, a special federal program to supply additional housing facilities for older

* (Since approved. Eds.)

people. Senator John Sparkman of Alabama has introduced a bill which provides that 15,000 public housing units will be set aside each year for the next five years for people 65 years old or older; and that special credit facilities be made available to older people who want to build their own homes.

While we are waiting for some new committee to review what *hasn't* been done, the Republicans on the Senate committee voted down last Tuesday the proposal, which seems to me eminently sensible, to work out a plan to make some of our government food stocks available to those, including the needy aged, who just haven't enough to eat.

Most serious of all, perhaps, are the medical needs of some of our older people. These needs have been estimated as from three to four times as great as those for younger people, and we know that the fear that plagues the older homes most insistently is the fear of an illness that cannot be financed.

. In short, I propose, for the benefit not only of the aged, but all of us, that in times of prosperity which the Republicans say we have—farmers and small businessmen to the contrary notwithstanding—that we invest some of our surplus—and our hearts and heads, for that matter—in life and health for all of us.

Last year, with 10 million American men and women suffering from heart disease, the federal government spent only $14.1 million on heart disease research—or $1.40 for each person presently afflicted.

One out of every seven of us, as things now stand, will die of cancer. Last year the government spent $18 million on cancer research—10 cents apiece.

With mental illness costing incalculable suffering, and a cash outlay of almost $1.5 billion a year for custodial care, we are spending $30 million a year in all to combat it—2 per cent of this cost.

Last year we invested about a penny a person for research on arthritic and rheumatic diseases—cripplers of 10 million Americans, most of them in the older group.

I don't know how much of this prospective $2 billion surplus in national funds could be directed helpfully to research programs into the cause, prevention and cure of crippling disease. It wouldn't *take* much to *do* a great deal. And last year the federal budget for research on cancer, arthritis, mental illness, neurological and heart disease combined was less than the Department of Agriculture research budget on plant and animal diseases. And only time and your patience preclude me from expressing my view on the fruit fly and the penny-wise pound-foolishness of this administration in cutting inspection at Miami—to save money for which it will now pay many times over in eradicating this menace to Florida's citrus economy.

But the point I am making is this: I would spend on these human health research programs every cent of our surplus that would speed up our war on these crippling and killing diseases, our probing for the secrets of life and death.

The same paralysis has been displayed in the unwillingness of the present administration even to make a start toward providing American families with greater protection against the financial catastrophe of serious illness—this in the face of our experience which shows that roughly a million American families will spend one-half or more of their incomes on medical care this year, that another 500,000 families will pay out more than their total incomes for illness. In fact, at the moment, 3 million American families are in debt for medical care, and many of them burdened with high interest rates.

Many of the victims of this special economic burden of expensive illness are older people. I think we should explore thoroughly and immediately the best ways of ensuring the ability of older people to participate in the private, voluntary medical insurance programs which are now becoming so common throughout the country.

These, then, are some of the lines along which I think we should proceed. It is not a matter of *security*—although this is part of it. It is not a matter of work *opportunities*—although this is part of it, too. Nor is it just a matter of *medical* care, or of *housing,* or of any other *single* thing. It is a matter of *fullness* of living. We have talked for a long time in this country of a program of full employment. I hope we are going to start *talking,* and *working,* toward a program of *full living.*

And in closing I want to emphasize again that I consider this the *problem,* the *opportunity*, not of any *one* group of us but of us *all.* I am sure that older people do not want to become, politically, a special interest group.

It should be as a people, all of us in our own mutual interest, that we should deal with this matter of our common concern.

We face the opportunity to make those who have served longest in our common endeavor full partners in the prosperity we now enjoy.

We have talked a lot in this country about conserving our natural resources. Well, the greatest natural resource we have is life itself.

I am determined, as the Democratic party is determined, to do my utmost to see to it that we can all live out the evenings of our lives with new opportunities to be active, to be useful, and to strengthen our faith in ourselves. This is part of what freedom has to mean.

5

Resources and Power

OUR NATURAL RESOURCES: PROGRAM PAPER

•

People and natural resources are all we really have for the building of a New America and a new world.

I have expressed already, in previous papers in this series, my deep concern that we provide for the full development of the greatest resource of all, the talent, skill and energy of human beings.

We need imagination and energy, also, to make full use of the natural resources with which this favored land has been so richly blessed. Our soil and water and forests and minerals, our great sources of power and areas of natural beauty, and now the energy of the sun and the power of the atom have been given us not to squander and destroy, but to use wisely, to develop, and to pass on enhanced and multiplied to our children's children.

To fulfill this trust we must have the vision to see, and the devotion to serve, the great needs of the future.

By 1975, there will be perhaps 210 million Americans.

By 1975, these Americans will require almost twice the water we need today.

By 1975, these Americans will be consuming 40 per cent more food than we now consume.

By 1975, we shall have made further great drafts on our minerals.

By 1975, we Americans will have more leisure than we do today, and we will need lands and forests and streams in which to hunt and fish and live with nature's restful beauty.

And by that interesting year, A.D. 2000, the forecasters estimate 275 million Americans—and the forecasters have often been caught short. The

Statement issued November 4, 1956.

world's population, meanwhile, will have been increasing, too; it is growing right now at the rate of 90,000 new mouths to feed each morning.

The Democratic administrations of Franklin Roosevelt and Harry S. Truman met these great future needs, with the achievements of the Tennessee Valley Authority, the Soil Conservation Service, the Rural Electrification Administration, the Bureau of Reclamation, the Bonneville Power Administration, with the expansion of forest, national parks and wildlife activities, and multiple-purpose river-basin programs providing flood control, inland waterways, irrigation, pollution control, and low-cost electricity in abundance.

But this progress has been stopped. In crucial areas we have lost ground.

The record of the Eisenhower administration in this most important area is one of abject and frightening failure.

I. THE FAILURE OF THE EISENHOWER ADMINISTRATION

The most obvious and distressing evidence of the failure of the Eisenhower administration to care for the public good is its giving away parts of the public domain to private interests: letting great natural sites for multipurpose public projects be exploited for private gain; repudiating public power projects; urging legislation that would transfer private rights in national forests to a privileged few; granting mining claims on public property to private exploitation, as in the Al Sarena hoax; allowing federal wildlife refuges to be invaded by hundreds of oil leases; encouraging legislation that would dispose of timber stands in our national parks and forests.

Behind this sorry record of giveaways is a still more devastating series of acts that jettison valuable and established policies, and even abandon the 50-year-old, bipartisan conservation policy. The Eisenhower administration replaced professionally trained careeer leadership of federal conservation agencies with unqualified political appointees. They appointed enemies of conservation to key resource posts, in both action agencies and regulatory commissions. They dismembered the regional action program of the Soil Conservation Service. They attacked the farmer-owned REA cooperatives and municipally owned utilities. They hit the TVA, by reducing its appropriation and by trying to undercut it in the devious Dixon-Yates affair.

This giveaway and anticonservation are tragic evidence of failure, but they are by no means the whole story, nor even the most important part of it. It is easy to publicize and make dramatic the evils of such backward steps; the greater evil of the unwillingness to take forward steps is harder to make plain. Yet this is the gravest failure of all—once more, as I have so often had to say, a failure of leadership.

This businessman's administration failed to provide—for our country— the same prudent planning for tomorrow's needs that any competent business would inevitably provide for itself. The Eisenhower administration abolished the National Security Resources Board and did not create any agency that would do what it had done, that is, make continuing and systematic surveys of our nation's resource needs. The administration almost completely ignored the excellent report made by the nonpartisan Materials Policy Commission, headed by William S. Paley. Many of the administration's acts even fly directly in the face of the careful recommendations of that commission's thoughtful survey. The administration has failed to give national leadership in the growing national problem of water, and forward progress in river-basin development awaits the return of a Democratic administration.

The Republican party has shown itself the servant of private exploitation, rather than of the public interest in the nation's future.

President Eisenhower's unsupportable claims of Republican accomplishments distort a sorry four-year record. Behind his platitudes lie the Hoover Commission Report and the Report by the Presidential Advisory Committee on Water Resources Policy—both outlining a national policy of retreat from responsibility.

Our Democratic resources policy will begin with a repudiation of the irresponsibilities of the Eisenhower administration.

II. The Framework of a New Resources Policy

We shall continue the proven policy of the past: the great American tradition of conservation, in which the names of a Republican Roosevelt and a Democratic Roosevelt stand side by side. From the time of Gifford Pinchot to the present day the foresight and wisdom of conservation leaders have served us well. We must not allow unthinking and irresponsible men to betray that noble heritage.

We must, instead, keep faith with the great men of that heritage by going beyond them; by matching the needs of our day with the foresight and devotion with which they matched the needs of theirs, commensurate with the needs of a population much larger and potentially much richer in the next half century.

We must, for example, have a new, and broader, conservation policy. Many of the guideposts for a new policy of conservation are provided in *Resources for Freedom*, the report of the Paley Commission. A Democratic administration will take the Paley Report out of mothballs, and review its recommendations carefully in the light of developments since 1950.

A. FEDERAL LEADERSHIP

The first principle of our policy will be a vigorous reaffirmation of the important responsibilities of the federal government for the nation's resources. The planning, construction and operation of comprehensive resource programs is a proper and legal, as well as a most necessary, function of the federal government, under a wide range of constitutional powers.

From an economic and engineering point of view, the federal government can and should assume the leadership in the task of harnessing our interstate river system for power, flood control, navigation, water supply, irrigation, recreation, pollution control, and for nurturing fish and wildlife.

B. COMPREHENSIVE POLICY

The new national conservation policy must acknowledge the rule that Nature herself provides: the organic unity of the seamless web of land, water, minerals, energy. These are not separate problems to be treated piecemeal, but part of one great problem, one great opportunity, that must be treated with comprehensive insight.

C. NEW INVESTMENT

We must increase the investment in our natural resources. It is folly to cut these investments. Yet President Eisenhower reduced them by 20 to 30 per cent even as the nation's income rose by 20 per cent. At the very least, our investment in natural resources should match our growth of national income. These investments, many of them self-liquidating, will more than pay for themselves in a fuller life for all our people.

III. WATER AND POWER

The New America must have strong material underpinning. Foremost among the requirements are increasing supplies of water and energy—particularly electric power.

Comprehensive development of our river basins will provide the maximum available supplies of both water and hydroelectric power. Scientific use and management of floodwaters—which, uncontrolled, are a constant menace to human lives, property and topsoil—is a key to such development.

As pointed out by the President's Water Resources Policy Commission in 1950, modern engineering has made it possible to store and use floodwaters for many purposes. Where conservation storage is feasible, the single-purpose flood-detention reservoir, which treats floodwaters simply as a menace, has come to be recognized as an unforgivable waste.

Release of water from multiple-purpose reservoirs is timed to prevent floods, provide domestic and industrial water supply, irrigation, navigation, electric power, recreational opportunities, and to aid in the abatement of pollution.

A. WATER

Of all the nation's resource problems, those relating to water are most critical and immediate. For the country as a whole, rainfall is more than adequate, but water is a resource for which national averages mean little. There are sharp limitations on its transportation.

Though good statistics are scarce, we do know that uses of water in households, industries, and agriculture are already huge and are rising every year. According to Department of Commerce estimates, water use in the United States increased from 40 billion to 262 billion gallons a day between 1900 and 1955.

In many areas the pinch of inadequate water supply is already sharp. As far back as the Second World War, plans to locate at least 300 industrial or military establishments had to be revised because water supplies were inadequate at the sites initially selected. And a survey in 1953 found that more than a thousand towns and cities had to curtail water use.

While the dry pinch of drought is felt on many a dust bowl farm and great areas of the Southwest are parched, the terrible surplus of water ravages New England, the Pacific Northwest and California in floods. Flood damages on large rivers and smaller streams cause hundreds of millions of dollars in damage annually as well as the loss of precious top-soil, the siltation of channels and reservoirs—and most of all the needless loss of human lives, sacrificed to our failure to learn that the best insurance against floods is their control.

In the Great Plains states, the Central Valley of California, and elsewhere drought has intensified drains on underground reservoirs of water. Somehow we must provide more water for the small family farm in the West. In many areas pumps are bringing brackish water and sand to the surface. There is great need for an adequate approach to the problems of water conservation in these areas. It must be geared not only to upstream and main-stem storage projects, to trap surface flows, but also to watershed protection. Intensified research is required to map, maintain and recharge underground reservoirs.

Furthermore, pollution, which destroys or impairs the usefulness of water that is available, is still increasing. Municipal pollution has not declined, despite the great expansion of treatment facilities, and industrial pollution has doubled since 1920.

A major step forward in pollution abatement was taken this year by the Democratic Eighty-fourth Congress with passage of the Blatnik Bill. This act provides federal grants-in-aid over a 10-year period to communities needing to build sewage disposal plants.

As water uses multiply and population pressures strain America's natural water supply, increasing attention and expanded research must be devoted to obtaining large new supplies of fresh water from brackish and salt water.

The success of such a program, begun during the Truman administration by the Department of Interior but given less than adequate attention by the Eisenhower administration, would relieve the extremely grave situation in such areas as southern California.

There are no easy solutions to the complicated problems of assuring ample supplies of water for the New America. But it is clear that the problems can be solved by full co-operation of local governments, joint water districts, industrial water users, and the federal government, if the federal government provides sound leadership. The federal government's responsibilities and opportunities lie in its constitutional authority over the nation's rivers.

These responsibilities have not been shouldered by the Eisenhower administration. Instead, the Eisenhower administration has issued a Cabinet Committee Report, the gist of which is that the federal government should abdicate its responsibilities to local interests.

The outworn issue of private versus public power is blocking development of large and small river basins. The only way to take advantage of modern technology is through an integrated effort to conserve rainfall and control the flow in a whole valley for all the many purposes to which water can be put.

B. POWER

The New America will require low-cost power in quantities undreamed of twenty-five years ago. To sustain its expanding activities, our electric utilities, public, private and co-operative, must provide 320 million kilowatts of generating capacity by 1970 and 600 million by 1980, compared with 116 million in 1955 and only 32 million in 1930. We must have this great supply of low-cost energy not only for an ever-higher living standard at home, but also to meet the challenge of the Soviet system abroad.

The typical home in the New America will have year-round electric air conditioning (heating in winter and cooling in summer), as well as the whole range of electric appliances, including dryers, dishwashers, hot-water heaters, food waste disposers, television sets and some that are still a gleam in the inventor's eye—providing low-cost electric power is available.

The typical farm in the New America will use more than five times as much power as it does today. In addition to a fully electrified house, the farmer will have electric feeding, milking, cooling, and cleaning in his dairy barn; electric chopping and handling of silage; electric curing of hay and drying of grains; electric pumping and heating of water for all purposes; and sprinkler irrigation to assure maximum growth of crops in spite of vagaries of the weather, to mention only a sampling of possible uses—all providing low-cost electric power is available.

The average worker on the New America's industrial production line will require 14 kilowatt-hours of electricity for each man-hour of labor, compared with less than 8 kilowatt-hours today and less than 3 kilowatt-hours in 1929.

This increased use of electricity will bring higher output for every hour of work, a rise of income, and more leisure.

Every mill (1/10 cent) saved in the cost of a kilowatt-hour of electricity will mean $1.5 billion annual saving to the country by 1970, and $3 billion by 1980. On the larger residential use of the New America, a half-cent saved per kilowatt-hour will save the average homeowner $100 in his annual electric bill.

1. A Power Program

The federal government, working with state and local governments and with private and co-operative power agencies, in a true regional partnership, can achieve adequate power at low rates.

By the policies we adopt today we shall decide whether we shall have to-morrow the abundant low-cost power we need; we shall determine whether the electric power industry will become a monopoly dominating our economic life and our political institutions, or whether it will be intelligently guided and controlled to serve the public interest.

The New Deal power program has been of great benefit to the American people and must continue. But we must go forward. Building on the proven policies of the past, we can devise a policy under which federal river-basin systems, privately owned power companies, federal and private atomic plants, state and municipal electric systems, and rural electric co-operatives can work together in assuring an abundance of the lowest-cost electricity for their customers.

This step forward would include:

The expediting of federal development of hydroelectric power through comprehensive river-basin progress;

Continued expansion of TVA power supply, including steam generation;

Federal construction of large demonstration atomic power plants;

A continuance of the preference to public bodies and co-operatives in the marketing of power from federal projects;

Legislation providing for authorization and regulation of regional wholesale power pools, whether publicly or privately or co-operatively formed or with mixed ownership.

2. Atomic Power

The program for the New America must include prompt development of atomic power as a major source of low-cost energy. The importance of atomic power as a major source of low-cost energy is well known. Yet the Eisenhower administration's rigid opposition to an effective federal large-scale demonstration program seriously endangers our leadership in this field. It does little good to offer atomic fuel to our friends abroad and to industry at home if we cannot provide practical plants in which this fuel can be used.

I believe that the federal government must take the lead in the development of atomic power—not surrender its rights to private enterprise, as it has since 1952. I take this position because the expenditures which are required are often too large and too risky for private enterprise; and because the development is replete with dangers. The current policy of leaving development to private utilities has resulted in our falling far behind other nations, including the Soviet Union.

With a vigorous program of federal demonstration plants, coupled with the projects of the utilities, American industry can move ahead rapidly to develop low-cost atomic power, compete successfully in the world markets, and demonstrate our international leadership in the peaceful uses of atomic energy. At home, the American people will reap more quickly the benefits of a great new source of low-cost energy, and areas with high power costs will especially benefit.

3. Restraint of Monopoly

The federal power program has been a curb on private monopoly in the all-important field of the nation's power supply.

In the Republican era which followed World War I the private power interests used their increasing monopoly power to rear holding company empires which milked millions of small investors, to mobilize lawyer-accountant-engineer teams to justify excessive electric rates, and to influence education, public opinion and politics in order to maintain their privileged position.

The Democratic party introduced the yardstick principle, which used public power to assure adequate service and fair rates. The Democratic party began the rural electrification program, the federal power developments in the Tennessee Valley, the Pacific Northwest and other areas, and supported the principle of preference for public bodies in sales and power.

Legalized monopoly was thus held in check, competition brought electric rates down throughout the country, use of electricity soared, and even the private companies grasped to some extent the possibilities for expansion in the electric industry. But with the advent of the Eisenhower administration, private monopolies reformed their lines and took quick advantage of the national government's abandonment of leadership.

The Eisenhower administration has undermined the preference right of municipalities to federal power. Thus, they have strengthened the position of private monopolies.

Enforcement of the preference clause and the Public Utility Holding Act should be the two keystones of a federal public utility policy.

IV. Minerals

Mineral resources are crucial for both economic expansion and national security. With a population of 151 million in 1950 each person used, on the average, 18 tons of minerals—14,000 pounds of fuel, 10,000 pounds of building materials, 200 pounds of metals extracted from 5,000 pounds of ores, 5,700 pounds of agricultural products, and 800 pounds of nonmetallic resources such as lime, fertilizer, and chemical raw materials.

With expanding population and constant extension of our requirements into new fields, the continued exhaustion of our basic mineral resources is forcing us to place increasing reliance on lower grade supplies, on importation, and on attempts of our technology to devise better uses of what we still possess or to develop substitutes.

All of our minerals are exhaustible. Drains upon them are increasing rapidly. And, as supplies decline and higher grade or more easily accessible mineral resources are depleted, then costs of extraction, of processing and of manufacture go up.

We need large and increasing supplies of food and raw materials from both domestic and foreign sources. Nevertheless, monopolistic tendencies often reduce our domestic output and interfere with imports.

By fully exploiting the almost unlimited potentialities of modern science and technology, we can greatly improve the utilization of known resources; we can better learn how to use those heretofore unusable; we can shift the pattern of utilization from extreme dependence on scarce resources to a greater reliance on those which are more abundant or renewable.

Thus, through modern science and its technical application, we can broaden the minerals base, while utilizing it intensively, and so avoid the economic penalty of rising costs.

This cannot be accomplished by unplanned, unorganized efforts. The problem requires socially organized, directed and financed research, designed to solve specific problems within the minerals field, with ample funds for large-scale pilot plant operation.

The present administration, with its big business orientation, neither understands nor approves the public interest role of science and technology in the natural resources area. This administration has not only failed to organize and support such a comprehensive research program in this area, but has actually abandoned promising research activities and reduced federal appropriations in this field.

An example of this shortsightedness is the abandonment of the government demonstration plant at Rifle, Colorado, which was well on the way to demonstrating economically feasible extraction of oil from oil shale. Oil shale constitutes an oil potential possibly six to eight times that of oil from our underground reserves. The possibility of our supplies of oil from the Near East being interrupted emphasized the nearsighted expediency of the Eisenhower administration's handling of our natural resources.

I propose that the federal government organize and support generously a comprehensive program of scientific research in this area of technological development of minerals.

The results of such research should be freely available to all and should not be monopolized by any special interests.

Our international economic policy must ensure a steady and adequate flow of raw materials from abroad. Capital and technical assistance will likewise be required for the so-called underdeveloped countries to expand the productivity of their natural resources industries.

The over-all effects of such policies would be to increase quantity and reduce costs of foreign supplies; to postpone exhaustion of domestic resources; to avoid excessive costs of marginal subsidized home production; and to strengthen both our own economy and those of other nations with which we trade.

Since our situation, whether we like it or not, is one of actual dependence on other countries for some of our most vital raw materials and minerals, it is imperative that the policies we adopt will make this interdependency mutually advantageous for all concerned.

V. Soil, Forests and Wildlife

A. FORESTS

America's forests occupy about a quarter of our land area; they are a great and—as we have learned in the past four years—vulnerable natural resource. We depend on our forests for vast and constantly increasing supplies of saw logs, pulpwood, and other essential timber products. Forests protect watersheds, and thus help to curb floods and to provide dependable water supplies. They give cover to wildlife and afford outdoor recreation to millions of Americans.

The so-called renewable resources, such as our forests, do not renew themselves automatically. Great gains in forest management were made in the presidencies of Franklin Roosevelt and Harry Truman. Unfortunately, the splendid rate of progress has not been maintained in the Eisenhower administration.

But the need is for greater effort, not less. Since 1940, timber prices have been rising much faster than the average for other commodities. The primary reason for the extreme rise is simply that of scarcity. The yearly harvests of timber have been short of the nation's demands. By the end of the century the nation's need for timber, pulpwood, and other forest products will be about double what it is today. And even today the supply is short. Already time is running out; it takes a human generation or two for a tree to come to maturity.

If we are to supply the lumber and paper, the water, recreation and wildlife in the abundance which our grandchildren deserve, we must take determined action today.

We must intensify the management of our public forests—national, state and local—through the building of adequate access roads and application of more intensive forest practices, including thinnings, improvement and sanitation cuttings where needed.

More intensive efforts are needed to improve our forest watershed management to reduce floods and provide dependable water supplies for irrigation and municipal uses.

There is great need for improved management of the nearly 300 million acres of forest lands held by private individuals in small tracts. This 60 per cent of all our commercial forest land is generally in poor or run-down condition. Yet increased productivity of these lands is essential to our future timber supply. The small size of many forest tracts aggravates the problem of management of these lands. I suggest federal aid in the establishment of a number of pilot plant projects to provide group management, and logging and milling facilities on a co-operative basis to these small forest landowners.

One specific aid to small producers, whether landowners or timber operators, would be in providing regular, localized market reports on prices for saw logs, pulpwood and other rough forest products. Market news has proven invaluable for other farm products. It would be just as useful for farm forest products.

Another service not generally available to small timberland owners and operators today is adequate credit on terms adapted to the special needs of their business. Insurance geared to the long-term risks in timber growing should also be made generally available to owners whose forests are well managed.

We must strengthen federal-state co-operative programs to protect forests from fire, insects and disease; and to provide assistance in reforestation. We also should push ahead with research in making more effective use of the products of our forests.

B. AGRICULTURAL AND RANGE LANDS

Our generation has witnessed a revolution in farm technology which has made the efforts of the man on the land more productive. But the gains we have made are overshadowed by a paradoxical situation—want in the midst of plenty. There would be no farm surplus problem, no need to reduce production, if only we devoted the imagination and the energy to it that we have given lesser problems. There should be no problem as long as great numbers of people in the world today are undernourished—even men, women and children in our own nation.

The existence of these so-called surpluses tends to hide that which we cannot forget: our population and the population of the world continues to increase. We can support a larger population in the United States on the current level of diet if we can continue to make the same kind of gains in agricultural technology in the future that we have made in the past. Continued progress along these lines will help to offset the loss of land to nonfarm uses. This loss has reached an annual total of more than a million acres and will probably increase in the future. Irrigation, improved drainage, and protection against erosion can greatly cut these losses.

Soil conservation efforts have suffered a setback at the hands of this administration. The abolishing of the regional offices of the Soil Conservation Service weakened this very effective action agency. The nursery program was abandoned, and now there will be less planting stock available to meet the heavy demands for young trees that the conservation reserve of the soil bank will bring, if properly administered. The research program of the agency was transferred elsewhere. Fortunately Congress thwarted the administration in its attempt to cut conservation appropriations.

Assistance to farmers has too long been denied on such undertakings as stream-bank stabilization and similar projects which cost too much for a landowner to carry out and yield no on-site benefits, but which if undertaken will create benefits downstream, particularly when such work reduces the siltation of reservoirs and the pollution of city water supplies.

Our Western public lands have been too long neglected. Range improvement to restore valuable native grasses which have been displaced by sagebrush and cheatgrass is important, not only to the livestock industry, but also in safeguarding the watersheds of the area that badly need water. We must, moreover, constantly be on guard against efforts to transform grazing permits on the public domain from revocable licenses to vested rights.

We must take bold and active leadership in restoring vitality to our weakened soil and range conservation programs. Individual initiative alone is insufficient for that task, a task which benefits the public more than the individual. The time has come for a unified land policy that will direct our efforts to those areas where the public need is the greatest.

C. IRRIGATION

In the West, irrigation of arid lands has produced a new economy, where before there was only barren sagebrush. Irrigation will play an increasingly important part in aiding the nation to produce an adequate supply of food and fiber.

For fifty years the federal government has pursued a bipartisan policy of treating irrigation and power as partners in the development of the West. Power revenues over and above the cost of operation and return of power investment have been employed to assist homesteaders in writing off the reimbursable irrigation costs of the project. The future of irrigation in the West depends upon the continuation of this policy, which is being effectively blocked by the Eisenhower administration's giving away of powersites. Multipurpose development is a condition for an adequate irrigation program.

Wherever practicable, we should adopt the principle of basin-wide pooled accounting as a logical extension of the nation's 50-year-old reclamation policy. This principle has already received approval in the Upper Colorado River Law.

D. WILDLIFE AND RECREATION

The overwhelming proportion of public land is available for outdoor recreation, but an accelerated access and facilities program is essential for its full enjoyment. The needs are substantial and growing.

A century ago, the total population was a small fraction of the present total and most of the people lived in the country, where the workweek averaged 70 hours and few people thought very much about vacations. Now, with the majority of Americans living in cities, and traveling about in automobiles and airplanes, with the workweek down to 40 hours, and paid vacations the rule, resulting rush to spend vacations outdoors has nearly swamped public recreation facilities—federal, state and local.

More than 50 million visitors come annually now to national parks—a fiftyfold increase since World War I. The trend is paralleled, with the numbers almost equally great, in recreational use of the national forests, and federal dams and reservoirs.

Every year more people will be seeking to use these facilities. Even the present overcrowding is so serious that the problem is not only how many more people can be accommodated, but whether present numbers will ruin the facilities that now exist. Only recently, and under the strongest kind of pressure from conservation organizations, has the present administration partially recognized the needs of the National Park Service for more roads and campground facilities.

The administration has prided itself on its Mission 66 program, a 10-year $785 million plan for our national parks. But this program is long on propaganda and short on action. President Eisenhower's national park budget request for fiscal 1957 was only $11 million. At this appropriation rate the so-called 10-year national park program would take more than seventy years to complete. The equally desperate situation for expanded recreation facilities in the national forests has not been recognized at all.

I propose that adequate steps be taken now—and not later—to modernize and expand the recreational facilities of our national parks, monuments, forests and other federal recreational areas to handle adequately the ever-increasing number of Americans who visit them. State, local and nonpublic recreational agencies, given federal government leadership, must without delay re-evaluate the recreational facilities, relate them to anticipated needs, and act co-operatively to provide the kind of recreational facilities that will add deep and rich nonmaterial satisfactions to our citizens. Here is a great opportunity for constructive planning and action. It is one of the great challenges of the New America.

E. FISH AND WILDLIFE POLICY

Effective administration of fish and wildlife programs depends upon freedom from political manipulation and political appointees to top positions. The career status of the Fish and Wildlife Service, disrupted by the present administration, must be restored.

Conservation and development of fish and wildlife will, therefore, constitute an important responsibility of the federal government in the New America. They will be treated as an important aspect of all multiple-purpose river-basin programs.

CONCLUSION

This then is our program:

—to reverse the retreat of the Eisenhower administration in almost every area of resource policy;

—to return to the forward march of comprehensive multipurpose developments for our river basins;

—to move forcefully ahead, under federal leadership, in the development of atomic power;

—to develop more and cheaper power;

—to assure abundant supplies of low-cost power available to all consumers;

—to bring a long-range forestry program to assure adequate supplies of timber at reasonable prices;

—to continue our irrigation policy;

—to expand our recreational facilities to match the expanding need;

—to protect our wildlife;

—to renew our program of soil conservation;

—to achieve a well-rounded mineral policy program inclusive of many of the recommendations of the Paley Commission: notably to advance research in new materials and to reduce waste, to pursue trade policies that will bring us needed materials from abroad.

In 1908, the Republican President Roosevelt opened America's first conservation conference by warning that "the natural resources of our country are in danger of exhaustion."

It is time to call another conference, for the second half of this century —a National Conservation Conference for the New America.

We will evaluate our whole resource problem for the New America. For, as Theodore Roosevelt said nearly fifty years ago when he announced the calling of his conference: "Unless we solve that problem, it will avail us little to solve all others."

CONSERVATION AND DEVELOPMENT OF
NATURAL RESOURCES

●

Today, I want to tell you what I think about the conservation and full development of our natural resources.

This is not a Montana issue, nor even a Northwest issue. It is a national issue of the highest importance. I talked about it at length the other day in West Virginia. And certainly it is an issue that clearly draws the line between the Democratic and Republican parties. The issue can be put very simply.

The Democratic party believes that our natural resources belong to all the people and it believes in conserving and developing them to the utmost and for the benefit of all the people.

The Republican party isn't so sure about conservation and strongly favors development for private profit.

I think Great Falls is a good place to talk about this subject. We meet today at a place where Lewis and Clark paused a century and a half ago while exploring the natural resources of the great West. We meet outdoors and in the great outdoors, where men know the value of the gifts of land and river, lakes and trees, that they have received.

When the first explorers traversed the broad face of America, they found a dense wilderness, rich and beautiful beyond imagining. In that early beginning, America was covered with a blanket of trees. The soil, not yet broken by the plow, possessed a capacity to produce that was unheard of in the older parts of the world. The earth was drained by mighty rivers, and beneath the topsoil lay mineral riches unimaginable.

All this had been put here in this blessed land for men to use as wisely as they might.

Swiftly men cut down the trees, plowed the soil, dammed the rivers, and mined the minerals.

Some of this was right and necessary, something that had to be done

From a speech at Great Falls, Montana, October 9, 1956.

if we were to civilize that land and ourselves.

Some was sheer waste.

Some was ruthless exploitation by greedy men.

And all of it wrought a change in the face of America.

Congress became alarmed at the swiftness of the change and determined to preserve a part of the original loveliness and richness for our children and our children's children. Congress set aside millions of acres of national forests and national parks.

Its first watchword was conservation—we had to conserve, to save, these public lands.

More recently, we have learned how to use them wisely. The parks are to be used by the public for recreation. The forests, too, are to be used by the public for recreation but they also may be used—under supervision—for selective logging, dam building, mineral prospecting, and grazing.

And for some fifty years, ever since Theodore Roosevelt and Gifford Pinchot took the lead in establishing the policy, both political parties have worked together to hammer out a bipartisan policy for the national parks and forests that would at once conserve them and use them wisely.

That policy has been scrapped by the present administration.

It was the intent of Congress that all the people should benefit from the use of the national forests.

It was decidedly not their intent that the public lands should be invaded by, and given away to, selfish private interests.

But that's precisely what the Eisenhower administration has been doing.

They gave a private mining company the right to cut the people's timber in the Rogue River National Forest in Oregon—and under such peculiar circumstances that the assay samples got dumped into Rogue River.

A Republican congressman introduced a bill which would have given the big lumber companies special privileges in the national forests—a bill which your great congressman, Lee Metcalf, correctly called a bill to permit "big lumbermen to trade stumps for trees."

A Republican congressman introduced a bill which would have given a few big-spread cattlemen—and no one else—what amounted to perpetual rights to graze their stock in the national forests. And though the bill was defeated, President Eisenhower nominated this same congressman to be Assistant Secretary of the Interior in charge of public lands—which sounded like setting the fox to guard the henhouse.

They gave the oil and gas interests about five times as many leases to explore and exploit the wildlife refuges as had been granted in the preceding three decades.

They got rid of the career conservation men in the Fish and Wildlife Service and replaced them with patronage appointees.

It is no wonder that Ira Gabrielson, the respected conservationist who was for years head of the service, told a congressional committee, "After spending most of my lifetime in an organization that was completely career service I see it all of a sudden turned into something political." And Mr. Gabrielson—he is a lifelong Republican—added, "I have told some of my friends sometimes that this administration and its action on conservation matters come nearer making a Democrat out of me than anything that Roosevelt and Truman could do in all the years I worked for them."

I think that not only Mr. Gabrielson feels that way. I think that the Eisenhower administration has made a lot of other new Democrats in the last three years.

Nor has the administration shown more regard for the Indians, who are its wards, than for the public domain. Their treaties have been scrapped, they have been coerced, not consulted, about their future, they are losing their lands at the rate of over 500,000 acres a year, and right here in Great Falls you have Hill 57, a miserable home for landless Indians that is a disgrace in a nation that calls itself rich. May I point out that in connection with the termination of government responsibility for the Indian's affairs, the Republican platform this year speaks only of consultation while the Democratic platform proposes to obtain their consent.

But in no other area has the Eisenhower administration shown its true colors more clearly than in its water policy.

America's water policy has and should rest firmly on first principles— the rivers belong to the people and should be developed fully for the benefit of all the people.

And this means developed to their utmost—for their hydroelectric power, for flood control, navigation, irrigation, and recreation. Water runs downhill. Water is just as wet and life-giving to farmers' crops after it has fallen through a turbine and twirled a hydroelectric generator as it was before. The water which flows as snow-melt out of a mountain forest can be caught behind a dam and put through generators for power, then recaptured and stored to prevent floods, then diverted to irrigate arid fields, then used to establish a navigable channel and carry off municipal wastes farther downstream—all the same water. And this is all that multiple-purpose development means.

Under Franklin Roosevelt the program of putting the people's property to the service of the people went forward as never before—and today in the great Northwest and down in the valley of the Tennessee and in other parts of this broad land you can see the results—new industries and fertile farms where once was wasteland, rows of houses standing safe where floodwaters raged, homes and factories and farms and vacation-lands that make America a richer and a better place for all of us to live. And all of it a result of twenty-five years of sound river policy.

But now suddenly the Eisenhower administration has scrapped this policy.

Of course, the Republicans don't talk out loud these days the way they talked in 1935, when a Republican congressman called TVA a step toward "Russianizing the United States." Nowadays, and especially in election years, the Republicans pretend they are in favor of public power programs. In fact, in an election year the Republicans pretend they are in favor of developing our resources for all the people. That's what they say this year.

But look what they've *done* for the last four years.

They have taken the Hells Canyon damsite, the last great damsite on the North American continent, and handed it over to a private power company.

They have crippled reclamation and the Southwest Power Administration.

They tried to give away Niagara's power to five private corporations, and today all along the St. Lawrence the battle is hot.

They have endangered the Central Valley development in California.

In Georgia they have refused to sell power to co-operatives—even though the Attorney General himself has warned that such refusal is illegal.

Only Congress has saved the REA from the administration.

The President himself called TVA "creeping socialism," and personally ordered the signing of the odious Dixon-Yates contract, a backdoor deal to carve up TVA.

The Department of the Interior invited the admitted lobbyist of the Pacific Gas and Electric Company into Washington to help rewrite the federal regulations for transmission lines over public lands.

The Assistant Secretary of the Interior testified before a congressional committee that TVA is "a federal socialistic monopoly."

The Undersecretary of the Interior said that he was "sick and tired" of listening to the "political hogwash of socialists who want to federalize the nation's electric power industry."

The chairman of the Federal Power Commission is a former representative of private utility companies.

The Assistant Secretary of the Interior in charge of power as a congressman voted four out of six times against public power programs.

And the Secretary of the Interior himself summed it all up frankly when he said that "we're here in the saddle as an administration representing business and industry."

And all this, I suppose, is what we might have expected from an administration dominated by a single interest—big business.

The administration says it favors something called "partnership" between government and private power in water-power development.

But it turns out that one partner—the private company—takes the profit while the other partner—you, the people—pays the bills.

Back in my home town, Chicago, some years ago, we had a city planner who, when Chicago was young, drew up the blueprints that helped make Chicago the great city it is today. That man was Dan Burnham, and his favorite saying was, "Make no little plans."

I say to you we need that kind of bold planning, that kind of imagination and vision in the United States today.

A high dam at Hells Canyon built by the federal government means cheaper phosphate fertilizer for the farmers, cheaper power in the farmhouse, in the factory, and in city homes; it means life-giving irrigation for arid lands; it means flood control, new industry, new homes, new towns, an expanding economy in the great Northwest.

Yet a while back former Secretary of the Interior McKay referred to High Hells Canyon as a "white elephant."

Well, not many years ago other Republicans referred to Grand Coulee as a "white elephant," in precisely those words. But today Grand Coulee has spread its bounty over millions of acres—has made the desert bloom, the factories arise, the cities grow, the farms light up. When Grand Coulee was proposed, a private power company wanted to dam the Columbia with little dams, and waste forever the power of the mighty river. A Republican congressman said there wasn't any sense in building Grand Coulee dam because "there was no one in the Grand Coulee area to sell power to except rattlesnakes, coyotes and rabbits. Everyone knows that. There is no market for power in the Northwest." And the press agents for the private power lobby of that day used all the arguments we hear today. They said Grand Coulee was too expensive, an unfair burden on the U.S. Treasury; but today Grand Coulee is ahead of schedule in paying back the U.S. Treasury power investment in the future of the Northwest. They said Grand Coulee was a wild dream of woolly-headed professors; but today it is one of the wonders of the world. And of course they said it was socialistic.

But thousands of veterans have settled on land Grand Coulee made fertile; it has lightened the labors and brightened the lives of thousands of farmers, and it has provided employment for thousands of men and women who work in the industries created by its power, industries that wouldn't be there if Democrats hadn't had the vision to use what God gave us to make something better out there than coyotes and rattlesnakes.

And, you know, I have a feeling that all those people just wouldn't give up what they've got to prove to the Republicans how anti-socialistic they are!

I want to stop this erosion of our resources by the Eisenhower administration.

And I want to get on with the full development of our resources for the benefit of the people all over this great country.

The Eisenhower administration acts as if this generation of Americans were the last.

I want a government that will honor its obligations to generations yet unborn.

This land, these rivers, these forests and mountains—they were not put there for us to despoil.

They were put here for us to use wisely, and to leave in better estate for our children and our children's children.

This issue means a great deal to us alive today but it will mean far more to our descendants. We are shaping a federal conservation policy—or a federal giveaway policy—today that will mold our children's lives. Theodore Roosevelt said, "Of all the questions which can come before this nation, short of the actual preservation of its existence in a great war, there is none which compares in importance with the great central task of leaving this land even a better land for our descendants than it is for us."

I believe that. I think we all believe that.

But we have to do more than believe it. We have to fight for it, just as we have to fight everlastingly for every good cause.

6

Agriculture

FARM POLICY
•

Four years ago at the plowing match at Kasson, Minnesota, both Mr. Eisenhower and I discussed farm policy. I want to take up right where we left off that day four years ago. There were some chickens hatched that day that have been waiting a long time to come home to roost. Here they come!

I want to start with Candidate Eisenhower's own words at Kasson. Here is what he said:

"And here, and now, and without any ifs or buts, I say to you that I stand behind—and the Republican party stands behind—the price support laws now on the books. This includes the amendment to the Basic Farm Act, passed by votes of both parties in Congress, to continue through 1954 the price supports on basic commodities at 90 per cent of parity.

"And," Candidate Eisenhower continued, "a fair share is not merely 90 per cent of parity—it is full parity."

And Candidate Eisenhower said the same thing many times during that campaign. At Brookings, South Dakota, on October 4, 1952, he said: "The Republican party is pledged to the sustaining of the 90 per cent parity price support and it is pledged even more than that to helping the farmer obtain his full parity, 100 per cent parity, with the guarantee in the price supports of 90."

Those were not idle or casual words. They were careful, calculated words. They were meant to get farm votes. And they did! And on that I am an expert!

Yet the same man who uttered those promises to the farmer four years

From a speech at National Plowing Matches, Colfax (Newton), Iowa, September 22, 1956.

ago said in Washington three nights ago: "We must never in a spirit of partisan warfare treat the farmer as a kind of political prize to be fought for and captured!"

What happened to those words of four years ago—which could only have been designed to capture the farmer?

First, President Eisenhower installed as Secretary of Agriculture a man who did not believe in price supports. Then Secretary Benson put in charge of that program a man who, only a few months before, had condemned price supports as "modern socialism." A committee loaded with bankers, manufacturers and processors then went to work to see what should be done, or how little could be done. They paid no attention to Candidate Eisenhower's promises. Also, they paid no attention to the farmers.

I am not going to attack President Eisenhower's motives. I am sure they are good and sincere. I am even willing to believe that he did not fully understand what he was saying to America's farmers in 1952. He had been in the Army and living in New York and Europe at that time.

But the President of the United States must be a responsible man. Secretary Benson was the hired man, and if a farm is mismanaged the farmer is responsible, not the hired man. We know that. And so should the President.

On that day at Kasson, when Candidate Eisenhower talked about 100 per cent parity, prices actually were above 100 per cent. Today the parity index is 82—down 18 points. Then corn was 97 per cent of parity; it now is 82 per cent—down 15 points. Wheat was then 83 per cent of parity; it is now 79—down 4 points. Cotton was 110 per cent; it is now 87—down 23 points. Rice was 96 per cent; it is now 77 per cent—down 19 points.

President Eisenhower has said that he will run on his record. This is his record on price supports.

But there is one success in the record. Four years ago peanuts were 82 per cent of parity; now they have gone up to 88 per cent. This administration has a fine record on peanuts! It almost made me wonder if General Motors has gone into the peanut-oil business!

And something else has gone *down*—the price of hogs!

To sum up, your prices are down, your over-all costs are as high as ever, and your credit is tighter.

Two or three weeks ago at Sioux City, a farmer said it better than I can. "Governor," he said, "I'm a dairy farmer and I know how to milk cows. But those Republicans are smarter than I am. They know how to milk farmers."

I told him they were even smarter than that—only Republicans could keep the stock market up and the farm market down at the same time. They did it the last time they were in office with Hoover at the helm and they're doing it again now.

This talk about the Republicans not treating the farmer as a political prize reminds me of the delegation of Republican congressmen who asked the administration for a floor under hogs at $15.50 a hundredweight last January when they were selling for about $11. And a high official said: "Gentlemen, do you want higher prices now or next November?"

Why November? Well, the election is in November, of course. Do the Republican politicians want higher prices in January or at election time? That summarized pretty well, I thought, their attitude toward the farmer. First they say nothing can be done for the farmer but cut prices and reduce production—and also reduce farmers. Then, with an election approaching, they advance the soil bank proposal which they had rejected only a few months before. They fix the support prices at the higher levels they have long denounced, and they even offer $1.25 a bushel for unlimited corn production while hollering about "Democratic surpluses."

Now, after what happened at Kasson four years ago, I don't suppose we should be surprised about such brazen political expediency. But I must object when the President at the same time says from aloft—"we must never treat the farmer as a political prize."

But let's talk about the future, not the past. Let's talk about what lies ahead.

This year we have the best farm plank in our Democratic platform that any party ever had. It is a plank designed to establish not merely price parity but income parity—a fair share of the national income for farmers. It spells out ways and means. It is one that farmers can understand.

—We propose to support basic commodities at 90 per cent of parity.

—We propose to extend protection to perishables through a combination of direct production payments, marketing agreements, and production adjustments. In this connection I would like to try production payments to encourage earlier marketing of hogs in the years when the runs are heavy. This may be a good way to help end the anxiety and the anguish of violent price movements. We must have learned that it takes more than words and stopgap purchasing programs to end these periods of bankrupt prices our livestock producers suffer so often.

—We will administer vigorously the soil bank, a good Democratic idea. Most people think the Republicans adopted it when they had to do something with an election coming on. But it used to be called soil conserva tion, and I've wondered if it wasn't that word "bank" that made the Republicans like it better. And I would urge consideration of what could be called a "legume bank" to change the emphasis from reducing cash-crop production to increasing acreage of soil-building crops.

Senator Kefauver and I have many times talked about a broad program with a variety of methods to balance production and income; we are for them now; and we will be for them next January.

The first step is to stop and reverse the decline in farm prices.

But that is not enough.

We must go on to assure ample credit at fair rates to the farmer who has to borrow money.

We must protect REA co-ops by safeguarding the preference clause, and by assuring them adequate funds for transmission, generation and distribution.

We must preserve the greatest asset we have inherited—the soil. I feel very strongly about this because I have seen the frightful desolation of once-fertile areas from erosion, overgrazing, deforestation and overuse in many regions of the world. We must strengthen the Conservation Program and the Soil Conservation Service, restore the role of leadership to the conservation districts; we must restore the administration of agricultural programs to farmers, and take emergency measures when needed to prevent another Dust Bowl.*

And finally we must go to the root of the causes of farm distress today—the inability of people both at home and in foreign lands to buy the food that they need and that you can raise. In 1932, you remember, our grocery stores were bulging with food. Yet people were hungry. Today our warehouses are bursting, yet half the world goes to bed hungry. And in our own country, many people on social security and on public assistance don't have enough to eat. We speak of a surplus of milk—but the children who need milk are not all in Calcutta—there are plenty of them in Chicago, too.

Abundance is not a blight, but a blessing. At home, we can vastly expand our school-lunch program. Did you know that less than one-third of all school-age children participate in this program? And we can launch a new program that will put food into the mouths of the many who need it.

Abroad there is much we can do with food and fiber to the advantage of mankind and the USA. We can encourage voluntary relief agencies to distribute surplus foods, and we can create a world food bank and

* Also see the Paper on "Natural Resources."

materials reserve to help the people of other nations. The recent agreement to furnish agricultural products to India seemed to me like a step in the right direction—and I am glad the administration is moving at last.

Today we are confronted not with a breakdown of our agriculture, but with a breakdown of our imagination and leadership. What we need today is the concern and determination that wrought the agricultural revolution of the 1930's.

So much for our program. This is what I propose at Newton in 1956; this is what we will do in Washington. I am not ashamed of what I said at Kasson four years ago; and I will not be ashamed of what I have said at Newton today.

There is something more we can do right now, and I have done it time and again and will do it every chance I get. I mean explaining the farmer's problems to the rest of the country. And this, I think, is one of the farmer's greatest needs. Politicians tell him all too often what he wants to hear about his troubles and their remedy, but all too seldom are his troubles explained to other people—the city people.

As I have traveled around this nation, I have been deeply disturbed by the lack of understanding of the farmer's problems. The farmer's story needs telling because too many people think of farmers as selfish malcontents forever demanding handouts from the sore-pressed taxpayers.

This feeling has been aggravated by the administration's setting city against country and country against city.

For four years the administration has dinned it into the ears of city people that their high living costs are the result of high rigid farm support prices. For four years now our government has accepted the proposition that the farmer is getting too much. In fact, last year one of Mr. Benson's personal assistants said that the years of Democratic prosperity on the farm were—and I quote him—"a dream world, and no one expected it to last."

I think it's time somebody told the rest of the country the truth about farming. I think we should talk *for* the farmer as well as *to* the farmer!

I want to tell the housewife that it isn't the farmer who is getting the high prices she has to pay. She ought to know that, while her market basket has been costing more and more, your share of her food dollar has fallen from 47 cents in 1952 to 38 cents in 1956.

I don't need now to tell the man who works in the farm equipment factory—or used to, before it shut down—that without a decent farm program, his job is gone.

The man with the hardware store on Main Street knows that when the farmer can't buy a new stove for his wife, his store is in trouble. But

I want to say to the businessman who distributes stoves and shoes and wallpaper, and the manufacturer in a distant city who makes them, that the same thing applies to him. Every American has a stake in farm prosperity.

I want to say to the American people that the farmer just isn't getting a fair share of our national prosperity.

Many people don't fully understand the uncertainties of farming and the necessity for price stability. They never stop to think that a farmer doesn't know what price he will get when he plants a crop, or when he harvests it, or even when he loads it on a truck and takes it to town.

General Motors has built-in price supports. Suppose General Motors' production depended on the weather; suppose it had to sell all its automobiles in three weeks; suppose it didn't have the capital to hold its products off the market. It would need protection too—and from this present administration it would get it!

There are many other facts lots more people should know about agriculture. They should know that for every $4 a farmer got in 1952 he now receives less than $3. They should be told that asking farmers to accept less than a fair parity price is like asking wage earners to accept less than a fair minimum wage. They need to know what a tight money policy really means to farmers—that when dollars are scarce, they always leave the small town first.

Our people need to understand that farmers, because of their isolation and other disadvantages, have lagged behind American standards for schools, medical care, libraries, and many other things. They need to know that the per capita income of farmers has never caught up with that of city people—a quarter of all farm families have to get by on cash income of less than $1,000 a year. The ramshackle tenant house on worn-out land is a disgrace in the richest country on earth, just as is the city slum, and the time has come for an all-out attack on farm poverty.

Finally, there is another thing that our people need to be told about farming, perhaps the most important thing of all. They hear about farming as a lot of cold facts and figures about prices and surpluses. They don't realize that farming isn't just a job, it is the way many Americans live, and that the family farm is the backbone of American agriculture, as it was once the backbone of American society.

They don't realize that on a family farm the most precious thing that's raised is not corn or cattle, but children—children who go to rural schools and rural churches and who will inherit the earth they live on and work in. People don't realize that when the family farm is in trouble, more, much more, than dollars and cents is involved. What is involved is the whole fabric of American rural life.

The real tragedy of a farm depression like this one is the human tragedy of young people forced off the farm, of cherished belongings up for sale, of human heartbreak, of the end of a family's chosen way of life. It is the tragedy of mounting debts, of ill-clad children, of men and women searching the skies for rains that never come, of black dust clouds in the western sky. And all this is an American tragedy that we who travel the backroads can see too plainly.

It is high time our growing urban population understood the economics and the realities of the farmer's situation. And I'm not sure a government as preoccupied with big business as this one can tell it, or will tell it, or can even understand it. I have tried to tell it because I think it is important that Americans understand one another; and I think that is the very special responsibility of candidates for public office, especially the only office elected by all the people of our blessed land.

Let's present a true picture of America to the world: the picture of these peaceful fields; the picture of the love of peace in the schools and churches of this tranquil, friendly land; the picture of the desire of all Americans to live in harmony with every neighbor. And let's do more; let's use the resources that we have to build the true conditions of peace. In doing that, nothing we have is more important than the great abundance of the peaceful, productive fields of Iowa and of the great heartland of America.

Our God-given abundance is a strong weapon in our hands for spreading democracy and freedom at home and abroad. You who open the soil to the seed know the urge to abundance in nature's vast resources. Let us work together to spread its benefits, to build a higher and more meaningful standard of living for the generations which will follow us on this good land.

7

Depressed Areas

REPUBLICAN POLICY TOWARD SURPLUS
LABOR AREAS

•

It is October now, and the campaign is beginning to pick up speed. For a time it looked as if the Republicans thought they could win with smiles and TV. It is all changing now. Every day we hear announcements of new tours and new broadcasts—because we have the Republicans on the run—and we mean to keep them that way until November 6.

And, as the Republican campaign develops, their whole approach to the problems of America throws into sharp outline the issue between the parties.

That issue can be defined in many ways. But I think one simple way to state it is that you are choosing this November between a party whose whole history and purpose has been one of caring primarily about people and a party whose whole history and purpose has been one of caring first of all for property.

Well, we Democrats say that the right answers are going to come only from the belief that every person, every individual, every American, is worth caring about. I just don't believe we can measure America's progress, or even its prosperity, on an adding machine—or by leaving anybody out. . . .

We should be thankful for the prosperity and well-being we enjoy, and we are! But let's not exaggerate, and let's not leave these people out and forget about them.

And are we just supposed to forget about the textile workers in New England, about mills that are closed, about others operating three to four

From speech at Providence, Rhode Island, October 6, 1956.

days a week, about skilled workers who have given fifteen or twenty years of their lives and are now middle-aged and unemployed or half employed?

These people can, I know, in good Republican theory, just pull up stakes and learn new trades. Well, it isn't that easy—especially if you're along in years. New jobs don't come easy after you're forty-five or fifty. And many people don't want, naturally enough, to move away from the community in which they have put down their roots.

You may remember that the Republican presidential candidate visited Lawrence, Massachusetts, four years ago and promised the workers around there that the federal government would take special steps to increase the number of jobs in their cities. Has anything happened? When the election was over, nothing was done—except to reduce further the tariff on textiles. In the words of one of President Eisenhower's advisers, the textile workers could enjoy the right to suffer.

And something else has happened, too, since those special efforts. Instead of more jobs, textile workers lost thousands of jobs in the next years—more than 100,000, or about 10 per cent, in a single year. And, when Democratic senators proposed a strong area redevelopment bill to help localities with a high degree of unemployment, the Republicans put in a weak bill of their own, fought the Democratic bill in the Senate and finally prevented it even from being brought up for consideration in the House.

I want to speak frankly about the question of tariffs. My party has always believed in the liberalization of trading and the reduction of trade barriers. I believe myself that the policy of keeping other countries out of American markets leads, in the end, to isolation and disaster. I believe in trade and more trade, and trading means buying as well as selling. So I am in general opposed to tariff increases which discourage buying, and therefore selling, abroad.

But I believe equally strongly that tariff reduction must be applied with human concern, with intelligence, and with a sense of the nation's long-run interests. And I don't share the Eisenhower administration's unfeeling attitude toward the troubles of the textile industry.

Let me put it concretely. I believe in a policy of gradual tariff reduction. I do not believe that the brunt of this policy should be borne by weak industries or by parts of the country under special economic strain. I do not believe that we can allow the New England segment of the industry which has lost more than 40 per cent of its jobs in eight years to be exposed, through further tariff cuts, to destruction from abroad. The problem of increasing world trade and of relieving the dollar shortage is a national problem. The burden of solving that problem should be allocated among industries and regions of the country as equitably as possible.

Now, I know that after years of indifference the administration has made its election year gesture toward the textile industry. It has done the same for farmers, for schools, and so forth. Every four years the Republicans get concerned about the people—a sort of leap-year liberalism. Just a few days ago Sherman Adams suddenly announced that the administration is working on an agreement with Japan to reduce the flow of textile imports. Almost at the same time an increase in woolen tariffs was announced.

Is this political cynicism a month before the election all the administration, after four years, has to suggest for the most troubled industry in America? What about those promises made in 1952? What about the merger problem, what about really doing something with government contracts for areas with surplus labor? What about really doing something with government contracts for small business? What about the bill for federal aid to distressed areas—the bill the Republicans killed this summer in Congress? What about a flood insurance bill that does not saddle the states hardest hit with an unreasonable share of the costs?

The prosperity of textiles involves people, and it can only be handled by an administration which sees economic problems in terms of homes and families and communities.

I make no sweeping promises about solving the problem. But I pledge you the sympathetic and compassionate concern of a Democratic administration dedicated to finding a place for this indispensable industry—in a regional economy which will continue to grow so long as thrift, craftsmanship, hard work and intelligence count in the affairs of a nation.

And what goes for textiles goes for small business. We have seen an administration so dominated by the big and strong and rich that it has had little concern for the little man—the vanishing man. It has amiably stood by while the merger movement has acquired new momentum. It has watched the failure rate in small business reach the highest points in years. It has assigned men to jobs who have little belief in the future of small business. Its tight money policy makes it hard for the small man to get the money he needs, and leaves the big man, with his ample reserves, in a still more favored position.

We Democrats believe in small business—because small business has been the foundation of American initiative and enterprise. We think he can be helped to survive in this age of bigness—by helping him to get the capital and credit he needs at reasonable terms, by making the tax laws more equitable for him, by a larger share of government contracts, by more attention to our merger and monopoly laws, and by putting the Small Business Administration in the hands of men who really care about small business.

And the government's concern for basic industry and small business goes for other national problems, too, such as flood insurance and flood control, for which New England's leaders, Democrat and Republican alike, have fought so hard.

The difference between the two parties can be stated very simply. When the Republican leaders think of economic problems, they see a ledger and a cashbook. When Democrats think of economic problems, they see men, women and children.

8

Civil Liberties and Civil Rights

CIVIL LIBERTIES AND CIVIL RIGHTS

•

You will have to find even in the abruptness of my greeting the measure of its warmth. For I have become painfully aware that, if television is to be a candidate's servant, he must accept it even more as his master. Not silence, but talk, has become golden.

So I shall come directly to the point.

I have come to New York to ask support for my candidacy for the office of President of the United States.

But this is too large a thing for any man to seek or ask on a personal basis. And I do not. I come to you rather in the deep conviction that, if there is to be peace in the world and freedom in America, the reins of our government must be returned to those with the passion for progress and the dedication to the ideal of human dignity which are the qualities of the Democratic faith—of your faith and of mine.

I spoke in Washington on Saturday of peace in the world.

I want to speak tonight of freedom in America.

Yet these are not really two issues, but rather two parts of one.

There can be no lasting freedom in America unless there is peace in the world. And there will be peace in the world only when we here in America prove that freedom means what we say it means. We must show that freedom is the servant of the poor as well as the rich—for most of the world is poor; that it protects change—for most of the world is in revolution; that it is color-blind, for most of the world is nonwhite. We must prove that freedom contains that full measure of justice without which it could be freedom for the strong to oppress the weak.

From a speech at the Tribute to Stevenson Dinner, New York, April 25, 1956.

I see freedom in the world today as the great life-giving river of which America is the source. It will be whatever we are, not more, not less. So, if we hope to make the principles of freedom meaningful in the world, we must first make sure they have mighty meaning for ourselves. We must—in our land, in our own communities, and in our own hearts— live up to the values of individual freedom and individual right which are the basis of our American socity.

Yet we must do this not just because it may exalt our leadership in the world, but above all for the sake of these values themselves—the values which give life and power to the great experiment in self-government to which we as a people have been so long committed, and to which so many others in Asia and Africa now urgently aspire. Our task is all the harder and the purity of our example all the more important because these peoples who know about *national* freedom know little about these values of individual freedom and rights which lie at the root of free society.

Let me speak first about the issue of freedom which is today causing greatest concern among us—civil rights for our minorities. The achievement of equal rights for all American citizens is the great unfinished business before the United States.

This would be just as much the case had there been no Supreme Court decision on desegregation in the public schools.

There remains, however, the abiding responsibility of the executive branch of the government to do its part in meeting this most fateful internal problem and the rising tensions that have followed in its train. The present administration, in my judgment, has failed to meet this responsibility; it has contributed nothing to the creation of an atmosphere in which this decision could be carried out in tranquillity and order.

The immense prestige and influence of the Presidency have been withheld from those who honestly seek to carry out the law in gathering storm and against rising resistance. Refusing to rise to this great moral and constitutional crisis, the administration has hardly even acknowledged its gravity.

It is the sworn responsibility of the President to carry out the law of the land. And I would point out that this office is the one office in the democracy, apart from the courts, where the man who fills it represents all the people. Those in the Congress bear particular responsibilities to the citizens of the states they represent, and on what is in some ways a regional problem their views are naturally divided. Not so of the Presidency. And where the nation is divided, there is special demand on him to unite and lead the people toward the common goal.

As president, if that were my privilege, I would work ceaselessly and with a sense of crucial urgency—with public officials, private groups, and educators—to meet this challenge in our life as a nation and this threat to our national good reputation.

I would act in the knowledge that law and order is the Executive's responsibility; and I would and will act, too, I pray, in the conviction that to play politics with the Court's decision and the basic rights of citizens and human beings is wicked.

It is, for me, another point of central principle that one of the most important guarantees of equality is the right to vote conferred on all citizens by the Fifteenth Amendment. Political freedom underlies all other freedoms. Wherever any American citizens have been denied by intimidation and violence the right to vote, then the right to vote of all American citizens is imperiled.

There are laws on the statute books giving the federal government authority to protect citizens' voting rights. These laws should be enforced. And if they are inadequate, they should be strengthened. And I believe that all responsible citizens, south and north, would go along with a determination to assure the right to vote under the law.

But again I say that the responsibility and the opportunity of the President in matters such as these go beyond the execution of the law. For his office is the repository of moral authority as well as legal, and it is from our chosen leader that there must come to our hearts, our heads and our spirits the common impulse to honor in our daily lives the principles we proclaim to all the world.

The protection of minority rights is in the forefront of our minds. But it is only part of the larger problem of protecting the Bill of Rights from the grievous assaults that have scarred and stained this interval.

The flood stage of hate and hysteria among us, so alien to our nature, reached its crest in 1953 and 1954, the first two years of the present administration.

Those were the days when our government quaked before the Junior Senator from Wisconsin, and White House aides spoke of the President's "passion not to offend anybody in Congress."

Those were the days when books were banned and even burned in American libraries abroad.

Those were the days of the "numbers game"—a sleight-of-hand operation intended to make the country believe that the Eisenhower administration had ousted from government a whole horde of Communists hired by the Democrats—when in fact not a single one was a Communist and almost half of those discharged (on what were called security grounds) had actually been hired by the present administration itself!

Those were the days when some American citizens demanded that the Girl Scouts rewrite their manual and denounced the tale of Robin Hood as Communist propaganda.

And those were the days when an emotional pressure toward a spurious conformity silenced tongues and shuttered minds throughout the land of the free and the home of the brave.

The 1954 rejection of the Vice-President's campaign appeal about Communists in government, the election of a Democratic Congress, and the senatorial censure of the man who described the great Democratic interval of victory over depression and Hitlerism as "twenty years of treason," marked the turning of the tide against the high point of the flood of hate, hysteria and fear.

But if the flood has receded, the evidence of the damage it did to the soul of America remains. There is much to be done today to restore respect for the foundation of freedom under law—the Bill of Rights.

Who can best clean up the wreckage? Who can best rebuild the structure of our Bill of Rights?

Is this a task to be entrusted now to the party whose leaders shouted treason and Communism for partisan advantage?

Is it a task to be entrusted to those who were indifferent to national dignity and individual freedom at home, while posing as champions of liberty in the world?

It is rather the task, I suggest, for those who tried faithfully to defend our liberties even as the flood mounted and rolled toward its crest.

Let us never forget some of the landmarks of sanity in this shameful period. There was President Truman's courageous defense of freedom of speech in his forthright veto message of the Internal Security Act, the McCarran Act, of 1950. There were the speeches of Democratic leaders against all that Senator McCarthy stood for at a time when he was still his party's hero. And I remind you that, finally, the Democratic senators voted to a man for his censure in December of 1954, while half of Senator McCarthy's own party still could not see that he had done anything wrong.

This is our job—yours and mine—a job, if you will, for Democrats. We must first stop playing partisan politics with internal security. Political debate must once again be pitched on the great issues of our time, not on impugning the loyalty of any group of Americans. Communism is not an issue, for both parties are dedicated to the struggle against it at home and abroad.

Our security system must be reconsidered. Today there are loyalty-security tests for between eight and ten million Americans. Federal employees, many state and municipal employees, servicemen, multitudes of workers in private plants, Coast Guard employees, and others have their private lives put under the microscope of investigation in the alleged interest of our national security.

We must, by all means, take the strongest possible measures to prevent espionage, and strengthen our counterintelligence activities and agencies in every useful way. But let us, too, weigh clearly and carefully the balance between these necessities and the equal necessities of protecting the rights of free speech and association guaranteed by the First Amendment.

I am glad to see that the administration itself has belatedly recognized that its security program has been actually endangering our security by holding back scientific progress, and that it is relaxing its requirements with respect to nonsecret research programs.

The time has come to restore to our security procedures the fundamental principle of the Bill of Rights, that no man shall lose his life, liberty or property without due process of law. The discharge of an employee by governmental edict without the right to face his accusers offends that principle.

The idea that a man's right to a commission in the armed forces or to an honorable discharge may be challenged because of his mother's or his sister's actions or associations denies the principle of personal responsibility and imitates the totalitarian doctrine of family guilt. I never thought we would live to see in America the day when not being good to one's mother was a sign of virtue.

As we defaced the American image when we defaced the Bill of Rights, so we can restore that image only as we enshrine again the Bill of Rights.

I wish there were time tonight to talk of newer frontiers, of the tasks we face if we are to give freedom the breadth of meaning it can have in this age of abundance in this most blessed of countries.

Freedom isn't complete for families living in slums, for men out of work, for children in overcrowded classrooms, for people who are sick and can't afford help, or for men and women who have worked long and faithfully only to find old age a time of fear.

All of these must be our concern as we think forward to the enrichment of freedom and to putting it in a setting of life where it will mean the most. As Senator [Herbert H.] Lehman has said, "we must work to restore Freedom to her hallowed place in our hearts and in the practices of our country."

For "the trouble is," Senator Lehman said, "that we have lost the passion for the full right of freedom."

But have we really lost it? What we have lost, I think, but only for this moment in history, is the leadership that passion for freedom demands; leadership in the majestic, vital tradition of the great champions of the American ideal—Jefferson, Jackson, Lincoln, Wilson, Roosevelt and Truman.

Only by such a rekindling of this nation's passion for freedom can we persuade the world that America is genuinely the hope of free peoples everywhere. For, in the end, democracy will triumph or go down, and America will stand or fall, not by the power of our money or of our arms, but by the splendor of our ideals.

CIVIL RIGHTS AND ECONOMIC ISSUES OF THE UNDERPRIVILEGED

•

I am proud to come to Harlem tonight as a candidate for the Presidency of the United States.

I am proud because I come as the representative of the party which through history has been dedicated to the people of America—the Democratic party.

From the beginning of this republic, the Democratic party has worked, worked hard, yes, and worked successfully to improve the condition, confirm the rights, and enlarge the opportunities of the Joe Smiths of our land.

In the last generation, the Democratic party has achieved social and economic and spiritual gains which have transformed American society— and it has done so under the leadership of two greathearted Americans, Franklin D. Roosevelt and Harry S. Truman.

Our party has fought valiantly for the plain people of America through its past—and I am here tonight to tell you that, so long as I am its spokesman and leader, it will fight as hard as ever for the people in the years ahead.

We have come a long way in the battle for human dignity and opportunity in America. But we still have far to go. The Democratic party

From a speech in New York, October 4, 1956.

has led the fight against poverty and discrimination—and it is our purpose
to carry on that fight as long as those ugly specters still haunt American
life.

We are the richest nation in the world—the richest nation in history.
And it is an indictment of our intelligence and humanity if we cannot
provide every family in the country a decent opportunity to earn a living,
a decent school for their children, a decent roof over their heads, and a
decent prospect of security in old age.

We have had four years of Republican rule—four years of shuffling
and postponement—four years of "time out" in the battle for expanding
human dignity.

The time has come to resume our onward march.

There are still miles and miles of slums in America. And every American family wants to escape from misery and squalor. We need new houses
—millions of them. We need a sound and imaginative public housing
program. Every American who has taken the trouble to see how other
people live in our country knows that these needs exist—and must be met.

How have the Republicans met these needs?

Well, the Republican leadership has fought and licked every good public
housing bill proposed in these last four years—and the bills were always
brought forward by Democrats.

I doubt if there will ever be much hope for an adequate public housing
program under an administration which takes its policy from the real
estate lobby.

But I say to you that under the Democrats we will have public housing
and urban renewal programs which will help provide every American
family with an opportunity for a decent home in a decent neighborhood.

You have already seen here in Harlem how public housing can begin
to transform a community and make it a place where you can be proud
to live—but then you have had Democratic mayors here in New York!

The battle for housing is only one part of our Democratic battle for a
New America, but in every field Democratic proposals to help the people
are met by Republican indifference, obstruction and opposition.

Take the minimum wage. Over the strenuous objections of the Eisenhower administration, the Democrats in the last session of Congress raised
the minimum wage to $1. But this is not enough; and it is the Democratic
platform pledge to raise the minimum wage—if you will make sure that
there are enough Democrats in Washington next year to help us do it.

Over the strenuous objections of the Eisenhower administration, the
Democrats in the last session of Congress lowered the age at which women

and disabled persons became eligible for social security benefits.

In particular, it is our determination to carry out a program which will make the last years of life more serene and happy for our older citizens. But food and dress and shelter are not all that matter to a good life. Man's highest fulfillment comes in the realm of the spirit—in the fulfillment of his inward sense of his dignity, his responsibility, and his freedom.

America has made progress toward that fulfillment, too—and that progress has come in the main, I am proud to say, through the leadership of the Democratic party.

Yes, we have seen nothing more brazen in the entire record of Republican misrepresentation in this campaign than the Republican effort to seize partisan credit for progress in civil rights.

They have claimed credit for ending segregation in the armed forces.

Well, you know, I happen to have been in on that story right from the start—and these Johnny-come-lately Republican claims make me pretty disgusted.

In 1941 and 1942, I was assistant to the Secretary of the Navy. And it was then that we took the first and the hard steps toward removing the racial barriers in the United States Navy. My part in that was small— and we only got the job started then—but we *did* get it started.

Then, on July 26, 1948, President Truman issued his Executive Order No. 9981. It was that order that sounded the death knell of segregation in the armed forces.

That order was issued despite the testimony of Chief of Staff Dwight D. Eisenhower before a Congressional committee on April 2, 1948, that complete desegregation in the armed forces would, as he put it, get us "into trouble."

But, four years later, Candidate Eisenhower admitted, in a speech at Chicago on October 31, 1952, that—and these are his words—"Now, so far as I know, there is nothing in the way of segregation in the Army, Navy, Air Force or Marines left—at least as a matter of official record."

Why, then—why—did President Eisenhower tell the American people on Monday of this week, in listing the accomplishments of his administration, that one thing the Republicans have done since 1952 is to end segregation in the armed forces?

I don't mind the President's trying to make off in broad daylight with the Democratic platform—he always returns it right after election day anyway—but he better stop trying to run on the Democratic record!

The Republicans have claimed credit for stopping discrimination in employment by government contractors—though all they did was to continue the work begun by the Fair Employment Practices Commission under President Roosevelt and by the Committee on Government Contract Compliance under President Truman. For that we are grateful.

They have even claimed credit for ending segregation in the District of Columbia—though the case which meant the end of segregation in many public places in the district was initiated at the time President Truman was in office and while Mr. Eisenhower was still a private citizen.

And, finally, when the President was presented with an opportunity for great national leadership in this field, he was virtually silent. I am referring to the Supreme Court decision on desegregation in the public schools.

Surely the gravest problem we face here at home this year is this issue of civil rights. We have faced it continuously for many years in varying forms and changing urgency. I faced it when I was Governor of Illinois. During that interval, we desegregated the National Guard; we used the National Guard to protect the safety of citizens in the Cicero riots; and we came within an ace of passing a fair employment practices act—and were prevented from doing so only by a close vote in a Republican legislature. We eliminated all racial designations in the employment service of Illinois and on drivers' licenses, and so on.

Yet, despite the progress we have made, the achievement of equality of rights and opportunities for all American citizens is still the great unfinished business before the United States. The Supreme Court decision on desegregation in the public schools was an expression of our steady movement toward genuine equality for all before the law: it expressed in a new field the old principle that the American heritage of liberty and opportunity is not to be confined to men, women and children of a single race, a single religion, or a single color.

I have spoken about this decision many times. Last week I spoke about it in Arkansas, and I am glad to have the opportunity to say here what I said there:

"The Supreme Court of the United States has determined unanimously that the Constitution does not permit segregation in the schools. As you know, for I have made my position clear on this from the start, I believe that decision to be right!

"Some of you feel strongly to the contrary.

"But what is most important is that we agree that, once the Supreme Court has decided this constitutional question, we accept that decision as law-abiding citizens."

And this statement, I am heartened to tell you tonight, brought applause from those who heard me in Arkansas.

I continued: "Our common goal is the orderly accomplishment of the result decreed by the Court. I said long ago, and I stand now squarely on the plain statement, adopted in the Democratic platform, that 'we reject all proposals for the use of force to interfere with the orderly determination of these matters by the courts.' The Court's decree provides for the ways and means of putting into effect the principle it sets forth. I am confident that this decision will be carried out in the manner prescribed by the courts. I have repeatedly expressed the belief, however, that the office of the Presidency should be used to bring together those of opposing views in this matter—to the end of creating a climate for peaceful acceptance of this decision."

The President of the United States recently said of the Supreme Court decision, "I think it makes no difference whether or not I endorse it."

As for myself, I have said from the beginning—and say now—that I support this decision!

We have a code in this country—a design by which Americans live with one another. It is called the Bill of Rights. It should not only be obeyed, it should be respected. The Bill of Rights is the moral spine of our nation.

I pray that all Americans, no matter what their feelings, will collaborate in working to sustain the Bill of Rights. No other course is consistent with our constitutional equality as Americans or with our human brotherhood as children of God.

The profound questions of our time remain questions of conscience and of will.

And the answers will come, at the last, "Not by might, nor by power, but by Thy spirit."

For ours is a time like that of which the prophet Amos wrote: "Let justice roll down as waters, and righteousness as a mighty stream."

TREATMENT OF PUBLIC SERVANTS

•

A basic complaint about this administration that you encounter all around the country is that it so largely represents a single interest—the big people, the rich and the powerful.

But I think our government should represent all the people and especially the ordinary people, the man in the street who has no one save his elected officials to represent him. The strong can look after themselves

From a speech at Walnut Hill, Virginia, September 15, 1956.

—they have their lobbies and captive spokesmen galore. But the weak have no one.

I say we need an administration which is interested in farmers, not just in surpluses; in the small businessman, not just in abstractions about free enterprise; in a young couple trying to get a house, not just in the rediscount rate.

I recall a remark by the chairman of the Civil Service Commission, who was asked at a Senate hearing whether his commission was furnished any names of persons who are declared security risks, and he replied, "No, we don't have any names. We just deal in numbers."

Well, maybe numbers are enough for the Civil Service Commission, but they are not enough for a people's government. And I say it's time for this administration to stop dealing in numbers and start thinking about people.

And a good place for it to start is with its own employees.

The United States government ought to be a model employer, fair, considerate, and generous. I know from my own experience as Governor of Illinois that it is not easy to attract good men and women to government, and no wonder. When I became governor, I found that Civil Service had become no more than a figure of speech, that the employees of the state had been exploited ruthlessly and the public payrolls loaded with political agents.

During my term we took the state police out of politics and put it under a merit system for the first time; we resumed examinations and strengthened the Civil Service in many ways; we extended the career idea to new areas of state government and we lifted salaries all along the line up to levels both of competition and of self-respect. I did everything in my power to improve the morale, the repute and security of state service so that it would be more attractive to good men and women.

And I am sure that the personnel, objectives and standards of our great federal services must be the very highest.

But what has happened in Washington in the last four years?

Although those of us who had worked in our federal government here in Washington were pained, we were not surprised when during the 1952 campaign the Republican leaders damaged callously, if unwittingly, the public reputation of the government service by their crusades against "bureaucracy" and what they like to call "government red tape."

If we winced at the wild Republican charges that the government was full of Communists and spies, we were at least used to it.

But everyone, I think, was surprised when the administration's war of nerves against its own employees continued after it took office. Secretary Weeks, you will recall, called civil servants "Trojan horses left behind to try to hamper, hoodwink, and wreck the new Administration." And Attorney General Brownell struck a more sinister note which we were to hear often when he complained of inheriting "more than our share of odd characters, log rollers and misfits."

Since then the guerrilla warfare on the people who serve the government from our responsible officials has continued.

The administration, it is true, has increased the total number of employees covered by the Civil Service. But at the same time it has removed from Civil Service and in practical effect placed at the disposal of the Republican National Committee a large number of career jobs to which employees have advanced through years of outstanding service. Time and again it has forced men out of government employment just a few months short of retirement age. Thus it has penalized precisely the ability, initiative and devotion to duty which it ought to encourage.

Worst of all, perhaps, the administration, for partisan political purposes, has pilloried innocent men and women under the pretense of conducting loyalty and security investigations.

The history of this shameless political trickery goes back, as I say, to the 1952 campaign. You remember they modestly called it a Great Crusade and the orators made so much noise about "Communists in government" that when they got into office they evidently felt obliged to find some, even at the expense of innocent government workers. So they invented and popularized the term "security risk," pretended that all security risks were "subversives," and soon were able to boast—just in time for the 1954 Congressional campaign, of course—that they had cleansed government of security risks by the bushel—or was it half a bushel?

Government workers were summarily suspended without pay on the basis of vague charges of ambiguous offenses, made after inadequate sifting of unevaluated information by untrained personnel officers—and then were forced to defend themselves at great expense before prosecutor-judges without being able to confront their accusers; and often without even knowing the real nature of the charges against them.

But soon a Congressional investigation disclosed that 90 per cent of the persons the administration claimed to have fired as "security risks" were never determined to be "security risks" at all; that others were not even fired but were merely transferred from one agency to another; and that half of those who were fired as security risks had been hired by the Eisenhower administration itself.

And finally the administration admitted, after about three years of such demoralizing harassments, that not a single person was fired for being a Communist.

As the *New York Times* said a couple of months ago, "The Administration deliberately used misleading statistics about the program for political purposes. The political approach has damaged the President's asserted attempt to clear the air of 'unreasoned suspicion.'" And now the Supreme Court has ruled that the Eisenhower administration violated the intent of Congress by its application of the security law.

The abuse of the security policies under this administration during the last four years is a shameful chapter in American history which began in consecration to individual liberty. The lives of decent and devoted government servants lie buried in the wreckage it wrought. The wider consequences are incalculable. Government always needs good men worse than good men need government jobs, and now sorely needed men have deserted a government that played fast and loose with the Bill of Rights, and government has been unable to attract young people with new ideas. Government needs men of imagination and courage, men with fresh ideas and the vigor to fight for them. We don't want to turn our public servants into a collection of weak and spineless conformists.

What shall we do?

Let me say to you that a first objective of a Democratic administration will be to restore dignity and honor and self-esteem to the public service. Those who prefer to serve the commonwealth rather than themselves deserve the respect of their fellow citizens. Under a Democratic administration they will have that respect once again.

We must, of course, vigorously oppose legislation intended to override the court decision—we must hold the line where the Court has fixed it.

We mean to reconstruct the present security system and devise a program which will safeguard the state without degrading those who serve it. Already, I am glad to say, the AEC has begun to move in that direction, and even the Army is talking about it. But it is shocking that the necessary broader reforms in the security system have been so long delayed. Recently the New York City Bar Association proposed broad changes which represent a long step in the right direction. The continued hesitation of the administration about this problem reveals all too clearly both its attitude toward the public service and its reluctance to concede the wrongs it has committed.

The way a government treats its employees, it seems to me, says a lot about that government. A democracy should not treat them as game for

partisan advancement or public ridicule, but as upright, decent, con-
scientious citizens devoted to the high calling, the unending task, of
making the government better serve its proprietors, the people.

It is in this spirit that they serve their country; it is in this spirit that
the people you elect should serve them.

SUPPRESSION OF NEWS

•

I'd like to talk with you about a problem that is as much in your line
of business as in mine.

There is a very serious issue in this country today that probably won't
count in the political campaigns at all—although it ought to. I mean this
business of the suppression of public information by the present administration in Washington.

I think it is pretty plain that there is today greater suppression of public
information by the national government than there has ever before been
in the history of this country, except in time of war.

I think it is plain, too, that the reason for this is not a special concern
of the present administration about the security of the country, but a concern, rather, about the security of the political party now in office. For
there has appeared recently not only revealing evidence of the needless
suppression of information, but equally revealing evidence of the distortion and manipulation of the news—not *by* the press, but *to* the press.
And invariably this manipulation is revealed as having been in an attempt
to cover up some administration blunder or to put a good face on a bad
situation for partisan political advantage.

I realize the seriousness of these charges, and I want to be sure that
they are not presented in such a way as to appear to be just politically inspired. I ask your consideration, accordingly, of these facts:

Last fall the convention of Sigma Delta Chi, your professional jour-
nalistic fraternity, found that "there has developed today the worst
abridgement of the American's right to know about the federal government in the 168 years of the American experiment in freedom."

One of the leaders of this organization, Mr. V. M. Newton, editor of
the *Tampa Tribune,* pointed out that a year ago President Eisenhower
had asked the press to report any officials who "strangle the news," and
Mr. Newton said: "I do not know whether the President was talking out

From a speech in Pittsburgh, April 18, 1956.

of one side of his mouth or whether he is ignorant of what is going on in federal government."

According to a recent report of the American Civil Liberties Union: "It is the fair consensus of Washington press correspondents that abuses of the power in federal agencies to suppress information were never so rampant as now, that this widespread abuse of power is exercised in the great majority of instances on matters having nothing whatever to do with national security, and that these abuses have curtailed the power of Congress and the press to be of service to the people and have advanced to the point where the civil liberties of the people are now threatened."

And there came just a few days ago, as startling evidence of this, the statement reported by a reliable columnist to have come from one of the members of the all-important National Security Council. "Policy decisions of the National Security Council," he said, "are not a fit subject for public discussion."

A Special House Subcommittee on Government Information has been set up under the chairmanship of John Moss of California.

The Moss Committee reports that since 1953 some thirty classifications of restricted information have been created—in addition to good old Top Secret, Secret, and Confidential.

This committee called before it Chairman Philip Young of the Civil Service Commission. He was one of those chiefly responsible for perpetrating the "numbers game"—concerning security discharges by the administration—on the American public. Young told the committee that he has an inherent right to withhold information about his agency's activities from the general public. Plainly, Mr. Young does not regard the public business as any of the public's business.

The Department of Commerce has established an Office of Strategic Information for the purpose of suppressing even unclassified data. This is done in the name of security, but its inevitable effect will be to prevent the American people from receiving information about technological developments in American industry.

The Secretary of the Department of Defense has ordered that nothing be said in Pentagon press releases which does not constitute a "constructive contribution to the primary mission of the Defense Department." And this directive instructs military officers that in talking to reporters they are to consider not only military security, but also what effect their information might have on American industrial power, morale, and—believe it or not—"other considerations (anything you can think of)"—and that last is a direct quote. As the *Tampa Tribune* editor said: ". . . virtually all Department of Defense news today is censored, regardless of whether or not it affects national security."

Congressman Moss points out that one government agency refused to tell how much peanut butter the armed services were buying on the ground that the information might enable an enemy agent to deduce the size of the armed forces. Yet at the same time another agency in Washington only a few blocks away was reporting regularly on the precise number of men in the armed forces.

Leading American scientists have declared in recent months that the present security system in our federal government is actually hindering the defense development of the United States rather than strengthening it. One of them, noting that we have steadily lost ground in the international competition for technical leadership, said: "An important aspect in this loss of supremacy in certain vital fields of technology stems from our present widespread practice of technological secrecy." Only recently the Massachusetts Institute of Technology declined to undertake a research study for the Atomic Energy Commission because it could not see how such a project could be carried out effectively under the prescribed security regulations. In view of such evidence as this, and in view of the disquieting reports that we are lagging behind the Soviet Union in certain areas of military power, I think we need to take a new look at our policy of controlling scientific information.

Turning to the matter of actual distortion of information, I call attention particularly to the statement made to the Moss Committee by James Reston, respected *New York Times* correspondent. There is, Reston said, "a growing tendency to manage the news." He added, by way of illustration: "I think there was a conscious effort to give the news at the Geneva Conference an optimistic flavor. I think there was a conscious effort there, decided upon even perhaps ahead of time, for spokesmen to emphasize all the optimistic facts coming out of that conference and to minimize all of the quarrels at that conference with the results which we all have seen."

This is a grave and serious charge. That the government of a free democracy should seek deliberately to manipulate the news to its own advantage is indeed shocking.

Then Mr. Reston went on to tell the committee that "There was, after the Geneva Conference a decision taken in the government that perhaps this was having a bad effect, that the people in the Western countries were letting down their guard, and therefore a decision was made . . . that the government should strike another note. So that after the Geneva smiling, the new word went out that it might be a good idea now to frown a little bit, so the President made a speech at Philadelphia, taking quite a different line about the Geneva Conference. That is what I mean by managing the news. . . . While it is bad to suppress a bit of information, it would seem to me even worse, if all the newsmaking powers of the Federal Government were to blanket the newspaper situation with the theme which *perhaps they did not believe was quite true, but might be an instrument of their thought."* (Italics added.)

I submit that the American people want neither smiles nor frowns, but only the truth. As the Freedom of Information Committee of the National Editorial Association said in convention at Chicago last year:

"The right of the people to know is basic to the preservation of our freedom and fundamental to our American way of life. The infringement of this right, whether by government or by groups or by individuals, no matter in what measure it may begin, will lead to tyranny, and to the death of liberty."

Very early in this administration a high administration official, C. D. Jackson, said: "We're going to merchandise the living hell out of the Eisenhower administration."

I think the record is clear that they have done precisely what they set out to do.

They have merchandised the American people—tried to sell them a bill of goods, to put it in language the advertising business can understand. And their method of doing it has included suppressing and distorting the news upon which the people must depend.

I've got two answers to these abuses by this administration of the people's right to know.

One answer is more and better leg work by the working press. You cannot depend on government handouts. You have got to find out the truth for yourselves. Now, more than ever before, the burden of informing the people rests upon you.

The other answer is in some ways simpler. I shall be grateful for your support in next Tuesday's election.

IV

CHOICE BETWEEN THE PARTIES

1. Broad Issues of the Campaign

2. Executive Leadership

3. Single Interest Government

4. Liberalism and Responsibility

Broad Issues of the Campaign

ACCOMPLISHMENTS OF THE PARTIES

•

On Monday of this week, the real issue in this 1956 election campaign was joined—and I felt it was important to get before you—squarely and promptly—the Democratic position on this issue.

The Republican candidate for the Presidency said on Monday that this election will hinge on the question, as he put it, of "which party, in these recent years, has done more to help all citizens meet the problems of their daily lives."

This is a proper statement of the issue. Of course, what matters is which party will do more in the future to help people meet the always new problems of their daily lives. But I'm sure that is what the Republican candidate meant. And he is right that each party's past record offers the best test of its future performance.

So, if the record is to be the test, let's get the record straight!

I think it is too bad that the President indulged in such gross misstatements of the record. He is an honorable man and could hardly have deliberately intended such misrepresentations.

Fortunately, the facts to set the record straight are at hand. Now let's look at them.

The President's speech referred to our Social Security program, and he claimed credit on behalf of the Republican party for its enlargement.

The fact is that this program—which so vitally helps almost all our older citizens and others in need meet the problems of their daily lives—was developed by Democrats against bitter Republican opposition.

The fact is that in this very year in Congress the Democrats proposed

Telecast from Pittsburgh, October 3, 1956.

that Social Security benefits be paid to employees fifty years old or older, who become permanently disabled, and to reduce the age of eligibility for Social Security for women to sixty-two. The fact is that 85 per cent of the Democratic Senators voted for the change on disability and 84 per cent of the Republicans voted against it.

The President reported in his listing of what he called Republican progress, that—and I quote him—"the minimum wage was increased."

The fact is that he himself, as well as his Congressional leaders, ardently opposed the successful Democratic effort to raise the minimum wage to $1.

The President even took credit in his speech for seeking a program to help distressed areas suffering from chronic local unemployment.

The fact is that the only adequate bill to help these areas was introduced in Congress by Democrats, was passed by the Senate over strong Republican opposition, and was killed in the House by the President's own leaders.

The President tried to claim that this Republican administration was the first to take up the cause of the needy farmer.

The fact is that the Democrats initiated the program of federal aid to the family farm with the Farm Security Administration nearly twenty years ago.

The President even listed farm prices in his summary of Republican progress. The fact is that farm income declined by one-fifth during his term of office.

"The cost of living," the President went on to say, "has been remarkably stabilized."

The fact is that, by the statistics of the Department of Labor, the cost of living reached, this July, the highest point in history.

The President gave the Republican party credit for helping small business. The fact is that last year the rate of small business failures was higher than at any time since 1941. The further fact is that the Eisenhower administration proposed no program for the relief of small business until this year, on the eve of the election, and even then after Congress adjourned.

The President gave the Republican administration credit for progress in civil rights—and the areas of progress he enumerated were all areas of federal responsibility and were all initiated by Democratic administrations.

The fact is that the President has taken no clear position and exercised no leadership in connection with the pressing present problem of school desegregation.

The President gave the Republican administration credit for a $12 a week increase in wages since August, 1952. The fact is that a substantial part of that increase took place under the Truman administration.

The President implied that the Republican tax cut of 1954 benefited everybody. The fact is that 91 cents of every dollar of that tax cut went to corporations and to families with incomes above $5,000 a year.

The President even claimed that the Republican party had ended "special favoritism and laxity" in Washington—but the facts are written otherwise in the record of the Dixon-Yates contract, the natural resources giveaway, and the resignations under fire of his Secretary of the Air Force and other top level officials of his administration. And I won't mention the numerous loopholes in the tax law sponsored by his administration.

The President said that he and the Republicans wanted federal aid to education—and that the Democrats defeated it. The facts are:

First, that the only bill that came up for passage and which would have provided $400 million a year for school construction was defeated by the Republicans in the House, and

Second, that during the first two years of his administration, when he had a Republican Congress, he proposed no legislation for federal aid for public schools other than in relation to defense areas.

These are the facts!

I have no way of knowing whether the President knew them when he spoke, or whether he didn't. But someone did.

Yes, and the American people knew these facts—from their own lives.

Are you a crippled miner, totally disabled, fifty years old, with children to feed and no way to do it—until the Democrats in Congress this year made you eligible for social security benefits?

Are you a working woman of sixty-two who can now retire—because of the action of this Democratic Congress?

Are you a man who almost lost his home in the depression—until the Home Owners Loan Corporation saved it?

Do you work in a steel mill here around Pittsburgh? Do you remember what the corporations did to your union—until the Democrats passed the Wagner Labor Act?

Are you a storekeeper, a businessman, who would have lost your business in the depression if it hadn't been for Franklin Roosevelt and a Democratic policy?

Are you an auto worker in Detroit who worried about temporary unemployment—until the Democrats established unemployment compensation?

Did you almost lose your Iowa farm twenty years ago—and did the Democratic farm program help you to save it? This made a difference in your life—and so does this administration's attitude toward agriculture.

Do you live in a part of the country where REA power lines, brought in during Democratic administrations and against Republican opposition, have transformed life's whole pattern?

Or are you a veteran from Minneapolis raising a family in a house in the suburbs—because we Democrats made it possible for you to buy a home with a GI loan?

I won't ask tonight if you are a mother with a five-year-old wondering what kind of school he'll go to next year, or a housewife worrying about high prices.

Run down the list of the measures which in what the President calls "these recent years" have strengthened the framework of economic security, social welfare and personal freedom. Ask yourself which of these measures originated with the Republicans, which with the Democrats. And I haven't even mentioned TVA or the great industrial development in our great river valleys.

I rest my case confidently on your answer.

I say in all soberness that nearly every governmental program in our time—in this generation—which has helped citizens meet the problems of their daily lives more effectively, which has enriched, enlarged and brightened their daily lives has been a Democratic program.

And I further say that this is no accident.

There is a deep and continuing difference between our parties—a difference in composition, in tradition and in ideals.

This is as it should be; this is why we believe in the two-party system. But let us not exaggerate these differences. Both parties share a profound belief in our nation, in our Constitution, in our legacy of political freedom and economic enterprise, in our commitment to the dignity of the individual, in our passion for peace, in our faith in divine Providence.

Let us never forget, even in the heat of a political campaign, that the things which unite us are still far more important than the things which divide us.

Yet within the framework of agreement there exist notable differences —differences which have existed since the founding of the Republic.

Thomas Jefferson defined the fundamental difference nearly a century and a half ago when he said that men are divided into two parties: "those who fear and distrust the people" and "those who identify themselves with the people." And Alexander Hamilton replied for the opposite tradition that the nation should be governed by the "rich and well-born."

President Eisenhower's administration has reflected the philosophy of his party.

But the Democratic party has had different values and a different tradition.

Our faith has always been in the people—that their welfare is the paramount obligation.

Our hope is to build a society—a New America—where the ideals we inherited from our forefathers will find a new fulfillment in a land of freedom and justice; where our abundance will serve, not just a few—not just what Hamilton called the "rich and well-born," but all of us.

CHOICE BETWEEN THE PARTIES

•

There have been remarkable changes in the political scenery [since 1952]. Four years ago the Republicans rallied the country against the egghead menace. I was pictured then as the leader of the longhairs—despite all surface evidence to the contrary. President Eisenhower defined an intellectual as "a man who takes more words than necessary to tell more than he knows."

Things are different today.

President Eisenhower no longer ridicules intellectuals, and I note with some amusement that his supporters have organized a committee devoted to the care and feeding of the egghead vote. It even includes college professors. Moreover, a ranking departmental official in the Eisenhower administration has not only read a book but has even written one. And one of the speakers at the Republican Convention was a writer whom Henry Luce periodically loans to the administration to inject some life—and perhaps a little time, too—into the Grand Old Party. I do not know how this gentleman's remarks were received; but he fared considerably better than did Joe Smith. He got the floor instead of the door.

We are entitled to expect good things from this blood transfusion. Already it has been announced that the Grand Old Party's vision has been restored. And perhaps through its new bifocals it will be able to fix more clearly on some matters of policy that have so far seemed to dance strangely—and dangerously—before its leaders' eyes.

It was only a few months ago that the President was saying that neutral-

From a speech at the Liberal Party Convention, New York, September 11, 1956.

ism was fine, the Vice-President was saying that it was terrible, and the Secretary of State was saying with his characteristic flair that, while neutralism was indefensible, most neutrals were all right.

When the Russians recently said they were going to reduce their army by 1.2 million men, the Secretary of Defense said it was "a step in the right direction"; the Secretary of State said it was a step in the wrong direction; Mr. Stassen said it was just what we wanted—and the President blessed everybody and appointed a committee to decide what we thought.

And only recently the President and the Secretary of State met head-on on the Suez Canal. On August 3, President Eisenhower said: "All of us, of course, appreciate the tremendous importance of the Suez Canal. Its continuous and effective operation is vital to the economies of our country."

To which Secretary Dulles added a few days later: "The United States is not dependent to any appreciable degree at all upon the Suez Canal. . . ."

Sometimes, disagreement settles in a single breast. Thus Senator Knowland recently said, "The people know that Dwight D. Eisenhower visited Korea and a peace ensued under which the Communists gained not one foot of ground." This was the same Senator Knowland who said in 1954, "Granting the Communists an armistice in Korea was a mistake . . . I think the armistice is a farce."

The infiltration of the intellectuals into the Republican party may or may not change these things. But it must certainly be recognized as a minor triumph of mind over matter.

But 1956 is not 1952. Perhaps the most striking change of all is the new face being worn by the Republican vice-presidential candidate. I know of no instance in which a man has so energetically tried to convince the electorate that everything he has said and done in past years bears no relation to himself, and that, until further notice, he is to be considered a new man.

You may not agree with him, but you have to be awed by the lack of conviction which makes so swift a transformation possible.

I don't wish to deprecate the Vice-President's new personality. But I do wish that we might hear some word from him repudiating the irresponsible, vindictive and malicious words so often spoken by the impostor who has been using his name all these years.

I am compelled to confess that I still prefer Joe Smith!

But one thing about this campaign is unchanged. Now, as in 1952, the Republican presidential candidate will speak in the accents of progressivism. There will be grand new talk about his design for "rebuilding" the

Grand Old Party. But the Old Guard will take this quadrennial verbal excursion in stride; for it knows from long experience that a few campaign speeches do not change the Republican party—and that any connection between Mr. Eisenhower's oratory and his administration is purely coincidental.

One of the curious facts in this curious year is that the new liberal Republican party seems to have room for everybody except the liberal Republicans.

Reflecting today on Harold Stassen, if his numbness has left him, we can note that in this new Republican party liberal Republicans are like opera singers: when they are stabbed they don't die; they sing.

Up in Wisconsin today the Republicans are choosing between Senator Wiley, who is an Eisenhower Republican, and Congressman Davis, who is a McCarthy Republican.

And, so far as President Eisenhower is concerned, well, he's neutral. This, I suppose, is what the Republican press means when it talks about President Eisenhower reconstructing the Republican party in his own image.

But I don't want to be unfair, for certainly neutrality in Wisconsin today is a triumph of political courage compared to 1952, when candidate Eisenhower deleted a defense of his benefactor, General Marshall, to make Senator McCarthy happy.

Of course, liberal Republicans in New York, like Mr. Javits, are more fortunate than Senator Wiley—or perhaps I should add "as of this moment."

For this was the fearless phrase with which the President rallied to Mr. Javits' defense last week.

Let me say that I admired Alex Rose's generous statement in defense of Mr. Javits last week. And I also share Mr. Rose's regret over Mr. Javits' latter-day admiration of the Vice-President. The discovery by the Republican candidate for senator that Mr. Nixon is a great liberal seems to me to sum up the fate of liberal Republicanism.

On the whole, it seems painfully clear that the new Republicanism is no different from the old as far as its leadership is concerned. The label has changed, but not the stuff in the package. Much as many Americans hoped otherwise, official Republicanism remains a policy of indifference to much except the aspirations of property. It remains the spokesman of big business and wealth. Nor should we complain. That is a wholly legitimate function.

But it is not the proper function of government, of the executive branch, in this beloved country of ours.

America needs today, and needs badly, the restoration of government which recognizes the existence of people—which will seek to meet their needs, to guarantee their rights, and to enlarge their opportunities. It is the nature and tradition of the Democratic party and of the liberal tradition to care about people—and care about them not as statistics in a market survey, but as individual men and women and children. And that is why we will win in 1956!

It is this dedication to the ideals of human welfare and individual liberty which makes us all so sensitive to the crucial importance of what is happening today in the desegregation of our public schools.

I share, I know, with you grave concern that there are today 3,000 school districts in this country where doors are closed against children for a reason—the color of their skins—which the laws that govern us and the dictates of our hearts say cannot matter.

I share, I know, with you great satisfaction at this week's report that this condition has been changed now in 723 school districts, 186 more than last year.

The things that bind us all together as Americans make us want tonight to speak our admiration for those citizens of Southern communities and those governors, mayors and local officials who are upholding the rule of law, sometimes even against their own personal feelings, sometimes in the face of violence.

I think of the mayor who, having lost his battle in court against integration, has called on all citizens to "obey the law," saying, "We are Americans before everything else."

I think of the Southern editor who has written: "Yesterday is gone; tomorrow is before us; the question is what shall we do with it?"

I think of the minister who has said to his townsmen, "I wonder if this critical period should not be looked upon as a marvelous opportunity to learn to be a Christian toward every other person and every race."

As a candidate, I want to say again what I have said from one end of this country to the other, that we must, of course, support the Supreme Court decision. All who voted for my nomination knew where I stood.

I stand squarely, beyond this, on the statement in the Democratic platform, adopted unanimously: "We reject all proposals for the use of force to interfere with the orderly determination of these matters by the courts."

Freedom is not a treasure to be hoarded; it is a faculty to be used and to be constantly renewed through use. This is as true of our civil liberties as it is of our civil rights.

A few years ago we ran the risk of letting the fear of Communism stampede us into weakening our hold on our legacy of freedom. But you in the Liberal party were wiser. You challenged the Communist fraud long before most Americans. And you knew both Communism and the Constitution; so you understood that we could fight Communism best by keeping our heads, not by losing them; and you never doubted that we could meet the Communist threat within the framework of our basic freedoms.

Many Americans, I think, have come to these same conclusions. But the best way to guard against the recurrence of what we went through is to make these conclusions explicit.

Freedom's struggle is not won. Nor will it ever be. Civil liberties may seem a much less urgent issue than it did a couple of years ago. But that is no reason for us to be the less vigilant or work less hard to establish our freedoms on the solidest of foundations.

As we fight to make freedom secure at home, we reveal once again to the world the true face of America—the nation which has fired the hearts and minds of ordinary people everywhere.

We need our military strength as we need our economic power; and these are all essential instruments in our foreign policy. But America's sharpest sword is the power of our ideals. And there could hardly be a better time for America to use her idealism. For the new disenchantment within the Communist empire offers exciting possibilities to the legion of freedom. The myths are shattered; yesterday's idols are today's devils; and throughout Europe and Asia there is a great yearning for a humane alternative to the exploded Communist delusion.

No nation is better equipped than ours to offer hope, inspiration and leadership in this time of turmoil. We have thus far failed to do so. We have failed because a business-dominated administration simply cannot comprehend the nature and complexity either of the revolutionary thrust of our time or the human longings which animate it. We cannot capture the souls of discontented people by boasting that *our* stomachs are full or that *our* arms are strong. We can do so only by reviving the original American mission—the conception of our nation as the bearer of hope and freedom to oppressed peoples everywhere on earth.

This seems to me the particular mission of liberalism in our day.

All of us here tonight call ourselves liberals, whether with a large or a small *l*. No man can precisely define liberalism without getting into an argument with another liberal; that is the nature of our creed—and our breed. We hold that no doctrine is so sacred that it must reject conflicting evidence; we do not hold with the old judge who was often wrong but never in doubt. We hold that life is unpredictable, varied and complex and that those who tell us it is all very simple are lacking either in wisdom or in candor. And I hope you will forgive me for reproaching those liberals who regard another's liberalism as genuine only when it coincides with their own opinion.

You of the Liberal party have been subjected to the charge that you are idealists.

I hope you rejoice in the accusation, and that you will always prove worthy of it.

Surely this is a time for idealists—a time for men and women who refuse to concede that this uneasy peace and this uneven prosperity are the best of all possible worlds.

I say there is a yearning for new vision in our country and our world; that we can imagine tomorrows more abundant and more serene than any mankind has known; and that we are reaching out now for better quality in our living, for higher purposes and richer values of mind and spirit.

It is in this spirit that I accept your nomination tonight.

"BREAD AND CIRCUSES"

●

I've made so many speeches in the last few days that I marvel that I have anything more to say. But I have! And the text of my lecture tonight is "bread and circuses." You rememeber how the Romans in their declining years tried to keep the uneasy populace satisfied and their minds off their troubles with food and games, gladiatorial combats and spectacles.

Well, I thought of bread and circuses not long ago when I read about the great Republican bandwagons that were going out all over the country, complete with movies, jeeps, girls and gadgets of all kinds—to sell Eisenhower and Nixon again to a docile, complacent, carefree people all happily chanting, "Peace, Prosperity and Progress—ain't it wonderful!"

The whole aim of all this ballyhoo and 30-foot balloons, those streamers

From a speech at St. Louis, September 27, 1956.

and bands, is not to excite thought or provoke discussion. It is, in the finest advertising tradition, to get at our electoral subconscious and persuade us to vote, blissfully and blindly, for things as they are.

"Politics," as the organizer of the Republican Convention put it, "is moving closer to show business." It certainly is, as they present it—balloons, not arguments; the chorus line, not the political issue. Don't think, just feel—feel it's all fine and the product is splendid. Pour out the money. Forget that mushroom cloud! Don't mention Suez. The world stops at the waterfront. And whatever the gales of change and upheaval and revolution roaring around the world, take it from us that this is no time for a change. Just vote Republican and take it easy!

How remote this all seems from the classic symbol of American political maturity—the Lincoln-Douglas debates, where, before rapt crowds, the two men hammered out, with all the rational conviction and controversial skill they possessed, the real issues facing a nation in crisis.

Well, bread and circuses didn't save Rome, and it won't save the Republicans either!

With each passing day it is more apparent that people understand what's going on better and better, and banners can't obscure realities much longer, nor slogans hide the truth. And that's why we will win in November!

Yet, of course, all this is in the Republican tradition. In the long decades of Republician dominance before the First World War, social problems at home and problems abroad grew steadily more dire while the Republican party careened along on slogans of "peace and prosperity" and "the American way of Life."

The chance of being "the party of the future" was thrown out with Teddy Roosevelt. It was the Democrats—Woodrow Wilson—who began, with the policies of the New Freedom, to bring America up to date and get the arthritis out of its political joints. But Republican arthritis is not cured so easily. The twenties saw another decade of "peace and prosperity" and "chickens in every pot," and once again it was the Democratic party, under Franklin Roosevelt, who had to bring the nation back into the broad currents of human progress after its twelve years of Republican boom and bust.

Today, in spite of the President's attempt to paint the Republicans as a young party, bursting out all over with new ideas, the pattern is not much different.

Where are the fresh, new ideas and new policies? The achievements to which President Eisenhower points with such pride in the past and such hope for the future consist mostly of not repealing what the Democrats have done. The innovations were Democratic ideas, molded by a Democratic Congress, and involving the federal action which, on other occasions, the Republicans always denounce as Big Government, creeping socialism, and bureaucracy—statism, and sometimes worse!

As for the specifically Republican ideas—tax reductions which favor the well-to-do, the "partnership" approach to power projects in which the private partner gets the profits and the public foots the bill, collapsible price supports, backing away at conservation, REA and TVA—these are hardly new ideas. They are as old as the Republican party and represent its lasting principle—to help those who can also help themselves.

Yet there never was a time when new ideas were more needed. In the past, the outside world was remote, safely removed from us across the oceans. Our own society was more loosely knit, and change in one part did not affect all other sections with the same speed.

In days when we were a self-sufficient distant land surrounded by seas, the periods during which the Republicans sat still on top and everything stirred underneath could last perhaps rather longer and with less devastating effect.

But the great caldron of the world is now seething to the boil, while our Republican friends say all is well and don't bother even to look at the stove.

I say we must look at the facts—they've got to be faced. We must not let them become stale even before they have become real.

The competition the Soviets offer is not simply for today and tomorrow. We must reckon on it for decades.

Today, with only one-fifth of the Communist Bloc's population, the American economy is producing almost twice as much in such key products as steel, petroleum and electricity.

But we have to look ahead. The Soviet planners intend to pull level with America by 1965 and ahead by 1970. During that period China is to build up a steel industry comparable to that of Western Europe and probably much greater than that of it chief Asian rival, India.

We must face squarely and responsibly the prospect that twenty years from now, if present rates of development continue, the balance of productive power may well have swung away from the side of freedom.

The Communists reckon that this growth will have all the more effect on the uncommitted peoples in Asia, the Middle East, in Africa and even Latin America. They are people who detest the memory of European colonial control. They sense a rising nationalist fervor and ambition. They have envious eyes for Western wealth. With these powerful emotional forces working on their side, the Communists reckon that their resources in capital and arms can be far more effectively deployed than those of the West.

Now, none of these risks will appear in Republican electoral speeches. Or, if they do, they will be dismissed as defeatism, as lack of faith in America, its way of life, but there are solid reasons for looking our dangers straight in the face, clear of cant and slogans and streamers and balloons and ballyhoo.

Complacency is not only dangerous, it is worse. It is unworthy of a great people, above all of a people as committed as we are to the pioneering of new opportunities and the dreaming of new dreams.

The breath-taking fact about America today is that for the first time in history we have the material instruments for accomplishing virtually any goal we set ourselves. Raw materials, managerial genius, skilled labor—all these means are lavishly at America's disposal. We have begun to master the techniques of keeping our great economic machine in high gear. We are learning to even out its earlier tendency to swing from bust to boom and back.

Here, in this gloriously endowed Republic, the only limitations are those we impose upon ourselves by lack of thought or lack of generosity or lack of vision.

In the last four years, a number of essential needs, particularly in defense, have been cut back on the grounds that there were more than the country could afford. Budget cutting took priority over security. Foreign aid was cut—again for budgetary considerations.

The question that has not been asked is whether the economy is expanding speedily enough to meet essential demands.

We need to know whether the projected capital expansion in the basic industries is great enough to take care not of the program we can "afford," but of the program we actually need. Of this kind of forethought we have seen no trace these last few years.

But failures of compassion and generosity are much graver than failures in forethought, for here we reach the soul and spirit of our community, the emotions that can save us from brash materialism, the feelings that redeem wealth and power by getting them to serve the humblest human needs. It could be tragic if the prosperity of some were to close their hearts to the needs of others who, even today, do not share in the general growth of wealth.

And in spite of all the Republican "pointing with pride," the sloganizing and the smug self-satisfaction, there are millions of Americans who live in privation, on budgets that barely feed them, in houses that are dirty and dangerous, in congested slums that cut out the living daylight, in debt for furniture, in debt for the doctor, in debt for any emergency that may strike. We cannot say today that their poverty is inevitable and unavoidable.

To leave people in misery in America today is a matter of policy, not of destiny.

Above all, Republican complacency blinds America to its historic vision of the broader, better life for all that our new instruments of wealth make possible. Once the mass of mankind has bread, we can really begin to learn that man does not live by bread alone. We in America are the first human community to reach this new threshold. Now that physical security has been so very largely achieved, we are reaching out for more spiritual values, for better quality in our living, for a higher purpose and a richer life.

We meet new needs as soon as we seek to open this new door.

There is the need for a greatly expanded program of education—to train mind and spirit for its wider environment and for the longer leisure which technological advance brings with it.

There is the need for better environment—homes where children can grow up in health and happiness, gardens and parks where they can play away from gang warfare in the streets, towns rebuilt and decentralized.

When new Democratic plans for better education, for improving the urban environment, for helping the millions of substandard families, are advocated, the Republicans set up a double roadblock; they protest that this means increased taxation and increased government intervention.

But this is only the obstruction of narrow vision. The way to meet new needs is to expand the economy fast enough to meet them. We've got to do this anyway, to have jobs available for the one million new members each year of our labor force. If we can secure a steady increase in our national product, there will be funds available from this increased revenue to build the schools we need and to meet these other needs.

And the Old Guard Republicans aren't really opposed to intervention by government, but only to intervention by government in the support of the general welfare.

Mr. Hoover may get up at the Republican Convention and talk of saving the country from the Democratic policy of "legalized socialism—twin sister of Communism." Yet there is no single greater prop to American industry than the government-imposed tariff system. And no

Republican calls that "legalized socialism."

The magazines and newspapers which denounce government intervention most lustily are all subsidized by the U.S. Post Office—but that is not, it seems, "legalized" or even "creeping socialism."

Nor do airlines, for example, complain of the assistance they get as mail carriers.

The private power companies—surely among the most active critics of governmental activity—have no objection to the billions of dollars' worth of government investment available free to the private builders of atomic power plants. Nor has any private company blushingly returned its tax write-offs for accelerated plant construction on the grounds that it is robbing the citizens of their tax money.

Government intervention is not government intervention so far as the Republicans are concerned when it is in aid of industry, particularly large-scale industry. In short, "giveaway" programs are sound government, assuming the right people are the beneficiaries.

The Republicans' real distaste in the past has been reserved for "giveaway" programs directed to those who really need them—social security, federal assistance for health and education, a fair share of the national income for farmers, minimum wage legislation—this is all part of the "legalized socialism" which for twenty years the Republicans denounced as a threat to the American way of life. These are the measures they will attack again when Democrats propose new advances in educational, medical and housing standards and new horizons for the life of the nation as a whole.

To make an ogre of government, to denounce its faithful officials as half-wits or traitors, to keep up the traditional Republican tirade against a mythical evil known as "Democratic socialism" weakens our whole American system and undermines the essential instrument in the partnership of all our people for wealth and growth and progress—which is the federal government.

By our long history as a party we Democrats have shown that ideals and vision and the forward march are the center of our inspiration.

We have not, before the work starts, stultified and undermined the essential federal instrument we need for some forms of further progress.

I believe with all my heart that, under democracy, this country is going forward to an uplifting of all its citizens, not just in terms of new goods and gadgets, but even more in terms of a broadening and deepening of the mind and heart of the nation.

This uplifting will not come if we wait for the good things of life to trickle down to the people from the top of the financial pyramid. It will come only as we work to assure a fair distribution, not only of the nation's wealth and production, but of the nation's opportunities.

It will come as we start measuring prosperity, not just in terms of cars and television sets, but even more in terms of the greater goods of education, health, security and peace of mind.

When we talk about ending poverty, when we undertake to extend the education, improve the environment and raise the dignity of all American citizens, we are promising to finish business we have ourselves begun.

And when we say that we will apply forethought, compassion and vision to foreign policy, we are only promising to recapture the leadership and imagination of the world which is America's historic tradition.

When, in short, we claim to be the party of tomorrow, we are only claiming to be what we have always been—pioneers of America's forward march, architects who build the future from the blueprint of America's hopes and her ideals.

ISSUES OF THE CAMPAIGN

•

I am particularly glad to be here at Woolsey Hall tonight because I always enjoy my visits at colleges. Now, whenever I say this I can see most of my entourage wince—particularly those eggheads who surround me, all of whom are hardboiled now.

You know that word "egghead" is interesting. Some people think it means that you have a lot in your head and some think it means that you have nothing on your head. In the latter respect I qualify as an egghead for obvious reasons. But it is when I am deemed to qualify in the former than I am happiest. And curiously enough that is usually around universities, and especially around university faculties, which I suppose proves something about the gullibility, credulity and innocence of teachers compared to undergraduates!

But I would say to the thinkers, the eggheads, that I think their prospects are improving, that I really don't believe they are as unpopular as they suppose; nor do I think that many Americans regard association with them as a criminal offense any longer.

It has been an interesting campaign, and I welcome the opportunity Woolsey Hall provides to reflect for a moment about it.

From a speech at Yale University, October 5, 1956.

The Republican sales managers thought that the President's endorsement would be enough to make their product go. But now they are having to reconsider their sales campaign—I think they call it "agonizing reappraisal." For they have discovered that the people aren't satisfied just to see the Republican leaders. They also want to hear what they have to say.

This discovery has caused a serious intellectual crisis in Republican ranks. And it is, of course, why the Republicans recently issued their Macedonian cry for intellectuals. I understand that at this very moment Republican talent scouts are beating the darkest recesses of Time, Inc., the Ivy League and the *Partisan Review*.

And I say: more power to them! I have never felt that it was fair for only one major party to know how to read and write, as well as cipher! But I say, too, that liberalism—or humanity in government, or real concern for people, or whatever you want to call it—is not something that a political party can pick up like an acquired accent.

It isn't something you can buy by the speech, or on Madison Avenue. We've been working on it in the Democratic party for 150 years now. We're not going to claim any patent infringement, for we're trying to improve the product ourselves and we're glad for any help or new ideas. But we're frankly pretty confident that we can beat any competition that relies on words as a substitute for action.

The Republican candidates can't say with much vigor and enthusiasm what they want to do—because they don't want to do anything very much.

Hans Christian Andersen has already written the story of this campaign. He called it "The Emperor's New Clothes." All that Estes Kefauver and I have been doing is to tell people what they already know: that the emperor really doesn't have any clothes on at all.

I think one of the most interesting and significant questions in the campaign will be whether the shock over this revelation will not drive our Republican friends into new excesses.

Denied his favorite device of associating Democrats with Communism, at least while traveling a higher road, Mr. Nixon has reverted to the familiar technique of associating Democrats with socialism.

This is standard operating procedure in the newly self-styled "party of the future." Only the other day Ezra Benson, the Secretary of Agriculture, was calling the leaders of the northwest grain co-operatives socialists. And, of course, the Republicans have opposed nearly every social advance within the memory of man as "socialistic."

I would commend to the Republican leadership—and especially to Mr.

Nixon—the wise words of Mr. Nixon's fellow Californian, Chief Justice Earl Warren.

"I think a lot of Republicans have been careless and politically foolish," Chief Justice Warren has said, "in the way they have confused social progress with socialism. In my opinion it does the party harm to yell about socialism every time a government, federal, state or local, does something to serve its people in the fields of health, job security, old-age security, child care, conservation, intelligent use of water resources or in any other general fields in which government today must operate because individuals can't do what is needed for the greatest good of the greatest number."

I do not think the American people are going to be much more impressed in 1956 by the Vice-President's threadbare shouts about socialism than they were two years ago by his loud shouts about Communism.

I really believe we have outgrown this kind of politics.

I am not opposed to a hard fight. Indeed, there are some who seem to think I have been fighting too hard in this campaign.

I was somewhat consoled the other day, however, when an old friend, comparing the 1956 campaign with 1952, said—a bit sourly, I thought—"I am glad at last to see the declarative sentence begin to triumph over the subjunctive."

Hard-hitting, factual debate is the essence of democracy. Innuendo, smear and slander are not. They debauch the language of politics; they defile the dialogue which is the means by which free society governs itself. George Orwell once said that, if you want to corrupt a people, first corrupt the words in which they express themselves. The English language can take a lot, especially in election year, but there are limits to the burden of deceit and infamy which it should be asked to bear.

This is a point in the campaign when it seems worth recalling the ground rules of political responsibility—and I mean in terms of self-reminder as much as criticism. I can only say that in the heat of battle even the obvious sometimes becomes blurred and worth reasserting.

Perhaps there is too much of the commonplace in the old injunction that victory is, after all, not an end in itself. Yet I often think that the single greatest difficulty about running for responsible public office is how you can win without, in the process, proving yourself unworthy of winning.

Don't misunderstand me: I mean to win in November.

But the perception that you can pay too great a price for victory—that the means you use may destroy the principles you think you cherish—is fundamental to Democratic responsibility.

If the rule itself seems overobvious—that there is something more to political accomplishment than electoral victory—then let me suggest two propositions that are both its corollary and its test.

First, I don't believe any victory is worth winning in a democrary unless it can be won by placing full trust in the members of the democracy.

I mean giving people the hard facts and the hard decisions—trusting their sobriety and their judgment—regarding them not as the customers of government, to be sold, but as the owners of government, to run their own affairs.

I mean resisting today's temptations to rely on soft soap, slogans, gimmicks, bandwagons, and all the other infernal machines of modern high-pressure politics in this age of mass manipulation.

The promise of such manipulations is contempt—contempt for people's intelligence, common sense and dignity.

The second corollary is that the political party can never be considered an end in itself. It is only an agency for a larger purpose.

Again, let no one misunderstand me. I believe in party loyalty and party responsibility. I am a Democrat, a good party Democrat, a very proud Democrat. But that very pride depends upon my heartfelt conviction that this party is an instrument for carrying out certain principles for the establishment of certain values. What is of fundamental and lasting importance is the ideals a party incarnates, and the purpose of the party is to make government serve our lives as it should serve them.

It is easy and proper and very right to assert that the fortunes of our party are, in the long view, closely and integrally related to our national welfare. Our long history of public service—its many contributions to that welfare in time of crisis, domestic and foreign—can leave no doubt of this. What is more important is to be sure we keep it always in mind that the fortunes of our party even in the short run are of infinitely less importance than the national interest as it is conceived by all our citizens in and out of direct party affiliation or allegiance.

Surely it is appropriate for us to consider the issues that face us in those terms.

The most important fact about any year, including the quadrennial one of national election, is its own identity, its standing apart in its own niche in time, its own remoteness from the years that have gone before, its uniqueness as the only gateway through which we may enter into the years ahead.

At Chicago a few weeks ago we Democrats were given a most timely and eloquent reminder of this fact by a great lady who, more than most, is entitled to recall the glories of years which have dropped over the far horizon.

"The world," Mrs. Roosevelt said, "looks to us again for the meaning of democracy, and we must think of that very seriously. There are new problems. They must be met in new ways. We have heard a great deal, and we were fired with enthusiasm by the tradition of our party. Thus, the new problems we face cannot be met by traditions only, but they must be met by imagination. . . . And it is a foolish thing to say that you pledge yourself to live up to the traditions of the New Deal and the Fair Deal—of course, you are proud of those traditions—but our party must live as a young party, and it must have young leadership. It must have young people, and they must be allowed to lead . . . they must take into account the advice of the elders, but they must have the courage to look ahead, to face new problems with new solutions."

Is it not the very essence of greatness, in a person as in an institution, to face squarely the often uncomfortable fact that the world moves on with the inexorable succession of the years? New problems arise, new challenges are presented, and, most important of all, new opportunities are provided which, if not seized upon with courage and energy and imagination, are shouldered aside by the relentless cycle of time.

I do not believe that we Democrats have the answers for 1956 simply because we had them for 1932. No more do I believe that the Republicans have them for this present moment in time simply because the country turned to them in 1952. And the greatest mistake we as a people could make would be to confuse 1956 with 1952 simply because the same two individuals are carrying the party standards.

As one of those individuals, I am peculiarly exposed to the temptation of thinking that the issues are the same because the faces are the same. But I try to resist it because I know that to yield is to defy the overriding law of life, which is change. And the way I resist is by continually asking myself: What is this election really all about this year? What are the watchwords of the past which have no relevance for the present? What should we be thinking, planning, initiating, doing—now?

I think the central issue in 1956, particularly for the uncommitted voter, is that complacency contains the seeds of decay, not of growth. It is at war with our national genius. It falsifies the tradition which has taken shape in sharp and glowing outline throughout our 180 years as an independent people. In the few periods when its siren song has been heard most loudly in the land, it has been a prelude to a harsher melody in which the saddest note is one of mourning for what might have been.

We have heard a very great deal and we are going to hear much in the weeks ahead about prosperity and peace. But surely the uneven measure of prosperity we now enjoy and the restless and uneasy peace in which we now find ourselves were not achieved by standing still and admiring them. We have become the world's envy because we never stopped raising our sights, because we constantly set new goals for ourselves even as we gained the old, because pretty good was never good enough.

In our hearts we know we must be up and doing, probing ceaselessly for new breakthroughs in our endless striving for solutions for today's problems and for the new ones that tomorrow will find on our doorstep, searching always for better answers than the ones we have been able to come up with thus far. We know that the gospel of discontent is the prophet of progress.

It is our mood that is the issue in this election. From whence is to come the energy to quicken it, the vision to excite it, the courage and will to lead it—to goad it, if need be—forward toward the greater fulfillment it has always demanded?

The essence of our faith is the determination to measure today's problems, not against yesterday's fears, but against tomorrow's hopes.

To you the young among us, I say that your generation confronts a baffling and difficult world. Your problems are not those of my generation. Your task is infinitely more difficult. It is not just to find a job for yourself—it is to save a world, a world in revolution. Your task is not to recover a faith, but to give that faith reality.

There have been revolutionary intervals before. They are times of danger and of opportunity—grave danger and exhilarating opportunity.

You know that America can conquer crippling disease, can discover creative uses for the new leisure which will come in the wake of abundance, can transform our surpluses into a blessing to mankind rather than a burden to the farmers, can strike a mighty blow at the ancient curse of poverty, and can achieve for all Americans that individual freedom, that equality of opportunity, and that human dignity which belong to them as American citizens and as children of God.

You know, too, that America can restore its position in the world, that it can become once again a trusted and inspiring leader, dedicated not to keeping things as they are, but to making the promise of our own revolution a light for all mankind. You know that we can lead the peoples of the earth away from the false beacons of Communism and slavery to a new age of human abundance and human fulfillment.

Our national purpose is not just to have an election and get it out of the way. Our purpose is not to watch a horse race in which all we care about is victory and at almost any price. Our purpose is to show how a great nation rises to the responsibility of self-government—and how it emerges from the experience purified in purpose, strengthened in resolution, and united in faith.

At least, speaking for myself, this is why I am here, and—if you think hard—that is why you are here at Yale. We know our goals: education will help us find our paths.

WHAT ARE THE REPUBLICANS FOR?

•

We are now approaching the end of the campaign. I had hoped that by this time issues would have begun to emerge in a responsible national debate.

But it hasn't worked out that way. My opponent has now made more than a dozen speeches. He has had a televised birthday party. He has received tributes from assorted groups of citizens at so-called television press conferences. He has ridden around in a bubble-top car. But we're all still in the dark about what he means to do if re-elected.

He says he's running on his record. What record? The legislative record? Well, that was just about zero, during two years of a Republican Congress (and he's asking for another!)—the record is what a Democratic Congress accomplished in two years over the opposition of most of his own party leaders and often of the candidate himself.

Or is it the record in foreign affairs? Surely not, when we're in trouble and losing ground from Iceland to Japan; when our blunders in the Middle East have cost the West the Suez Canal and given the Communists a toehold the czars could never get; when our alliances are shaken; when neutralism is spreading and Communism probing every recess of the globe.

The President remains a shadow candidate—as he has been a shadow president.

What has he said in this campaign?

He is in favor of national unity. Anybody here against national unity?

The President says he's in favor of good government. Anybody here against good government?

From a speech at San Francisco, October 27, 1956.

My opponent has come out foursquare for prosperity, national strength and national security. And you've got to respect his clear and forthright opposition to inflation, deflation, fission, fusion and confusion, doubt, doom and gloom, and fog and smog.

Also he is fearlessly for health, right thinking, happiness, and golf.

Now, these are worthy sentiments. We all applaud them. But do they add up to political leadership in a time of gigantic crisis? In fact, do they even fulfill the normal obligation of any candidate to tell the people what he'll do if he's elected.

In all the words he has uttered, my opponent has told you almost nothing about the issues of the campaign.

If he has anything on his mind to propose to Congress in January, he is certainly keeping it a secret.

If he wants to do anything at all—except to win re-election—he has managed to conceal his objectives from most of the voters.

Do you know what he wants to do about the Taft-Hartley Act?

Do you know what he has in mind to improve the system of medical care for our people?

Do you know how he means to help out our older citizens, so many of whom are living today in want and neglect?

Of course, you don't know.

What about his housing program? His conservation program? His education program? His defense program? His immigration program? His program to develop atomic energy for peaceful purposes? His program to keep the cost of living down—which is now at the highest in our history?

Not a word—not a word.

The Republican campaign of 1956 is very simple. It is this: Trust Ike, and don't ask questions.

It is very simple—and it is based on a profound contempt for the intelligence of the people, or maybe it's not contempt but hope that the people won't use their intelligence.

All they offer you is a blank check—and ask you to sign on the dotted line.

Well, we're going to take a long hard look at that check—and a long hard look at the cosigners.

"Just trust Ike" isn't enough. There's another question: Who are we supposed to trust when Ike isn't there?

Are we supposed to trust the man whose blunders brought us once again to the brink of war in Suez—Secretary Dulles?

Shall we trust the farm problem to the man whose policies made it so much worse—Ezra Taft Benson?

Shall we trust the Defense Department to the man who trusts what is good for General Motors most?

Shall we trust our financial policies to the man who is trusted most by the biggest interest, the Secretary of the Treasury, George Humphrey?

Shall we trust the health of our children to a Department of Health, Education and Welfare which couldn't "foresee the demand" for the Salk polio vaccine?

Shall we trust our liberties to an attorney general who impugned the loyalty of President Truman—Herbert Brownell?

Above all, are we seriously asked to trust the destiny of America—the future of our children—the decision over the hydrogen bomb—to Richard M. Nixon?

And when they say "trust Ike," do they mean trust the Congress to Knowland, Bridges, Jenner and McCarthy—who are for Eisenhower every four years, during the political hunting season?

They don't say—for they're afraid to say—"trust Nixon," "trust Benson," "trust Dulles," "trust Wilson," trust the Old Guardsmen in the Congress.

They know they can't persuade the people to trust the Republican party. And so they say "Just trust Ike."

Of course, a lot of "the team" has gone underground for the duration of the campaign, and a number of others are putting on amiable Halloween masks.

This happens every four years.

The hands that struck down better schools for the nation's children, more homes for the ill-housed, a better break for the farmer, fair play for the workingman, and tax relief for the American family are suddenly extended to all in eager fellowship.

The Republicans seem to love the people today. But just try to follow up on some of these cordial greetings after the election—and be careful someone doesn't bite your hand!

They have painted the cupboard door, but when you open it there's nothing inside but the same old china—the Benders, the Brickers, the Dirksens, the Capeharts, the Welkers, the Kuchels, and all the rest. Put a new idea into these obsolete jugs, and they will explode in a shower of clay.

Yet they wield the real power in the Republican party. They do so today—and they will wield all the more power as their protégé, Mr.

Nixon, the heir apparent, takes over the leadership intended for him.

No, the image of a "New Republicanism" has been fabricated overnight, for campaign purposes only, out of Old Republican whole cloth.

There is something that doesn't quite ring true in the story that Mr. Eisenhower married the Republican party in order to reform it—that it was not a love match, but an act of duty.

A man who really wanted to reshape the Republican party would not have been scared by Senator McCarthy and his friends out of backing Alexander Wiley in the Wisconsin primary.

He would not have driven Wayne Morse from the Republican party, nor would he have sought to ram Douglas McKay down the throats of the voters of Oregon.

And he would hardly be singing the praises of Everett Dirksen, of George Bender and of Thomas Kuchel as emblems of the New Republicanism.

They can tell us that Mr. Eisenhower is remaking the Republican party in his own image—but all he is really doing is mentioning his connection with it as little as possible in public.

I want to know one thing: who is making over whom in whose image? Something had to give—and I don't think it was the Republican party. Instead of remaking the Old Guard, he joined 'em.

We know what the Democratic party stands for. Since the beginning of the Republic, it has been the party which believes in the people, trusts them with facts and with decisions, and seeks day in and day out to strengthen their rights and to enlarge their opportunities.

Our candidates don't change their faces or their principles.

You hear much talk of the "new Nixon" versus the "old Nixon"; but no one would ever dream of talking about the "new Kefauver" and the "old Kefauver."

That is because the Democratic candidate for Vice-President is a man of integrity, who preserves the same face and the same principles in prosperity as in adversity, in 1956 as in 1950. I am proud of our candidate for Vice-President—and so, I know, are you.

Above all, the Democratic party has been the party of social progress. We have constantly sought to move forward, redefining our goals in terms of the challenge of each new generation.

The challenge to forward movement has never been more ringing than today, when modern technology puts us on the edge of undreamed-of abundance.

It is a challenge to break with the obsolete ideas and obsolete leadership of the past—to move ahead to a New America where no one wants for food or shelter; where everyone has the freedom to speak, think and worship as he chooses; an America dedicated to the fight for peace and justice in the world; an America that has at last realized the promise of our destiny and of our faith.

The Democratic party summons you to fight for the New America. It is to meet this challenge that I ask your support today.

Let's get up and moving again!

THE WAR PARTY?

•

I understand that certain members of the opposition party here have been engaging in the growing and desperate Republican habit of suggesting that one of our two great parties is a War party and the other is a Peace party. May I say quite bluntly that so far as I am concerned any man who talks this way is hardly worthy of being a United States senator.

I believe that the things that unite Americans are more important than those that divide us. One of the things that unites us is our hatred of war, and our great overriding hope for peace. I say that a man who talks of any war in which this country has ever been engaged as a partisan political affair dishonors the brave men, living and dead, who fought and won those wars. We have, not as Republicans or Democrats, but as Americans, sought always to avoid war. When, in spite of all we could do, war has come, we have fought—not as Republicans or Democrats, but as Americans. We will cheapen our political debate, yes, and we will make infinitely harder the remaining job of winning the real peace, if we start playing politics with war and peace.

And I want to read to you—because this seems to me so terribly important—the judgment about this of that great Kentucky statesman whose patriotism knew no party lines, that revered and beloved son of Kentucky —Alben Barkley.

In one of the last speeches he ever made, Alben Barkley in April of this year talked about this very question. This is what he said:

"For a generation Republican politicians have sought to beguile and deceive the American people by referring to the Democratic Party as the 'War Party' and Democratic Administrations as 'War Administrations.'

"I am old enough," Alben Barkley said, "to remember the campaign

Excerpts from remarks at Louisville, October 19, 1956.

of 1916 in which Charles E. Hughes . . . then the Republican nominee for President of the United States, bitterly criticized President Wilson for not pursuing a more aggressive and belligerent attitude toward German submarine warfare against American commerce, the American flag, and the American people.

"I recall with what solemnity President Wilson asked Congress in April, 1917, to accept the status of war forced upon us by the central powers of Europe and I could never forget what he said—'It is a fearful thing to lead a great peace-loving nation into war'—but he and the American people recognized that sometimes a righteous war is better than an unstable and humiliating peace. Who was the peacemaker and the peace-lover of those days?

"We did not make a political issue of the second effort to organize the world for peace. We asked the Republicans in equal numbers to sit with us and draw the framework of the charter of the United Nations at San Francisco—(and I was there)—and President Truman appointed a great Republican, Warren Austin, to head the first permanent American delegation to this world's organization to preserve peace.

"Let the shallow critics answer. Let them answer to the American people, or accept as men the obligations and responsibilities that go with statesmanship and leadership."

Those were Alben Barkley's words. As he so often did, he summed up the issue so that all could see the truth. Let us remember his great words when we hear the sinister, derisive words of men who value political success higher than American unity.*

We have another choice this year—a choice between the party of youth and the party of age, between the party with new ideas and the party with old ideas, or no ideas! And this is particularly important here in Kentucky this year, where you have lowered the voting age. I am told that already in Louisville you young people have, on your own initiative, been interviewing candidates and studying the issues in preparation for the vast responsibilities and the exciting opportunities of democracy's most precious privilege, the ballot.

I came across, the other day, a yellow copy—I have it here—of a political speech my grandfather gave in Bloomington, Illinois, in 1878. It ends with this little poem about the ballot:

> The ballot—which falls as lightly
> As the snowflake falls upon the sod,

* (We have deleted part of this speech dealing with the effects on the Senate should the Republicans capture the Congress. Eds.)

Yet executes a freeman's will
　　　As lightning does the will of God.

I have thought often, recently, of Woodrow Wilson. Wilson was fighting to awaken the country to the absolute necessity of finding new and
better paths to peace. He found it tough going. New ideas are never popular at first, even when their purpose is peace. Wilson said it was not easy
for him to speak when, as he put it, he thought of his clients in the case.
And he added, "My clients are the Children. My clients are the next
generation."

These are my clients too—our children and our children's children. It
is the young who will inherit the earth, who will build the New America.
Let's give them a chance to do it.

And I would say another word to you young and first-time voters. The
power of the secret ballot is the greatest power on earth. It is at once a
blessing and a burden. It is your right to think as you please; it is also
your duty to think how you vote.

To vote is a simple act—pulling a lever, marking a piece of paper. But
to vote is to shape the future.

And I would say to you, as you face this new responsibility, the words
that were said by a very great and a very wise man who was born here
in Louisville a hundred years ago this year. "Sometimes," Mr. Justice
Brandeis said, "if we would guide by the light of reason, we must let our
minds be bold."

Think—think boldly—and then vote.

2

Executive Leadership

THE PRESIDENCY

•

My friends, I have one point to make tonight. That's not many, but it is one more than is made in some political speeches—and that includes some I have delivered myself.

The point that I'm going to make tonight has to do with responsible political leadership.

And I think Missouri is a mighty good place to make this point.

Above all, this is the home territory of the man who rose with all the ruggedness of Missouri to meet the greatest responsibility on earth—Harry Truman.

The point I want to make tonight is one that President Truman has made both by word and by historic deed. It is, very simply, that in the United States the President cannot—in Mr. Truman's language—pass the buck. I know that is his language, because he used to have on his desk a sign that said: "The buck stops here."

And it did.

When the time came to make the great decisions—dropping of the first atom bomb, the Berlin Airlift, the Marshall Plan, the Truman Doctrine, etc.—he made them, himself.

And when the criticisms came in from his opponents, he took them—himself.

He did not believe in the delegation of presidential authority and the diffusion of presidential responsibility.

It is no secret that Mr. Truman and I have sometimes disagreed. And I hope it is no secret that I have often said and repeat now, in his presence,

From a speech at Kansas City, Missouri, September 26, 1956.

and along with millions of other Americans and millions of citizens of the world, that we know a strong president when we see one.

And that's a very important matter to every one of us. For, if the President of the United States does not lead, our system cannot work effectively and every American citizen will suffer.

The framers of our Constitution thought—to quote the words of the Federalist Papers—that "energy in the executive is a leading characteristic in the definition of good government."

The President is the only executive officer chosen by all of us. He represents every section, every faction, every racial group and economic interest, every American citizen. He—and he alone—can execute the great common purposes of the nation.

When the President is weak, and when he does not fight relentlessly for the public welfare, then the cause of public welfare loses its greatest champion. Politics, like nature, abhors a vacuum. When the public interest moves out of the White House, the private interests move in.

But, when the President is strong, there is no limit to what America can be.

Now, the Democratic party has always believed in a strong Presidency and has produced most of our strongest presidents—because it has always advocated the cause of the people and a strong Presidency is essential to that cause.

And the Republican party has most often been the party which believed in a weak Presidency—because, after its radical Civil War period, it fell progressively under the influence and control of special interests which can find other champions than the President.

And what has been true in the past, by and large, has never been more true than today.

Let me make it completely clear that, when I speak of the need for a strong Presidency, I am not talking about the President's health or any personal aspect of the situation in Washington. I am talking about the limited concept of the Presidency that Mr. Eisenhower has announced publicly and followed in practice. And I am not "attacking" the President, as the newspaper headlines so often say. I am talking, rather, about what has seemed to me his philosophical attitude toward the office and his consistent rejection of the positive responsibilities of leadership—a rejection that began not last fall, but in January, 1953.

Let's look at the record.

In 1953 and 1954 Republicans were in control both in the Congress and in the White House.

But, although President Eisenhower asked Congress to enact legislative programs that looked good on paper, he did little to get them enacted. The Republican Congress tore the Republican President's "State of the Union" message into little bits and pieces and scattered them to the winds —and the President watched in silence, at least public silence.

Then, while President Eisenhower declined to exert presidential leadership, Republican Senate Leader Knowland carried on his personal—and belligerent—foreign policy.

Republican Senator McCarthy conducted, unhampered, his career as national bully.

Republican Senator Bridges rallied Republican senators in a fight against the Republican President's own nominee as ambassador to Russia.

Republican Senator Bricker pressed his amendment to cripple the Republican President's control over foreign policy.

Eighty-four per cent of the House Republicans voted against the President's position on housing.

We know how, from a book written recently with White House help from White House sources, that the President was so discouraged with the Republican party that he began to talk of forming a third party.

And yet, despite Mr. Eisenhower's own privately expressed dismay at the Republicans' behavior, the President soon let it be known that he "favored the election of every Republican over every Democrat for every office any place."

Fortunately for the President and for the country, you voters did not take his advice too seriously in 1954. You returned the Democrats to the control of Congress, and they helped him get things done. He ought to be out today campaigning for a Democratic Congress.

But even with a Democratic Congress the problem of Republican irresponsibility remained.

Republican Senate Leader Knowland kept right on with his personal— and belligerent—foreign policy.

Republican Senator McCarthy kept right on trying to be the national bully, even though the American people, with the aid of television and such senators as Missouri's Symington and Hennings, soon thereafter found him out and the Senate called his bluff.

Republican Senator Bridges kept rallying Republican senators against the Republican administration—this time against the Republican President's desire to send aid to Yugoslavia.

And Republican Senator Bricker kept right on plugging away at his amendment to cripple the Republican President's control over foreign policy.

The President said he wanted a school bill. Sixty-one per cent of the House Republicans promptly voted against federal aid to the schools.

And on and on, up to the present moment.

But there were exceptions to this rule. The White House was most certainly not passive and indifferent on every issue. Far from it. For example, when the Hells Canyon project was before the Congress, the White House exerted vigorous pressure to kill the bill so that the great powersite could be turned over to a private utility company.

And the same was true in the Congress on the tax bill for the benefit of the corporations and the well-to-do.

Let me say it again: when leadership moves out of the White House, the special interests move in.

And it is not just that the President has had trouble getting the Republicans in Congress to do what he wants. He has had just as much trouble with the men he appointed to lead his own administration.

In fact, a typical scene in the last four years has been the President's efforts to repair the damage done by his own lieutenants—the farm policies of Mr. Benson, the foreign policies of Mr. Dulles, the conservation policies of Mr. McKay, the defense policies of Mr. Wilson, the monetary policies of Mr. Humphrey.

The President said he was against book burning, but he couldn't quite convince Mr. Dulles—and he ended by calling Mr. Dulles the greatest Secretary of State he had ever known.

The President was against making Communism an issue in the 1954 campaign, but he couldn't quite convince Mr. Nixon—and he ended by writing Mr. Nixon a letter commending him for his campaign.

In fact, many people have wondered how much President Eisenhower has to do with the Eisenhower administration. Sometimes the President seemed to wonder himself.

Everyone understands that no Executive can be held morally responsible for every act of every subordinate. But the American people have always assumed that the Presidents were responsible for the important acts of their administrations.

Harry Truman thought there was only one place for the buck to stop.

But when President Eisenhower's Secretary of State boasted—in a magazine—that he had three times led the American people to the brink of war without telling them, the President said he had not read the article and knew nothing about it.

When the Yalta papers were released over Winston Churchill's objections, Mr. Eisenhower's press secretary said that the responsibility was not his, but the State Department's.

When his attorney general impugned the loyalty of a former president in a formal speech, Mr. Eisenhower was content to say that he had not seen or approved the speech.

When Edward Corsi was forced out of our Refugee Relief Program, Mr. Eisenhower's Mr. Hagerty said that it was someone else's responsibility.

When the Dixon-Yates deal was proposed, Mr. Eisenhower fought hard for it. But now that the Department of Justice has finally admitted what the Democrats had been saying from the start—that the whole thing was illegal—it doesn't seem to have been the responsibility of anyone.

There is only one question to be asked about the Eisenhower administration. That is: who's in charge here, anyway? Who, in this businessman's administration, keeps the store?

And there is nothing abstract or remote about this question either. The difference between weak leadership and strong leadership is the difference between direction by a few strong men who serve the interests of a few most of the time and firm direction which serves all the people all the time.

You who live on the Great Plains understand the difference that positive national leadership can make in your lives. Let us look at one set of problems with which you here are necessarily much concerned—problems having to do with water, the disastrous cycle of drought and flood.

The Republican approach to the national water problem has been to chop the Truman flood-control budget in half, drag their feet on drought relief, and cripple the Soil Conservation Service by closing down many of its important operations, breaking up its regions, and splitting teams which had been working together for years on soil and water problems.

Why, the Republicans ask, should the people of California or Connecticut be concerned about the flood that swept over Kansas City, for example?

Why, they ask, should the people of Ohio or New York be concerned about the drought that now spreads its parched and withered fingers across so much of the Great Plains regions that I have flown over in the past few days?

Well, let's answer that question. Let's say straight out that all Americans must be concerned with the devastation of massive floods and massive droughts—because we are one nation and one people; because catastrophe anywhere weakens us everywhere and its costs should not be borne by one vulnerable section alone.

We Democrats have a strong historical belief in local action and local responsibility, and we believe in doing what needs to be done. In part at least that is why so many cities and states have been turning to Democratic mayors and Democratic governors in order to get strong local and state government that gets things done.

But there are some problems which local and state leadership cannot wholly meet. The problem of water is one. It is a regional problem and a national problem. Localities and states trying to deal with it are inevitably driven into conflict with each other over water supplies, flood control, and the location and type of dams, and so on. This is exactly the kind of problem that requires comprehensive regional thought and planning and forthright national leadership.

The Republicans, of course, complain that the national government is somehow the enemy of the people. But we Democrats reply: the people in the local communities elected the government, and if it doesn't serve them well, they'll get rid of it.

We say that it is the responsibility of leadership—national, regional, state and local—to meet our needs and rise to our opportunities—whether better water policies, better schools, better housing or better medical care.

We say that, while the want of funds may sometimes delay us, we cannot surrender to the frustrations of jurisdictional conflicts of leadership. And we say that where there's a will to get things done, there's a way. The history of this century is bejeweled with examples—from Bonneville Dam on the Columbia to the Everglades Canals—of great achievements—under Democratic leadership.

We Democrats acknowledge a national responsibility in all areas of national concern. We Democrats believe in strong and responsible leadership to make sure that the whole nation pulls together to achieve our goals and that the whole people enjoy the benefits.

We want to march forward now, all of us, into the land of freedom, justice and abundance which lies ahead—into the New America.

For the New America is, above all, a challenge to leadership.

Drift cannot lead us to it, nor smug complacency, nor fear of change, nor slick slogans and advertising arts, nor pious homilies and campaign promises.

Only the strength of a united American people can achieve it—and only effective leadership can concert that strength and make it effective.

Today we have reached a great divide in world history. Man now has the power to achieve unimagined miracles of abundance—or the power in a final holocaust to destroy humanity forever.

And it is of America's national leadership that all mankind asks today: What shall we do with the power unleashed in our laboratories and workshops? Shall we use it for man's salvation? or for man's annihilation?

These are some of the reverberating challenges of our time. I do not know—no one can know in advance—the precise form in which they will be met, for it will be a people's will—a people's judgment—by which they will be met. And yet I do know, and it humbles me, that it is the President's task in our system of things to unlock the people's judgment, and to carry it out.

And I submit that on the record it is the Democratic party that has by its basic principles and purposes given the Presidency the nobility of resolve and the strength of spirit to make itself the instrument of the national will—which alone can meet the awesome and exhilarating crisis of our age.

And I submit, too, that the American people know this—which is why the Democrats are going to win in November.

LEADERSHIP

●

I have spoken often in this campaign of the evils of indifference in the management of our public affairs, of absentee administration, of political administration, of administration without heart and without heart in its work. The farmer, the small businessman, the children and teachers in ramshackle and overcrowded schools, workmen in many places, the sick and the aged, and the government employee have all had a firsthand experience with this kind of government. To them a part-time president and an indifferent administration is more than a phrase. The lives of many have been altered in these past four years; the lives of some blighted. Ask the thousands who have been kicked around as security risks in the Republican effort to prove one of the calumnies of 1952—that our government was riddled with subversives.

Tonight I want to tell you first what this kind of leadership or lack of leadership means—both abroad and here at home.

And I want to talk about the effort made by this administration to cover up its errors—errors that result from abdication of responsibility.

In the last week the American people have watched anxiously the heroic

From a speech at Los Angeles, October 27, 1956.

efforts of the Poles and Hungarians to free themselves from the hard yoke of Moscow.

And the so-called Republican "truth squad" last Friday in Rock Island, Illinois, celebrated the event by announcing that the great revolts were "a clear-cut result of the new American foreign policy." We have said more foolish and insulting things about other peoples during the Eisenhower-Dulles period than we like to recall and at an expense in good will and respect we can ill afford, but this was a new low even for the Republicans.

If it was true, it would be shameful stupidity to say it; but as it is false, it was a gross effort to exploit the anguish of brave people to make votes in an American election. The credit goes where it belongs—to the heroic Poles and Hungarians who face the tanks and guns of their Russian rulers; it belongs to those who were willing to risk all—their lives, their fortunes, their families—for freedom. No credit goes to men who in recent weeks have exposed themselves to nothing more dangerous than their own campaign oratory. And, as a postscript, let me remind the Republican "truth squad" that truth might be an interesting experiment for them someday; that they could have announced more accurately that we were caught off guard, that when the fighting broke out in Poland, the American ambassador wasn't even at his post—he was visiting Berlin to see his dentist. And when the revolt broke out in Hungary, our envoy was not even in that country.

And you may gauge President Eisenhower's interest in this whole problem by another bit of history. In June of last year, by a vote of 367-0 the House of Representatives passed a resolution expressing its sympathy with the satellite nations and condemning colonialism. When asked about this resolution on June 29, President Eisenhower said: "I did not know about that. Maybe I was fishing that day. I don't know."

But this was not an isolated example. Let me give you another example where the issue of war and peace was at stake.

The winter and spring of 1954 were a time of deep trial and anxiety. Indochina was falling to the Communists. I saw that frightening war in the rice paddies and the jungles with my own eyes. The free world was divided, troubled and alarmed. Hasty voices—Mr. Nixon's, with characteristic volubility, was among them—were advocating armed intervention by American troops. On February 12 the *New York Times* reported that Senate leaders "alarmed by fears of possible U. S. involvement in the Indo-China war" had called high members of the administration to an urgent secret conference. On the same day the *Times* also reported that President Eisenhower had gone south for hunting with Secretary Humphrey and had bagged his limit of quail.

Two days later the alarm had deepened in Washington and the papers reported that President Eisenhower was leaving for a six-day vacation in California. On February 19, Secretary Dulles returned from the critical Four-Power Conference in Berlin. He couldn't report to the President. The *New York Times* said, "It was golf again today for President Eisenhower" at Palm Springs.

Later, on April 13, Mr. Dulles and British Foreign Secretary Anthony Eden met to explore the possibilities of joint action—joint military action —in Indochina. The *New York Times* reported that President Eisenhower had landed in the South "to begin a golfing vacation."

Next day it was announced that we would airlift aid to Indochina; and also that the President was playing golf in Georgia.

On April 17, the *New York Times* said in a headline that the United States "weighs fighting in Indochina if necessary." The President, it said, was still vacationing in Georgia.

The next day the country learned from the papers that Nixon had said that the United States might have to intervene with military force. Less spectacular news that day was that President Eisenhower had played golf in Augusta with Billy Joe Patton.

On April 23, it was announced that the last outposts around Dien Bien Phu, the French stronghold, had fallen. That day the President arrived in Georgia for a new golfing holiday.

The free world suffered a severe defeat in Asia and lost a rich country and more than ten million people in Indochina. And after it was all over Secretary Dulles boasted in an article in *Life* magazine that it had been a victory.

He also boasted that we had won this victory by our bold behavior and by bringing the country to the brink of war. And when President Eisenhower was asked his opinion, he replied, "I have not read the article."

I could go on. The President was away golfing when it was announced early last year that our Air Force had gone on a full war footing as a result of the Formosa crisis. He was shooting quail when we evacuated the Tachen Islands. He was golfing in New Hampshire in June, 1954, when the Soviets shot down a U.S. plane off Alaska. In the *New York Times,* it said, "There was no visible evidence that the President had anything on his mind other than having a good time."

In February of this year, the President was golfing in Georgia during the on-again, off-again, on-again mixup over the shipment of tanks to Saudi Arabia which so alarmed the Israeli people. Mr. Dulles, as usual, was out of the country. Mr. Herbert Hoover, Jr., was running the store.

The President was asked this year whether Russia was leading us in guided missiles. He answered, and I quote him, that he was "astonished at the amount of information that others get that I don't."

The President was asked on April 4th of this year about an urgent message on the Middle Eastern crisis that Prime Minister Eden had sent him ten days earlier. It developed that he didn't even know the letter existed!

The President is an honorable man. So when he smilingly assures us that all is well and America's prestige has never been higher, he just must not know that in fact the American star is low on the world's horizons.

And even what happens here at home passes the President by.

In 1953 and 1954 we had a serious drop in employment and economic activity. On February 17, 1954 the Department of Commerce announced that unemployment had passed the three million mark. The *New York Times* said the President would act if there was no upturn soon. It also said that he had just departed for five days' vacation at Palm Springs, California.

A year ago last May he was asked why Secretary Hobby had difficulty in foreseeing the great demand for Salk vaccine. He said he didn't know anything about it, and to ask Mrs. Hobby.

Last February, when the head of the General Services Administration was let out for using his job to help friends get government contracts, the President thought he had resigned for "personal reasons."

The President was asked if Republican leaders had told him why they killed an important bill to bring aid to areas suffering from unemployment. He said, "No, you are telling me something now that I didn't know."

When President Eisenhower's Secretary of Labor urged extending minimum wage legislation to employees of interstate retail chain stores, the President was asked where he stood. He said, "I don't know that much about it."

This list could go on endlessly.

I have left out of the list every case where the President's absence from Washington or his ignorance of crucial facts could be traced to his illnesses.

And I want to make it clear that I realize fully that any president will inevitably be gone on some occasions when a crisis arises. I surely don't begrudge the President either the recreation, the repose or the exercise necessary for health. I think even a president is entitled to enjoy himself occasionally.

But a president must assume the full responsibilities of that high post. He is the Chief Executive. And I say bluntly that I do not agree with President Eisenhower that the United States can be run by a board of directors, with the President presiding at occasional meetings.

Nothing could be more at odds with our constitutional system. The President was elected to the responsibilities of leadership by the American people. Dulles, Wilson, Benson, Weeks and the others were not elected at all. They are the hired hands, but the President runs the store.

And we know now that the Eisenhower system just doesn't work. The price of the President's abdication has been irresponsibility in our foreign policy. This irresponsibility has brought the coalition of the free nations to a point where even its survival has been threatened. And it has brought American prestige to the lowest level in our history.

Here at home, we are in the midst of a great social transition. We have come to see with new clarity the full implications of our Bill of Rights and of our democratic faith, and we are moving forward again to assure the equal rights of man to all Americans, regardless of race or color.

Throughout the nation many citizens of both races are working quietly, working hard, risking much, daring much to solve the stubborn problems that lie in the path of any great social transformation.

Who but the President could say for the whole nation that those participating in this great effort—sometimes even though they disagree with the decision itself—deserve the gratitude, the respect, the moral support of their countrymen? But President Eisenhower, far from rising to this challenge of leadership, has not even expressed his views on the decision and the goal itself.

Nor has he acted with decision to sustain even the most elementary right for all adult Americans—the right to vote. The assurance of this right to all citizens is written in our laws and must surely be the keystone of our democratic institutions. But here again Mr. Eisenhower has seen no challenge of leadership.

Nothing can be more essential to our system of government than affirmative presidential leadership. The President was elected to these responsibilities by the American people. He is the only officer of our government who is elected by all the people.

These four years of a part-time Presidency have been bad enough. But what would another four be like?

Well, I'll tell you. But I don't really need to, because yesterday, at the

Commonwealth Club in San Francisco, Republican Senator Malone of Nevada put it squarely and bluntly. The "greatest sin" the Republican party has committed, this Republican senator said, has been "carrying on what Democrats started." Then he added, "But we'll change that in 1957 and 1958 if you elect . . . President Eisenhower."

Why? Why will re-electing the same man president mean a whole new and different government policy—a policy of wrecking twenty years of Democratic building in America?

We know exactly why.

The reason is simply that, if the Republicans should be returned to office again, the powers of the directorate which has governed in the last four years will be shared and perhaps pre-empted by a man you know, and know well, too well. I refer to the heir apparent, hand-picked by President Eisenhower—Richard Nixon.

President Eisenhower will not be a more vigorous leader in the next four years than in the last four years. He will almost certainly be even less disposed to lead. He will have greater need to conserve his energies. The habit of total delegation once formed is not easily changed.

More important, he will not be allowed to lead. The Republican politicians, we now know, love their leader, the President, mostly at election time. They will follow him to the polls, but no further. For four years the Democrats in Congress have repeatedly had to rescue the President's program from his own party.

Beginning in 1957, if President Eisenhower should be re-elected, the Republican leaders in Congress will owe him exactly nothing. He cannot help them get elected again because, under the Twenty-second Amendment, he couldn't run again even if his age and health permitted.

We know from past experience that the President will not lead. We know that, if he should try, his party will not follow. And into this vacuum would come Richard Nixon—beloved by the most reactionary wing of Old Guard Republicanism.

That's why Senator Malone is so confident that a new term for Mr. Eisenhower will mean an opportunity to do a wrecking job. It's because a new term for Mr. Eisenhower will mean a new destiny for Richard Nixon.

In the last few weeks a plaintive note has entered the Republican newspaper discussion of Mr. Nixon. They say in effect: "Can't people see that this man has changed?"

Well, people prefer men who don't have to be changed. And even some mighty good Republicans don't think the Republican party ought to be in the laundry business.

A lot of people just don't believe that Richard Nixon is really at home in this role as the Little Lord Fauntleroy of the Republican party. They wonder if he doesn't yearn for his old tar bucket and his brush. And they suspect that, if the circumstances let him, he will make a fast grab for them again.

Common decency is at stake here. But more is at stake even than that. President Eisenhower does not lead because he won't. Richard Nixon cannot lead because the American people will not follow.

This is partly because Nixon has a long record against the people. He has voted against public housing, to weaken Point Four, against extending Social Security, against middle-income housing, against increased appropriations for school lunches, against increased REA loan funds and, of course, he voted repeatedly for the Taft-Hartley Act.

People mistrust a man who votes against the people. They have an additional reason to mistrust Mr. Nixon, for on several of these issues he has taken an equally firm stand on both sides.

Mr. Nixon's advertisers call him "adaptable." Well, that's just the trouble. For what "adaptable" means here is that this man has no standard of truth but convenience and no standard of morality except what will serve his interest in an election. The plain fact is that the people of this country just can't picture Richard Nixon as the leader of the greatest of the world's nations.

They can't imagine putting Richard Nixon's hand on the trigger of the H-bomb. They just don't trust him.

Our nation stands at a fork in the political road.

In one direction lies a land of slander and scare; the land of sly innuendo, the poison pen, the anonymous phone call and hustling, pushing, shoving; the land of smash and grab and anything to win.

This is Nixonland.

But I say to you that it is not America.

America is something different. It is a land of mutual trust and confidence, not suspicion and division, a land of neighborliness, of unity of purpose, and of common faith.

America is a tranquil land, where people seek fulfillment, not by the frantic service of themselves, but by the quiet and thoughtful service of their communities.

This we must be—a free land, where people speak their minds without glancing over their shoulders, where the right to think as one chooses, write as one chooses, and worship as one chooses is safe from inquisitorial arrogance and the wolf packs of conformity.

America is a just land, where people are safe from the hit-and-run politicians who ambush the innocent passers-by; a land where fact can overtake falsehood, and where the accused and the abused can count on a fair trial in a fair environment.

Above all, America is a growing land, humble not boastful, modest not arrogant, believing deeply that life means change, and that change is the product of the free contest of ideas.

This is our America. It is the America for which the Democratic party has fought before—and it is the New America that is our goal today.

I summon you tonight to join in the march to the New America—to the banishment of smear and suspicion and to the enthronement once again of reason and responsibility.

The tide of Democratic sentiment is rising through the land. As we remain steadfast in our course, I know the rising tide will sweep us to victory.

3

Single Interest Government

WRITE THE PEOPLE IN

●

It is the Democratic faith—mine and, I know, yours—that the government of a democracy must trust *all* the people it serves, that it must be made up of representatives of *all* the people, and that its obligation cannot be to any special interest but only to *all* the people.

It is apparently the Republican proposition, on the other hand—or at least it is the obvious belief of the present Republican administration—that the government of this nation can most effectively be vested in the representatives of a single interest, and that the welfare of the society can best be served by promoting that single interest—on the dubious theory that the benefits will then trickle down to people generally.

We have today, if you will, in the executive department in Washington, what amounts for most of us to government without representation.

Does this seem too broad a charge? Then let's look in for a minute at a meeting in the Cabinet room at the White House.

This is the table where decisions are made affecting the needs, the interests, the dreams, the whole future, yes, the survival of 166 million American men and women and children.

Every single one of these 166 million people is a consumer. Who speaks at this Cabinet meeting for these consumers?

Sixty-five million men and women in this country are members of America's work force. For six months in 1953 there was a representative of American labor at this table. But when he spoke up for American labor, he was silenced. Who from American labor speaks at this Cabinet meeting now? There have been sitting at this Cabinet table three men

From a speech at UAW International Education Conference, Washington, April 24, 1956.

from one corporation—and no one from the 18 million membership of the AFL-CIO.

Thirty-five million Americans—the pride of all the rest of us—are sitting this morning in schoolrooms. Thousands of these rooms are fire-traps. The roof of one fell in out in Chicago earlier this month. Everywhere I go, people, particularly women, say to me: "We want to do *something* about getting better schools and more good teachers for our children." Who represents the 35 million children of America—America's future—at the meetings of this Cabinet?

A gray-haired man came up to me on the street last week and said: "Governor, it isn't just social *security* we want. We want a chance to be somebody." Who at this Cabinet table represents the millions of older men and women in this country who want most of all an opportunity to make the evening of their lives not only secure, but worth-while?

Yes, and who at this table represents the interests of the 22 million Americans who live today on this nation's farms—and whose average per capita income has now dropped to $860 a year? And who represents the men who were farming—doing what they wanted to do—three years ago, but are now trying to get work in the cities—a thousand of them at a struck plant in Sheboygan, Wisconsin?

Every man at this Cabinet table has boasted of this nation's prosperity —without ever, so far as I know, suggesting the slightest degree of genuine concern about the fact that 30 million Americans are going to have to make ends meet this year on family income of less than $2,000. Who—certainly not the prosperity boasters—represents these 30 million Americans?

This isn't a meeting of a people's Cabinet. It is a meting of a corporate board of directors. What single interest government has come to mean, for most Americans, is simply, I repeat, government without representation.

And the consequences, in terms of the failure of this administration to meet the human problems of America, have become sharp and clear.

There hasn't been time, or energy, for carrying out this administration's promises to labor. And now the Secretary of Welfare in the businessman's Cabinet announces that this administration is opposed to the changes in the Social Security program which were last year endorsed overwhelmingly by the House of Representatives. This administration went all out to secure tax benefits for corporate stockholders. Now it opposes paying retirement benefits to a man who has worked for his living, paid his social security taxes, and then, at the age of fifty or more, becomes totally disabled.

And the highway program we need so badly has been held up because the administration tried to make it a bonanza for the bankers who would finance it. And children who needed it didn't get the Salk vaccine fast enough because even where the stakes were life and death it was considered more important to preserve the established commercial channels of supply.

This is what single interest government has come to mean. But it is not a government of or by or for the people.

You know, I remember reading, eight or ten years ago, a statement in your UAW magazine *Ammunition*. It was about collective bargaining contracts, and I remember especially the last line. "It's time," this statement went, "to write the lawyers out of the contracts and write the people back in." I propose an amendment to that statement. It is time, I suggest, to write the businessman's administration out of this government and write the people back in.

Let's see what this means.

In a collective bargaining agreement, "writing the people in" means a seniority clause that says plainly that a man's service gives him a right in his job; it means recognition and grievances clauses that bring democracy into the plant; and it means, or is coming to mean, thanks to the insistence of the UAW, clauses that give a man and his family the supplementary unemployment compensation they need and are entitled to.

What does it mean in government?

Well, it means giving first attention to the human problem that is uppermost in people's minds: the establishment of true equality of all opportunity in this country, regardless of race or creed or color.

It means recognizing that a mathematical, or "average," prosperity in this country isn't enough. If one family's income is $2,000 and another family's income $50,000, this doesn't put them both in the $26,000 class. Sure, America is prosperous. It's prosperous enough that there is no excuse for so many having so little. . . .

"Writing the people in" means, too, a recognition—which this administration has completely denied—of the essential role played in this society and government today by free labor unions and free collective bargaining. The provisions of the Taft-Hartley Act which limit union security, permit the so-called state right-to-work laws, make organization difficult, prohibit legitimate, peaceful bargaining pressure—these and other provisions like them must be changed. And the important question is not whether these changes are in the form of repeal and rewriting or in the form of basic amendment; the important thing is that these changes be made.

It is equally important that the NLRB be re-established as a fair-minded, nonpartisan administrative agency—administering the law as it is written and not according to the partisan views of either labor or management.

One other point. There is today in this country a growing restlessness and concern about whether these new machines that are coming in are to be men's servants or men's masters and their enemies.

There is a theory that "automation" is no business of the government's, that the only people who are to have anything to say about fitting automation into our industrial life are the corporations that buy these new machines. And the Secretary of Defense says not to worry about this anyway, that if a machine replaces a man there will be another job for him making that machine, and that if that new job happens to be a hundred miles away in another city, well, what of it?

The Secretary leaves some things out. What he forgets, of course, are all the human elements here. Does it occur to him that maybe that man, and perhaps even more his family, doesn't want to move, that the community they live in has become part of their lives, that a mother would like, if she could, to spare her children the uprooting that comes from a change in schools in the middle of the year? And it probably never crossed the Secretary's mind that when a man changes jobs he loses his seniority—the biggest capital he has.

It looks now as though within a few years, perhaps ten, possibly twenty, the coming of these new machines and the release of atomic energy for industrial use will mean that the nation's production needs can be met by three-quarters of the work force, or by all of the work force working 30 hours a week instead of 40; or, in the alternative, that we can increase the production of consumer goods so that the standard of living in this country can be raised to the level of people's dreams.

"Writing the people into government" means facing up as a people to the social as well as the economic implications of the second industrial revolution, for this is what is coming.

I believe with all my heart that, under democracy, this country is going forward to such an uplifting of its citizens as mankind has scarcely dreamed of.

I see this uplifting not in terms of technical advances alone, not in terms only of new consumer goods, but even more in terms of a broadening and deepening of the mind and heart of the nation.

This uplifting will only come as we stop waiting for the good things of life to trickle down to the people from the top of the financial pyramid, and as we work again to ensure a fair distribution, not only of the nation's wealth and production, but of the nation's opportunities.

It will come as we start measuring prosperity, not just in terms of refrigerator sets and television sets, but even more in terms of the greater goods of education, health, security and peace of mind.

It will come only as we set our course once again by the stars on the constellation of the general welfare, and by the beacon lights of individual freedom and human dignity.

4

Liberalism and Responsibility

LIBERALISM

●

I'd like to talk particularly about the continuing, yes, I think the in-creasing importance of what has been one of the deepest of democracy's taproots. I mean the idea, the concept, the attitude we have called "liberal-ism." Great and proper concern is expressed in these political campaigns about conserving our natural resources, about developing water and air and atomic power. I venture the belief that the natural resource we should today be even more concerned about, the source of our most essential and infinite power, is a militant, effective and responsible liberalism.

What do we mean by "liberalism"?

Perhaps you recall that a few years ago a national magazine had great fun when it posed the question: "*What* is a Liberal?" Its letters columns were filled with a rich variety of answers: answers from reactionaries say-ing that liberals were people who had formed a blood pact with the devil; answers from the liberals also, each one choosing his own terms of defini-tion. This filled the editors with great glee, and they drew the conclusion that a modern liberal didn't know who he was, or what he was, and hence was a vague, confused and ineffectual zombie wandering from point to point in a world he never made, and couldn't run.

Now, I had always thought that variety of opinion was supposed to be the great hallmark of the American Way—the unafraid and unfettered freedom to possess one's own political thoughts; *not* dictated by a party line, *not* cast in bronze, *not* chiseled in marble, *not* demanded by some commissar or Obergruppenfuehrer. But, no, this magazine seemed to think the variety of voices with which liberals spoke made liberalism a mockery, and that a variety of opinion was somehow either funny or silly.

From a speech at Town Hall Luncheon, Los Angeles, May 31, 1956.

If anyone had thought to ask the editors, "What is a Reactionary?" there would of course have been no such variety of opinion. I think the voice that answered would have said in a hoarse monotone: "See what the boys in the back room will have."

I have my own feelings about what is a liberal in today's protean world. I offer them to persuade, not to coerce. If someone else has different views, well, we might both be right.

First, he believes in the existence of the future as well as the past, and believes that it can be made a good future. If he is my age, he may often think of the past, and he may think of it with affection and nostalgia. But he rejects the idea that it was "better" than what we face now. In answer to the conservative's classic question, "Whither are we drifting?" the liberal says: "We cannot drift, we must *go*." Although he respects the past, he has no desire to tinker with the clock or turn it back. He does not try to force it ahead. But he does wind the clock!

He has never seen from on high any slightest indication that Heaven itself wishes to return to the good old days—and so he walks ahead, in courage and steadfastness, and with a minimum of backward glances, into the perpetually obscure, the perpetually dangerous, the perpetually unknown future. No wonder he cannot always tell where he is going.

In contrast to this, the reactionary can always tell you where he has been, so he has an air of authority. What he doesn't know is that the political house of his fathers, which he talks about so much but hasn't seen for many years, has now been condemned or torn down.

A second major belief of the liberal today is that *people* are all that is important, and that *all* people are equally important, and that such ideas as property and corporate business are only means, not ends.

You will recall that John Locke listed the inalienable rights of man as "life, liberty and property" and he went so far as to state that "government has no other end than the preservation of property." But when the Founding Fathers were at their desks drafting our Constitution they amended Locke's classical formula to read "life, liberty and the pursuit of happiness"; and Jefferson wrote that "the care of human life and happiness, is the first and only legitimate object of good government."

I think of a third element that gives the liberal faith its integrity and sets it apart. It requires no commitment to particular conclusions, but it demands of its adherents that they bring courage to their convictions. I am sure there are liberal Republicans as well as liberal Democrats. I am sure that true liberals can be in complete disagreement on any given point, that liberalism is a process for approaching answers rather than any given set of answers, that it never indulges itself the soft luxury of being absolutely sure the other fellow is wrong, that it is marked by tolerance, yes, and that its besetting sin is intolerance of tolerance.

But I am sure at the same time that the effective liberal is essentially characterized, too, by a commitment, something within him, which makes him restless and unsatisfied unless he can be doing something to advance that cause.

Woodrow Wilson spoke of a "fighting ardor for mankind." Herbert Lehman was talking about the same quality when he spoke in Washington last month not just of freedom, but, as he put it, of a "passion for full freedom." There is no connection at all between extremism and liberalism, but every really effective liberal I know is a dedicated person—who can be convinced, even converted, but who won't ever admit he's licked and therefore never is.

I'm sure there's much more than these superficial reflections to the anatomy of modern liberalism. But this is enough to let us ask now what these elements of the liberal faith mean in terms of today's more immediate political issues.

There is time to touch only one aspect, in this connection, of the infinitely important and central matter of the conduct of our foreign affairs.

I realize that a great many liberals, like a great many others who would disclaim this label, hold firmly to the simple belief that the heart of a better, wiser foreign policy would be simply a new address for John Foster Dulles.

There is, of course, much more to it than this. I have said that it is a part of the liberal tradition that conviction be coupled with courage. I think the most significant fact in world affairs today is that the administration of the nation which should be exercising leadership in those affairs is inherently unable to bring courage and consistency to the support of its convictions.

Why is this? What lies behind this aimless, erratic drift—which now disturbs every thoughtful American as much as it has disturbed America's allies for years?

Why, the explanation is simply that this administration has failed in its effort to unite behind it the two wings of the political party upon which it must depend for its support. America's drift is the inevitable consequence of a basic conflict, actual, factual and philosophic, that has divided the Republican party probably for a half century, since the tariff struggles, and certainly for thirty-five years, since the League of Nations struggle. . . .

But to turn to the problems and the prospects which face us here at home is to perceive even more clearly the importance of restoring to our political life the faith in the future, the ardor for mankind, the passion for full freedom, and the courage of conviction which are the stuff of the liberal tradition.

These are exactly the elements which must prevail to win the new advances toward racial equality, the recognition of what we know is right, and the full acceptance of what our hearts as well as our laws say to us.

Those of us to whom these answers are already so clear that we have trouble seeing another side to it will have a special responsibility here to guide wisely the course of this transition, to accept the scheduling the Supreme Court dictates in its phrase "with all deliberate speed," to bring to this problem the affirmative leadership which the Court has called for but cannot itself supply. I would count this a top responsibility of effective, responsible liberalism today.

There remains, too, a very large task for liberal leadership in the repair of the ravages of these past three years to our Bill of Rights. Nowhere were people more cruelly and needlessly subordinated to the system, or human rights sacrificed to political opportunism, and nowhere did we lose more grievously for a time our passion for full freedom than in these recent assaults upon individual rights in the name of security. And may America never again be subject to the international humiliation of such a squalid spectacle as the McCarthy-Army television show.

Today there is general agreement that, while security is obviously essential, it can be achieved without resort to those unfortunate extremes. And yet there is all too much evidence that the administration cares little whether this wound on democracy's face is closed or not.

I shall not review the "numbers game" and all the abuses of the innocent. But just this month a member of the Subversive Activities Control Board, a Republican and an appointee of the President, has called public attention to the continuing injustices in the government's personnel-security program and has condemned the political distortion by the administration of the actual facts regarding the hiring and dismissal of government personnel. He has called for the very honesty in government and the regard for human values which the President has repeatedly extolled. Yet the newspapers now predict that the response will be to get rid of Board Member Cain.

And the President, when he was asked about the most recent case of abuse in the name of security, said he was not familiar with it because, as he puts it, "They bring before me what has been going on, usually not in terms of names but in terms of numbers." I shall resist the temptation to comment on that.

I suspect that perhaps one of the most serious affronts to the liberal tradition today is in the suggestion of the Republican leadership that we have just about arrived at where we want to go as a people, and in the almost complete lack of realization—certainly of any enthusiasm—about the frontiers of human betterment this nation now faces. To really believe in the future and to have an ardor for mankind is today to be driven by the feeling that we are wasting precious time as a nation in not doing the things which are possible now for the first time in our history.

Surely, no one can suppose that even in our blessed land have we reached the limits of human welfare, or harnessed our abundance. Nor can we in a world undergoing revolutionary change hope to prosper by standing still. The most urgent need for new thinking springs from the fact that we are constantly, by our science, our techniques and our inventions, altering out of recognition the contours of the human scene. The old landmarks are going. We need new roadmaps in a world that is, whether we like it or not, being remade every day.

But free society cannot be content with a goal of mere life without want. It has always had within it a visionary spark, a dream that man, liberated from crushing work, aching hunger and constant insecurity, would discover wider interests and nobler aims. If quantity comes first so that men may eat, quality comes next so that they may not live by bread alone. Free society in the West has brought most of its citizens to that great divide. The next frontier is the quality, the moral, intellectual and aesthetic standards of the free way of life.

I see so many new tasks for this free, powerful, rich society of ours. It seems to me we sometimes get so concerned about our problems that we miss our opportunities. The shaping of a new society is not the function of government. And yet government is at the same time our only instrument for carrying out some of our common purposes, for realizing some of our common hopes, for reaping, if you will, some of the fruits of our abundance in this period of unparalleled plenty. And I suggest that it calls for the faith of the liberal, a faith in the future, a consuming passion for the interests of people, if these opportunities are to be seized.

I have talked too long and I'm afraid I may have imposed upon you. My days recently have been very long and very crowded, and there has been too little opportunity for the thought about my remarks here today which would have permitted more precise utterance. I can testify to the accuracy of a line in Froude's life of Bunyan to the effect that the exercise of perpetual speaking is not conducive to the highest thought!

It is hard, frankly, for a politician to concentrate, in the last week of four months' campaigning, on a nonpolitical speech. And perhaps you will in this connection permit me to add one note. I have leaned heavily today on a phrase of Woodrow Wilson's. Its broader frame, which I now quote, is this: "You will observe that whenever America loses its ardor for mankind it is time to elect a Democratic President."

THE DEMOCRATIC PARTY AND BUSINESS

•

The Republican party has a well-established reputation as the party of business. I understand that the Democratic party does not have quite this reputation. In fact, some businessmen are even said to regard it as anti-business!

I suggest to you that both the reputation of the Republican party and the reputation of the Democratic party are undeserved.

I would go further. I believe that the Democratic party is the best friend American business has; and I should like to tell you why I think so.

Certainly if we Democrats don't like business, we exhibit our dislike in a curious way. When the Democrats came into office in 1933, after a dozen years of Republican rule, the American business system was flat on its back. When the Democrats left office in 1953, the American business system was in more robust health than ever before in history.

In those twenty years, the gross national product of our country—the total of all the goods and services our nation produced—in current dollars, rose by more than 500 per cent. In stable dollars, the rise exceeded 200 per cent. Everyone—business, workers, farmers, professional people—benefited.

I have heard the achievement of the New Deal defined in a number of ways.

One is that the New Deal made America safe for capitalism.

The other is that it made capitalism safe for America—and safe especially for the responsible businessman.

What was ruining capitalism—and precipitated deep national misgivings—was the irresponsible minority in the business community, those people who supposed that anything was justified so long as it put another fast buck into their own pockets.

From a speech in New York, October 24, 1956.

It was these men who established sweatshops—and forced their competitors to compete in terms of cutting wages of labor rather than in terms of improving quality for customers.

It was these men who palmed off phony securities on a gullible public.

For the sake of the decent employers of the country, it was necessary to establish ground rules so that the responsible businessman would no longer be penalized because he would not cheat those who bought from him or those who worked for him.

During those years, a Democratic administration abolished the sweatshop. It abolished child labor. It ended the savagery of competition among employers as to which could work labor the hardest and pay it the least.

A Democratic administration similarly brought decency and stability into the securities market. It outlawed falsehood and deception in the investment world.

What the Democrats did was to show that the methods and aspirations of business could still produce profits in a society which recognized the obligations a modern state has to its citizens.

This, of course, is all in the past. But it bears upon the present and the future. For government and business will continue to be mixed up together in the common task of keeping the American economy strong and growing. Indeed, the whole history of American progress has been a history of constant government-business interaction—at its best, a creative interaction which has advanced the welfare of the whole nation.

I believe that the need for this interaction—for this balanced and reciprocal co-operation—has never been greater than it is today. For our society is in a state of transition. We have moved out of the bleak past, when our problem was scarcity and our task the hard one of distributing too few goods among too many people. We are finally entering that age of abundance of which we have dreamed so long.

Our national output is already reaching heights which would stagger the most starry-eyed prophets of a generation back. On the horizon are a number of new developments which will multiply our future productive capacity even more: the whole process of automation, harnessing to production the fantastic developments of modern electronics; the miracle of atomic power; the striking new advances in industrial and agricultural chemistry; and so much else, some of it still in the minds of our inventors, our scientists and our business leaders.

In the end, we will accomplish a second industrial revolution which will add far more to the productive power of the world than the original industrial revolution. And let us not deceive ourselves: just as an era of scarcity created one set of values and institutions, so an era of abundance will create new values and new institutions. Too much of our present controversy is conducted in an idiom which is rapidly becoming obsolete. We must rethink our economic policy in terms of the technological revolution—just as we have to rethink our defense policy in terms of the weapons revolution—and our foreign aid policy in terms of increasing hunger and political restlessness.

The task ahead is to take full advantage of the technological revolution while still preserving those sources of the creativity of American life—the free individual, making his own way in life; the family farm; the family firm; the small town; the small college; the small enterprise of any sort. This task will require imagination and ideas in the field of social policy to match the imagination and ideas in our business offices and our research laboratories. It will call on the co-operation of all elements in our society—the business community, labor, agriculture, the consumer and the government.

Now, I do not believe that the Eisenhower administration can meet the challenge of this new age.

One reason it cannot do so is that it does not represent—and cannot command the confidence of—all the groups in our diverse society. For this job we require a balanced government—and our government is badly out of balance today. The American tradition must be against government by any single interest, whether business or labor or agriculture. In particular, government in which big business has disproportionate representation cannot be expected to do what is necessary to control the march of bigness in America.

Another reason why the Eisenhower administration cannot meet the challenge of the New America is that it lacks imagination and recoils from new ideas. Neither in foreign nor in domestic policy has it had any new ideas. In both fields it has lived on its somewhat garbled memory of what previous Democratic administrations had thought and done

It has been well said that a new Republican idea is a Democratic idea at its twenty-fifth reunion! Indeed, we are given to understand that the Republican achievement in finally accepting the main outlines of the New Deal should be taken as a great intellectual and philosophical triumph. (Well, maybe it should be at that.)

There is one more reason why the Eisenhower administration can't meet the challenge of America's economic future.

The Republicans don't like to spend money in such fields as education, health, welfare, and the conservation of natural resources. They drag their

feet on every proposal to improve our school system, our system of medical care, our system of social insurance, our public domain, and so on.

But I say that money spent to improve the education, health and welfare
of American citizens and to develop the natural resources of the country
is not money for which there is no return; it is not money wasted. It is
money invested in the improvement of America—money which will repay
itself many times in developing a population which can produce more,
purchase more, and plan more for new expansion in the future.

It is no accident that the unprecedented economic gains of the last
generation took place in a period of unprecedented enlargement in the
government's social services.

Everything our society can do to improve the intelligence and energy of
its members contributes to the wealth of the nation and the productivity
of the economy.

Our Republican friends recoil from this challenge of the future, even
as they recoiled from the challenges of the past from which they have
profited so handsomely. The proof lies in the failure to attack our deficien-
cies in schools, health, care for older citizens, slums, distressed areas, etc.
It lies in the troubled condition of so many small businesses. It lies in the
exposure of our natural resources to private exploitation and waste.

And, if I may say so to this audience, it lies especially in the precarious
state of small business—squeezed by the growing giants, buffeted by the
merger movement, strangled by high interest rates and the difficulty of
getting capital and credit. Under the Republicans, the rate of small business failures has reached its highest level in fifteen years. American business—and America itself—cannot afford to lose this unique source of
inventiveness and enterprise.

We Democrats conceive of America as the land of opportunity. When
opportunity vanishes, America will suffer a fundamental change. And
opportunity means opportunity for all. We reject the idea of an America
in which everyone is on the payroll of a few giant corporations.

The fact is that the Republicans, taking over the country at a high point
of economic activity, have done nothing for such vital groups in the population as small businessmen and farmers—and have done less than
nothing to prepare for the difficult problems of the future. The Eisenhower administration seems to have confused genuine friendship for
business with snuggling intimacy toward a few of its giants. And meanwhile the big have become bigger and the small are disappearing.

I would ask businessmen to consider soberly whether the Democratic
party has not actually served the true interests of business far better this

century than the weary and rigid standpattism of the Republicans—and whether Democratic foresight and energy are not likely to be better for business in the long run.

It is the Democratic purpose to use our individual and social intelligence to keep opportunity alive for every American. Because we believe this— because our record for a century and a half has shown our devotion to this ideal—is I believe the reason why you American businessmen are here today—why you think the Democratic party is entitled to your support in this fateful election.

V

THE END OF THE CAMPAIGN

OVER-ALL LOOK

•

This 1956 campaign is now drawing to a close. It has been a long haul, and hard work. Senator Kefauver and I have kept our promise to carry the campaign to the home towns of America. We have talked sense.

We have faced the hard issues and faced them squarely.

On the age-old questions of justice and freedom, I think we have kept the Democratic faith.

And on the new and burning issues of our technological age, we have refused to be intimidated into silence.

All this, in my judgment, is the right way to conduct a political campaign in a democratic society. For it is by discussion that you decide what is right and wrong in a democratic society, not by dictation.

But it has been a strange campaign, a one-sided campaign, for, to every Democratic proposal, every Democratic criticism, every Democratic idea, the Republicans return but a single answer—"Trust Ike."

And to this we Democrats reply—"Trust the people."

And that is the difference between the two parties.

In all his speeches and telecasts and public appearances, the Republican candidate has told you almost nothing about the serious issues of the campaign.

If he has anything on his mind to propose to Congress in January, it must be a military secret.

He is fearlessly in favor of national unity and good government; but no one knows what he proposes to do about the school crisis, about housing, about civil rights, about restoring our farm income, about the conserving and developing of our natural resources, about medical care, about Taft-Hartley, about the peacetime uses of atomic energy; no one knows what he proposes to do about prosecuting the cold war, about taming the hydrogen bomb, or about rebuilding the crumbling alliance on which our security and freedom depend.

I say to you that it will be a sorry day for this nation and for popular government when we replace responsible political debate with a personality cult. An American presidential election is not a sort of beauty contest; it is a solemn, irrevocable decision about the direction in which the greatest democracy in the world wants to move, because we can't stand still.

From a speech in Chicago, November 3, 1956.

And I suggest to you that the Republican campaign—"Trust Ike, and ask no questions"—really means something else. It means: Trust the men around the President—trust John Foster Dulles, trust George Humphrey, trust Ezra Benson, trust Charles Wilson, trust Richard Nixon. What it really means is: Give the Old Guard Republicans a blank check for four more years.

And what does a blank check for Republicanism mean? They tell you it means peace and prosperity and progress, and they hope that, if they say it often enough, you will come to believe it. They have tried to sell Republicanism like cigarettes, soap and cars.

But I don't believe this is even good politics. I don't believe you can win an election that way. And I know you can't win the future for America that way, because it doesn't pass the first test. It doesn't fit the facts.

Just take a look at the Republican record of peace and prosperity over the last week.

On October 25, the government announced that the cost of living had reached a new all-time high. On October 30, the Department of Agriculture announced a new drop in farm prices. And, of course, on October 29 the outbreak of war signaled the total collapse of our policy in the Middle East.

What a glorious week of Republican peace and prosperity! How many more weeks like this one can we stand?

These failures are the consequences of part-time government—of government in which the Chief Executive has never had the inclination and now lacks the energy for full-time work at the world's toughest job.

They are the consequences of single interest government—of government in which the men around the President who make the big decisions and formulate the policies come largely from a single sector of society—big business—and, with the best will in the world, feel they serve the nation best by serving the interest of the rich and powerful first.

They are the consequences of government which denies the people the full facts and does not trust them with the decisions.

And they are the consequences of government by a Republican party which is so deeply divided over domestic and foreign affairs that any consistent strong policy would tear it apart.

So long as we continue to have part-time government in Washington, so long as we continue to have single interest government, so long as our government in Washington refuses to entrust the people with the truth, so long as it represents a party with a split personality, then all the problems which torment us—from the Middle West to the Middle East —can only get worse.

The tragedy in the Middle East is an example of the Eisenhower administration in operation.

In September, when asked by the press in Washington to express my views on the crisis in the Middle East, I declined in order to avoid embarrassing the administration. I had hoped that this issue might be kept out of politics. But President Eisenhower came along on a political broadcast and brightly reported that the news from Suez was good. He followed this later by assurances that he knew of no trouble with our allies. Then last Tuesday war broke out in the Middle East.

After the President made his political pronouncements, I began to express my views about our disastrous policies of provocation and appeasement, vacillation and deceit, which have contributed in such great measure to these tragic developments.

I am firmly opposed to the involvement of American forces in the Middle East, but I believe that our country must contribute to responsible leadership in this area.

And while I am on the subject of responsibility, I proposed at the University of Virginia a year ago that the United Nations patrol the borders to preserve peace between Israel and her neighbors. Canada is now making the same proposal in the United Nations and the newspapers report that Mr. Dulles has expressed his complete approval. If the administration is for it now, why wasn't it when I proposed it? Or was it "irresponsible" because it came from a Democrat?

And my comments about the Middle East are not the only instance in which the administration responds to truth with epithets and to serious proposals with derision. I am proud of having brought squarely before you in this campaign the issue of the hydrogen bomb.

I was warned that it would be hard in a political campaign to get a new truth across, and surely Mr. Eisenhower and Mr. Nixon have made it infinitely harder by their accusations and distortions. The President even called my suggestion that we take the lead to eliminate this menace a "theatrical gesture." But what are campaigns for but to advance ideas to help mankind?

And, my friends, this bomb, if ever used in war, will kill millions, and, if it is not used, could still injure all mankind in the testing. The poison from the test explosions will injure our children most of all. Let others, including the President, argue about whether these bombs are filling our bodies with 15 per cent or 10 per cent or even 1 per cent of the amount of radiation they can take. Over three hundred scientists have testified to the hazards, and only this week one of the most respected doctors in the country warned that the bones of today's children may already be imperiled.

Again, I have proposed that in order to strengthen our armed forces we investigate better methods of recruiting and retaining the skilled manpower we need in our armed forces. The draft is undemocratic, it takes only one boy out of eight; it is expensive and it is inefficient because of the rapid turnover. Certainly there is no sin in trying to do things better. This is not a political issue and President Eisenhower's attempt to distort suggestions that many of our military leaders approve may be smart politics but it is no service to our country, whose security depends upon the strongest possible defenses.

And so it has been. New ideas are dismissed with epithets, abuse and distortion.

Government which does not tell the truth cannot inspire the confidence of its own people or of people anywhere else in the world.

There is only one way to arrest the decay of American influence—only one way to push ahead in the fight for peace—and that is new management in Washington!

And the Eisenhower administration is no better equipped to deal with our affairs at home.

I have told the people from Arkansas to Michigan and from Florida to California that I think the decision of the Supreme Court on desegregation of the schools was inevitable and right. And I have said that force and violence must have no part in working out this great social adjustment. I think people respect honesty in a candidate even if they don't agree with him. Meanwhile the President has done nothing to exercise any leadership in this field nor has he ever disclosed his opinion of the decision.

Nor has President Eisenhower's leadership met the problem of enough school buildings and teachers for the children of America.

It has failed to maintain a decent level of income and livelihood for our farmers.

It has made no serious effort to wipe out the slums and give every American family the chance to grow in health and sunlight.

It has failed to provide an adequate system of medical care for its sick and ailing.

It has failed to offer a tranquil security in the evening of their lives to our older citizens.

It has failed to defend the Bill of Rights and it has thereby betrayed the spiritual essence of the American faith and tradition by abuses of our security system.

The Republican party has no program to offer America, no policy, no philosophy. In fact it seems to have little else but President Eisenhower—who in the next years would inevitably recede more and more from the picture.

The fact is that the Republican administration has taken everything from the Democratic past—and offers nothing to the American future.

Oh, yes, it has one thing to offer to the American future: it has the Vice-President of the United States.

Every consideration—the President's age, his health, the fact that he can't succeed himself—makes it inevitable that the dominant figure in the Republican party under a second Eisenhower term would be Richard Nixon.

Do you trust Richard Nixon to be fair to labor—or to the farmers—or to the children who need schools—or to the poor and unemployed—or to our elder citizens?

Do you believe that Richard Nixon will work to restore the Bill of Rights to the center of our life?

Do you want this man as commander in chief to exercise power over peace and war?

Do you want to place the hydrogen bomb in his hands?

Do you believe that Richard Nixon has the confidence of other countries—the sort of confidence necessary to re-create the coalition of freedom?

Yesterday he hailed our break with our allies as "a declaration of independence that has had an electrifying effect throughout the world." Perhaps the first electrifying effect it had was to embolden Russian troops to re-enter Hungary to crush the forces for freedom.

Somebody said there's only one thing about him you can be sure of—if you get Eisenhower, you also get Nixon.

But when you think of the Democratic party, you think, not of one or two men, but of thousands.

I came to you tonight not as a man alone, but as a man borne onward by the thousands in this hall tonight and millions across this nation—men and women who believe in the principles of the Democratic party.

Our strength is the strength of the Democratic tradition and the Democratic faith in our national life—a tradition and a faith that stretch back to Thomas Jefferson; a tradition and faith which have been responsible for nearly every step ahead in freedom and welfare in the modern history of our nation.

We live in a time of revolutionary change. Before our eyes, in the very headlines of our daily papers, a new world is being born.

In Eastern Europe, in Asia, in Africa, the rigid structure of the postwar world is crumbling. Stalin is dead, the long night is lifting in the satellite countries, the Middle East is shifting like the desert sands, the peoples of the underdeveloped world are struggling for dignity and equality.

Here at home, too, great changes are taking place. Our population is growing, a technological revolution is transforming our economic life, our quest for equal opportunity imposes new goals and new responsibilities.

This is a time for new ideas, for boldness, and for another great thrust ahead in our national life. And we know that only the Democratic party has the vision and the vigor to make that thrust effective.

Under Democratic leadership, we can win the fight against poverty and injustice. Under Democratic leadership, we can build a New America in a world of justice and peace.

The New America is an affirmation of faith—faith in our land, faith in ourselves, faith in our future.

It is also an affirmation of reality. For the New America exists already —in resources, in machines, in ideas, in hopes, in the hearts and minds of men and women.

The New America is here—today—within and around us. All we need is to awaken to what lies within our grasp. All we need is to arise from our slumbers. All we need is for America to be herself again.

With the courage and vision to summon a great people, to great deeds —with, above all, a prayer for the guidance of the God we love—we will proudly enter the gateway of the future.

THE FATEFUL DECISION

•

First of all, I want to thank you, my good friends everywhere, for all that you have done for me, during so many weeks and months—for having helped me find the means and the heart to fight hard for all that we of the Democratic party hold vital in this crucial election.

As Jack Kennedy has told you, this night marks the end of a long and thrilling journey. For four years now I have gone up and down the airways and rail lines and roads of this astonishing country of ours, and what rewards I have had!

Telecast from Boston, November 5, 1956.

I have traveled, too, all around the world: to Asia and the Middle East and Africa and Europe, and I think I have seen with open eyes the realities of this wonderful, precarious earth.

I have needed the strength of many men to get through these travels and this hard fight for what I believe—and I have drawn deeply on hidden sources of strength. I have seen millions of American faces as I have traveled. I have spoken with Americans of all conditions of life, of all ages and kinds, and I have been deeply moved and sustained by the warmth, the reliance, the confidence, the affection that they—that you—have so generously given me.

I think of the young people, boys with banners and girls with notebooks, college students and many kids too young to vote, who wanted to participate in the exciting process of our democracy.

And so many of you have come forward to tell me that you have gone into politics in the last four years. Volunteers, precinct captains, young women who have held coffee hours to raise money. Some of you are running for office—and you've told me this was all because of things you heard me say in the '52 campaign.

And then I've been moved by the simple, kindly phrases spoken by humble people who reach out from the crowd to say "God bless you," "I hope you win," "Don't get too tired," "We need you."

I have known—and really this knowledge has given me the greatest strength of all—that these words were spoken not so much to me personally, but because I was the Democratic candidate for President of the United States—and they trust the Democratic party which has fought the people's battle so long.

And so this simple trust and confidence was a gift to me, in a way, of their faith in themselves.

And what has given me strength has been my faith in them—in you. We are surely a good and strong people, of that I am sure. We are a people who combine generosity and idealism with a practical, down-to-earth realism that we learned the hard way, as we pushed back the harsh frontiers of nature and science and politics. Ours have been the legendary broad shoulders of Paul Bunyan and the restless seeking mind of Thomas Edison and the great heart of Abraham Lincoln. We Americans are Tom Sawyer and Justice Holmes and Jackie Robinson; in our best dreams we are carefree wanderers and noble thinkers, and men who can drive in runs when they're needed.

We in the Democratic party think there is nothing we cannot do if we want to do it.

The Democratic party believes we have not yet finished making our country, that we still have important work to do.

We of the Democratic party think of "the people" as living human beings, one by one, individuals with differing ways and talents and hopes, each worth in himself the whole weight of government.

We Democrats see in "the people" the strong young man at the loom or the press or the drill in the clatter of earning a wage, and we want for that young man fair work laws and a steady job and pride in what he does.

Or we see the grandmother with a broken hip or a heart attack or cancer, sitting in the sun on the porch in the thin workless evening of life, and for her we want security and medical care and some kind of bulwark against loneliness.

Or we see the mother pushing a wire cart in the grocery store, anxious whether she can buy enough for the children, yet not too much for the family budget, and for this mother we want prices within reach and a good life of her own and high hopes for her kids.

We Democrats see the slum dweller, the workman living in the shadow of automation, the teen-ager trying to find a moral footing—and we look for ways to help them all.

Now, I want you to listen as some of my colleagues in the Democratic party tell you very briefly about a few of the real issues of this campaign.

When they have finished, I want to come back and add a final word about the most important reason of all for casting your vote tomorrow for the Democratic ticket.

In the years of this Republican administration we have made little progress on the home front. All the things my friends have talked about are urgent—your child's health, your income, your child's school and teacher—how your child learns to live in this magical, dangerous world.

I have thought of that much this afternoon, here in Boston, where I've come to see my first grandchild—which I must confess must be the world's finest, fattest morsel!

But I've thought even more about what kind of world this baby will live to see.

For there is no use talking about a new and better America if we can't keep the peace, and also the freedoms we cherish even above peace.

Yet today America's foreign policy, our policy for peace, is in disarray in all parts of this world. Our alliances are unraveling; NATO is disintegrating, neutralism is spreading, we are helpless in Hungary's agony.

Our policy in Asia is rigid, militaristic and unresponsive to the great revolution where hunger is spreading and hope is rising.

Our policy in the Middle East is in ruins, and has furthered the Soviet design to penetrate this strategic area, to the great damage of the cause of freedom.

Israel, surrounded by enemies growing stronger with Russian arms, has lashed out in desperation, and, worst of all, Britain and France are going in one direction and we are going in another—in the same direction as the Communists.

And tonight we have seen the ironic culmination of the disastrous Eisenhower foreign policy in the Middle East—with the Communists now urging us to go to war with them against Britain and France!

We regret what our friends have done. We do not condone the use of force. And, as I wired the President last Wednesday, there is no reason for the involvement of America's military forces in this area. But the need for some positive American leadership is desperate everywhere.

I see no hope that the Republican party can retrieve the tragic situation abroad. It is split internally—as it has been since the fight over the League of Nations; and a divided party cannot regain the confidence of our allies or rebuild the coalition on which our strength and security depends.

Worst of all, this Republican administration has not taken the American people into its confidence. Either it hasn't known what is going on, which seems incredible, or it has misled us time and again, step by step, from President Eisenhower's early statement about unleashing Chiang Kai-shek to recapture China to his statement a few days ago that he had good news from Suez and that there was no trouble with our allies.

And now we have seen in this campaign a refusal on the part of the Republican candidates even to talk seriously about the great problems of the world. Constructive proposals have been dismissed with scorn and epithet.

So it has been when I propose that we take the lead to tame the hydrogen bomb that releases poisons, war or no war, which can permanently injure your child and destroy the whole balance of life on earth.

And so it has been when I say our economic aid system is still so tied to defense policies that it appears to Asia to be little more than a bribe to take sides.

And now one other matter.

Your choice tomorrow will not be of a president for tomorrow. It will be of the man—or men—who will serve you as president for the next four years.

And distasteful as this matter is, I must say bluntly that every piece of scientific evidence we have, every lesson of history and experience, indicates that a Republican victory tomorrow would mean that Richard M. Nixon would probably be president of this country within the next four years.

I say frankly, as a citizen more than a candidate, that I recoil at the prospect of Mr. Nixon as custodian of this nation's future, as guardian of the hydrogen bomb, as representative of America in the world, as commander in chief of the United States armed forces.

Distasteful as it is, this is the truth, the central truth, about the most fateful decision the American people have to make tomorrow. I have full confidence in that decision.

After tomorrow, in the months and years to come, we have great work to do together—to improve the lot of all Americans—in the home, the office, the factory, on the farm.

I said earlier there is nothing we cannot do if we decide we want to do it.

Man always can see further than he can reach, but let us never stop reaching. He dreams more than he can achieve, but let us never lay to rest our dreams.

I was in church yesterday, and there I read this responsive reading:

> Methought I saw a nation arise in the world
> And the strength thereof was the strength of right.
> Her bulwarks were noble spirits and ready arms . . . :
> All factions and parties were turned to one cause;
> The transformation of evil to good.
> Bitter words, the utterance of hate and despair,
> And envy and conceit were no more heard in the land . . .
> To the supreme good all the people were devoted.

Let this be our vision for America. Good night. God bless you.

STATEMENT BY ADLAI E. STEVENSON

•

I have just sent the following telegram to President Eisenhower:

"You have won not only the election, but also an expression of the great confidence of the American people. I send you my warm congratulations.

"Tonight we are not Republicans and Democrats, but Americans.

"We appreciate the grave difficulties your administration faces, and, as Americans, join in wishing you all success in the years that lie ahead."

And now let me say a word to you, my supporters and friends, all over the country.

Made in Chicago, November 6, 1956.

First, I want to express my respect and thanks to a gallant partner in this great adventure—Estes Kefauver.

I wish there was some way I could properly thank you, one by one. I wish there was some way I could make you feel my gratitude for the support, the encouragement, the confidence that have sustained me through these weeks and months and years that I have been privileged to be your leader.

Thanks to many of you, I have twice had the proud experience of being selected by the Democratic party as its nominee for the most exalted office on earth. Once again I have tried hard to express my views and make clear my party's hopes for our beloved country. To you who are disappointed tonight, let me confess that I am too! But we must not be downhearted, for "there is radiance and glory in the darkness, could we but see, and to see, we have only to look."

For here, in America, the people have made their choice in a vigorous partisan contest that has affirmed again the vitality of the democratic process. And I say God bless partisanship, for this is democracy's lifeblood.

But beyond the seas, in much of the world, in Russia, in China, in Hungary, in all the trembling satellites, partisan controversy is forbidden and dissent suppressed.

So I say to you, my dear and loyal friends, take heart—there are things more precious than political victory; there is the right to political contest. And who knows better how vigorous and alive it is than you who bear the fresh, painful wounds of battle.

Let me add another thought for you who have traveled with me on this great journey:

I have tried to chart the road to a new and better America. I want to say to all of you who have followed me that, while we have lost a battle, I am supremely confident that our cause will ultimately prevail, for America can only go forward. It cannot go backward or stand still.

But even more urgent is the hope that our leaders will recognize that America wants to face up squarely to the facts of today's world. We don't want to draw back from them. We can't. We are ready for the test that we know history has set for us.

And, finally, the will of our society is announced by the majority. And if other nations have thought in the past few weeks that we were looking the other way and too divided to act, they will learn otherwise. What unites us is deeper than what divides us—love of freedom, love of justice, love of peace.

May America continue, under God, to be the shield and spear of democracy. And let us give the administration all responsible support in the troubled times ahead.

Now I bid you good night, with a full heart and a fervent prayer that we will meet often again in the liberals' everlasting battle against ignorance, poverty, misery and war.

Be of good cheer. And remember, my dear friends, what a wise man said—"A merry heart doeth good like a medicine, but a broken spirit dryeth the bones."

As for me, let there be no tears. I lost an election but won a grandchild!

VI
CREDO

PRINCIPLES OF THE DEMOCRATIC PARTY

●

Being a Democrat is for me a very great deal more than just being on a particular side of a lot of different issues.

I suppose there's no question about the fact that one reason I'm a Democrat—and mighty proud of it, incidentally—my father and grandfather before me were Democrats. I often think how much it is a measure of my political prejudice that inheritance always seems to me a good enough reason for being a Democrat but not a good enough reason for being a Republican.

But there is a lot more to it than this. I am a Democrat because I believe deeply in what the Democratic party stands for, and has stood for for almost a century and a half. We sometimes forget that while other political parties have come and gone, we who are Democrats today are members of the party of Thomas Jefferson and Andrew Jackson. We have become the party of centuries because we *do* have a central belief—and time has proved its soundness.

I can't put it in one word—although if I had to, that one word would be "People."

I find the heart of this belief in three statements you'll find in the history of the Democratic party—two of them, incidentally, by Democrats from the South.

It was Jefferson who said, 132 years ago, that "Men . . . are naturally divided into two Parties; those who fear and distrust the people, and wish to draw all powers from them into the hands of the higher classes, and those who identify themselves with the people, have confidence in them as the most honest and safe . . . depository of the public interests."

Almost a century later, Woodrow Wilson said this: "When America loses its ardor for mankind it is time to elect a Democratic President."

And, just last month in Washington, a great Democrat of today, Senator Herbert Lehman of New York, spoke of what he called "the passion for the full right of freedom."

What is at the heart of Democratic policy and principle and faith and belief? Well, we identify ourselves with people and have confidence in them; we have a fighting ardor for mankind; and we have a passion for the full right of freedom.

And these aren't just words. It seems to me they offer clear and firm guidance to the most immediate and current problems we face today,

Telecast from Miami, Florida, May 26, 1956.

yes, and to most of the issues in this election.

The present administration went into office proclaiming itself a business-man's government. The President's Cabinet and most of the agencies of government have been filled with representatives of a single interest. I spoke in Fort Lauderdale last night of the policy of this administration not even to tell the rest of us, the people of this country, the truth about what is going on in our government and particularly in the handling of the issue of peace and war in the world. I say, with Thomas Jefferson, that this is wrong; that the government of this democracy cannot be one that distrusts the people and draws all powers from them into the hands of one class; that government in America *must* identify itself with *people,* have confidence in them, recognize *all* people—and no single group—as the only safe guardians of the public interest.

We are prosperous today as a nation. Yet in these last three and a half years the administration in Washington has done nothing—or at least nothing substantial—about the human uses to which most of us want at least some part of this prosperity to be put.

We want better schools, more teachers, the hospitals we need, removal of the slums and the urban blight that breed juvenile delinquency. We want to keep the family farm as an essential part of our society. But these are basically human rather than business concerns—and this administration is utterly lacking, it seems to me, in what Woodrow Wilson called a "fighting ardor for mankind."

We want a program to make our older age a time of meaning, of dignity, of opportunity.

We Democrats do have a "fighting ardor for mankind"—and what this means to us is using the fruits of our prosperity in this land of plenty in this age of abundance not to give tax cuts to large corporations, but to give us the things *we* want as *people.* Yes, and it means a program of dealing with the peoples of Asia and Africa and the Middle East in the realization that it is not war or military pacts that will defeat Communism there, but a program rather that shows those people, too, that our ardor for mankind extends to *all* people.

Yes, and we Democrats have a *passion* for the *full* right of freedom. That's why we spoke out so strongly against the political attacks by Senator McCarthy and Vice-President Nixon on the Bill of Rights. That's why we have championed the idea of *free* trade unions and *free* collective bargaining. That's why we have felt so strongly and have been so critical about the failure of the present administration in Washington to recognize that in the Middle East this past year not just one little nation, Israel, but the whole idea of freedom was being threatened by cynical aggravation of old tensions.

We don't just believe in freedom as an ideal; we've got a *passion,* as Senator Lehman puts it, for *full* freedom—that means what it's supposed to mean in people's everyday lives—here at home, yes, and in the whole world, for liberty knows no boundary lines, and tyranny won't stop at any border.